"Factor (*Love Maps*, 2015, etc.) chronicles life with [Felix, who is autistic and physically disabled . . . In t that vibrates with unconditional love, the author details what life is like with Felix and her other two children . . . Factor adeptly chronicles each step of the process, each moment of triumph when Felix reached a new goal, and the times when she and her husband felt dismay and even shame when he failed to advance like the other toddlers around him. Throughout, readers gain a sense of the complexity of Felix, whether he's happy, responding to music therapy, or engaged in some awful fit that forces him to scream and tear at his own body. Factor also discusses her other two children, who were born without such issues, her battles with the health care and educational systems, and her subsequent founding of the nonprofit community center Extreme Kids & Crew. The author's story demonstrates the need for more quality help for parents of children with disabilities, who will find solace in knowing that others have struggled and found joy in this type of parenting. A frank, compassionate, and highly detailed account of the roller-coaster ride of caring for a disabled, autistic child."
—Kirkus Reviews

"In this honest and loving book, Eliza Factor describes what it is like to raise a disabled child, and in doing so reflects on the meanings of parenthood itself: on how we put into words a passionate attachment that cannot be exercised in words. In evocative, vivid prose, she brings to life her own heart, the heart of her son—and, by extension, the hearts of her readers."
—Andrew Solomon, National Book Award–winning author of *Far From the Tree* and *The Noonday Demon*

"So moving and thought-provoking about the deepest things: the value of life, the varieties of communication . . . beautiful."
—Rebecca Mead, *New Yorker* staff writer and *New York Times*–bestselling author of *My Life in Middlemarch*

"An aching, raw, honest, exquisitely written memoir of art, parenting, and the unexpected places life takes you."
—Marie Myung Ok-Lee, author of *Somebody's Daughter*

"Strange Beauty draws no easy conclusions. Instead, it does the harder work of staring, with unflinching gaze, at the puzzle of how someone with severe disabilities fits into society and family. In Factor's care, we see 'disability' as a concept that is impossible to pin down: partly a social construction and partly an unbudging physical reality; partly an invitation into new worlds and partly a barrier to connection; and always a part of human experience, never a thing that can be escaped or 'cured' away.

I picked my nails as I read this book. I searched for hope, and did not find it. And then hope slapped me square across the face. As, I imagine, happened often to Eliza Factor in life. In short, the experience of reading felt like the experience of life, complete with the pain, fear, hope, frustration and surprise life throws our way. I'm not sure how Factor prevented herself from making easy meaning of her family's story, but she did, and in so doing, left the reader with a gift, as promised in the title, of immense and strange beauty, a vision of truth with all its messy tendrils of confusion, brutality, and hope left on display.

This book has lessons not just for those of us with loved ones with disabilities but for anyone seeking to think more creatively and expansively about ways of incorporating the beautiful neurodiversity of our species into society. There is inspiration in here for social thinkers, for designers, psychologists, parents, entrepreneurs. It's also, at times, a quite funny book. Factor shares thoughts of drinking gin in the morning, thoughts of death, thoughts of vengeance, and all the other things you usually hide in polite company. She is accused of child abuse, and called (most frequently by herself, though occasionally by others), a bad mom. In the ways she pulls herself through these challenges—with humor, social connection, business ideas, love, creativity—we can all learn a thing or two about perseverance.

Her command of the pen and understanding of the mechanics of the heart makes this a read ripe with riches. It isn't always easy, but I dare you to come out of this book unchanged."
—Lulu Miller, co-host of NPR's *Invisibilia*

Strange Beauty

Strange Beauty
A Portrait of My Son

Eliza Factor

PARALLAX
PRESS

BERKELEY, CALIFORNIA

Parallax Press
P.O. Box 7355
Berkeley, CA 94707
parallax.org

Parallax Press is the publishing division of
Unified Buddhist Church, Inc.

Cover and text design by Debbie Berne
Cover photo © Eliza Factor
Author photo © Micaela Walker

Printed in Canada
Printed on 100% post-consumer waste recycled paper

Names: Factor, Eliza, author.
Title: Strange beauty : a portrait of my son / Eliza Factor.
Description: Berkeley, California : Parallax Press, [2017]
Identifiers: LCCN 2017024577 (print) |
    LCCN 2017029242 (ebook) | ISBN 9781941529737 |
    ISBN 9781941529720 (paperback)
Subjects: LCSH: Factor, Eliza—Health. | Factor, Felix. |
    Autism in children—United States—Biography. | Children
    with disabilities—United States—Biography. | Autistic
    children—United States--Family relationships. | BISAC:
    BIOGRAPHY & AUTOBIOGRAPHY / Personal
    Memoirs. |FAMILY & RELATIONSHIPS / Children
    with Special Needs.
Classification: LCC RJ506.A9 (ebook) | LCC RJ506.A9
    F33 2017 (print) | DDC 618.92/858820092 [B]—dc23
LC record available at https://lccn.loc.gov/2017024577

ISBN: 978-1-941529-72-0

1 2 3 4 / 20 19 18 17

For Felix.
If ever you can read this, please forgive my blunders
and know that it was written with love.
Ehzoyhee!

contents

You can't go fishing, buy a car, or even have a baby without some form being thrust upon you. Before my son Felix came along, this paperwork annoyed me, but attending to it did not feel antithetical to my very being. I could decipher the "M" box for male and "F" box for female. I had the muscular coordination to maneuver the pen. I could check "F" without spiraling into an identity crisis. Filling out forms on behalf of my son is a different matter. Even being asked to record something as seemingly benign as his height makes me want to shout to no one in particular: How? He cannot step up to the height rod at the doctor's office. Even if we could get him there, and help him balance, only the balls of his feet would touch the floor, not his heels. So where would we measure from? The floor? The bottom of his upraised heel? Perhaps it would be better to lay him on a bed? Still, he cannot fully straighten his legs and spine at the same time. Shall we get one of those fabric measuring tapes used by tailors and measure along the curves of his body? That could give an accurate measure of his length, but not his stature.

No matter how I fill in the form, I feel that I misrepresent him. I started this book wanting to blast through all those boxes and numbers and lines, the bureaucratic tally of Felix that is so removed from the person he is. I wanted to create a portrait that would show off his depths, though I myself cannot fully plumb them. But in the writing, things changed. What emerged is a story about me, growing up with my son, discovering parts of myself through him, and entering a world more expansive, unpredictable, grueling, and gorgeous than the one I had once inhabited. It became a story of motherhood.

• • •

When you are writing or talking about a person like Felix, the inadequacies of language rear up immediately. Legally speaking, Felix is disabled. I use this term throughout the book because that is the way mainstream society views him, and because the disability movement has been instrumental in making life better for Felix and so many others. But disability is a knotty and confounding term. I suspect that its vagueness and accent on the negative are partly responsible for the disability movement's residence on the outskirts of American consciousness.

When I first grappled with it, my mind would spin for hours. What constituted a disability? We are all made up of cans and cannots. I can do a side kick, but I can't remember where I put my keys. I can write a letter, but I can't seem to make a phone call without heart palpitations. My husband Jason, lawyer that he is, pointed out that my weaknesses and oddities do not significantly hamper my ability to participate in society, and therefore they don't count as disabilities. But if the degree of one's participation in society is key, then how do you explain the likes of Stevie Wonder, Frida Kahlo, FDR, Van Gogh, Edison, Dostoyevsky? Not only did they and many other scientists, artists, and leaders with disabilities participate in society, they significantly influenced our culture. What's more, their contributions were shaped by their disabilities. Edison was considered slow and addled (his era's version of learning disabled) when he was a boy and his mother had to homeschool him. But the different

architecture of his brain led to the ideas and inventions that illumi-
nate and connect our world today. Frida Kahlo didn't start painting
until a near fatal bus accident left her bedridden for months; she
credits the isolation and pain she felt at this time for honing her
vision. FDR's bout with polio at the age of thirty-nine "plowed up
his nature," in the words of his biographer. The man who emerged
may have lost the use of his legs, but he had gained in empathy, complex thinking, compassion, courage, and flexibility, qualities that
would make him one of America's most enduring and beloved of
presidents. Furthermore, if disability is understood as a social dis-
advantage, shouldn't those people who are significantly overweight,
or marked by burns or scars, be considered disabled? Their appearance can have a more devastating effect on their chances of finding
employment or even being allowed into a restaurant or airplane
than many people with legally vetted disabilities.

The Americans with Disabilities Act defines disability as a
physical or mental impairment that substantially limits one or more
major life activities. Again, the language is so general as to be univer-
sal. Disability cannot be pinned down because it is not a thing like
a tree, or a face, or a broken bone; rather it is an idea, a perception,
a relation. My friend Victor Calise, the Commissioner of the New
York City Mayor's Office for People with Disabilities, thinks of a
person with a disability "as someone in need of a little more help."
Victor, who injured his spinal cord in a dirt bike accident when he
was young, speeds around Manhattan in a sleek wheelchair that he
can jump and pivot. He is one of the more dynamic people I know
and does not usually feel disabled. Why would he? He works in a
wheelchair accessible building, his position allows him a car and
driver, he is agile in body and mind. But last year, he got into a skiing accident and broke a shoulder. He could not dress himself and
had to use a bulky electric wheelchair that could not roll over the

curbs, bumps and ministeps so pervasive in our city. *Sotto voce*, he told me that he once again felt disabled, with all the indignities and frustrations that the term connotes.

• • •

His story illustrates how we move in and out of disability; its demographic is as shifting as its definition. According to the 2010 Census, 19 percent of Americans have one or more disabilities. So what do we call that other 81 percent who at the moment of filling out their Census returns did not feel impaired or were not officially impaired? People are far too complicated to be divided into "disabled" and "not disabled," and yet we are embedded in binary thinking. "Us" and "them" is a mainstay of our grammar. We organize people into groups and categories, and we identify with people with whom we share certain similarities. I could not have done my community building work without clumping people together under the flag of disability. But I readily acknowledge its slippery nature, its clunky, not-the-right-word feel.

The same goes for "normal." "Normal" is the word that usually appears in my mind when I have to find a corollary for "disabled." I find it to be an interesting term, as problematic and shifting as its mate. I remember being six or seven and saying "thank you" when a classmate told me that I was weird. She looked confused, and the discussion ended in my favor. I can probably recall this because it was one of the rare occasions when the right words came to me immediately. I didn't agonize later on, wishing I had said this or that. My response perfectly mirrored my inner thinking. Weird was the opposite of normal, and normal was predictable, obedient, lacking in imagination. Who wanted to be that? I felt this way into my thirties. The humdrum connotations of "normal" are sewn into the language. Imagine saying: "Congratulations! You did a normal job." "What a normal dinner party!" "Thanks, I had a normal time." Normal is boring.

But normal is also something we grab at when we feel insecure. Is this mole normal? This thought, this dream, this desire? Am I OK? Do I pass? When we are scared, being told that we are not normal is frightening. We feel that abnormality casts us out. Sometimes it does. One of the most painful parts of being confronted by a disability is the social and physical isolation that can come with it. Normal, on the other hand, implies that you fit in, that you are safe, that your anonymous position in the throng of likewise normal people will protect you from whatever it is that you fear. This is an illusion, but a powerful one.

• • •

One of the more unexpected and liberating things that Felix has given me is the chance to escape this parsing of words and language altogether for great chunks of time. Not that he and I are always silent. Felix likes to make noise. Sometimes words even come into the mix. He strings them into phrases which give him pleasure, and I babble, my words losing their meanings, becoming fun sounds to make with my mouth. But often we travel in silence, and in so doing step into a fuller experience of the wind, the quivers of nerves, the smell of chocolate and the rustle of cellophane. He has allowed me to plunge deep into the world below language—more often than most adults my age can. For this I am grateful. It is a wild and fertile place, shimmering with energy and unencumbered by conventional modes of thought. My hope is that through our story, you will be able to visit it, too, and share in its strange beauty.

The Beginning

Early in my pregnancy, when the tests were still normal, and a large part of me was simply a pouting thirty-four-year-old, bridling against prenatal restrictions and unasked for advice, a nice neighbor brought over a copy of *What to Expect When You Are Expecting*, and I almost burst into tears. This is the kind of book people are giving me these days? Sentimentalized pictures of mothers in rocking chairs? I tossed it in the recycling and reread Kenzaburo Oe's *A Personal Matter*, a black comic account of Bird, a Japanese intellectual whose first son is born with two heads. I loved that book; I still do. It is so open about the anxiety caused by otherness: Bird tries to starve his baby to death, but the baby won't die. He tries to run away with another woman, but he is drawn back to his own wife. When, at the end, he bows to his duty, there is no glory in the act, only a sort of submission. The book is a work of fiction, but it is directly related to Oe's personal experience. Hikari Oe, his first-born son, was born with severe brain damage. My friend Norbert was astonished when I told him what I was reading. "You dare to read that?" I was surprised by his reaction, as if curling up with Oe was somehow inviting mayhem into my pregnancy. But perhaps he was right.

I found Oe more comforting than *What to Expect* because Oe dealt with the dread of parenthood; whereas *What to Expect* assumed a reader who was, on some level, eager to become a parent, and more specifically, a mother. I was interested and at times amazed by the biological process taking place within me. I enjoyed playing with children. I liked the idea of a child pattering around our apartment, spilling flour on the floor, but the idea of being the person nagging this child to clean up the flour or sweeping it up myself? No. The word "mother" hit a powerful button in my psyche, the effect of which was to make me balk. When people congratulated me on becoming one, I would freeze, unable to respond in any sort of honest way. The word conjured a grotesquerie—a woman at turns smothering, cloying, judgmental, bent on improvement, knowing-better, disappointed, proud, smug, worried, oppressive, presumptuous, and embattled. It should be noted that my own mother, an independent, quirky, organic gardener more apt to go to an Amnesty International meeting than the PTA, bore little resemblance to this frightful tangle of character traits. You'd think that her example, along with that of my grandmother, and my feminist education, would have diminished the power of this mind-harridan. It hadn't.

It wasn't just the word mother. It was also the way people congratulated me. How could they be so cheerful? What was their optimism grounded on? What if I had the next Hitler? What if I absolutely loved my child, then ran her over as I was backing up the car? What if nothing dramatic happened, and I simply sank into a morass of boredom and suffocation, bickering and diaper-changing without any means of escape and no time to write?

You might be wondering why, if I felt this way, I was pregnant in the first place. The answer is al-Qaeda. Jason, on his way to work on the eleventh of September, had come out of the subway a block away from the World Trade Center. The building was burning like a matchstick, on the verge of collapse. When it imploded, he was caught up in a cloud of smoke and debris so thick that all light and sound was blocked out. He ran, then tripped and fell, burning his leg on an ember. Across the East River, in our Brooklyn apartment on Court Street, I paced in circles, doubled over, moaning, screaming, urging him to be OK.

I had met him two years before, after a jiujitsu tournament on the Upper West Side. I was thirty-one, a humble green belt, giddy with relief that the tournament was over. I hated getting up in front of people, but one of the rules of the dojo was that you had to participate in these things, so I had. I was heading home when someone invited me to the after-party. I was curious. I'd interacted with the people at the dojo for a year, but I'd only seen them clad in their gis, which look a fair amount like white pajamas. I wanted to check out their street clothes and hear their voices. Instruction at the dojo was done wordlessly, through mimicry, or hand-over-hand prompting. You weren't allowed to talk. But even at the party, with no such prohibition, voices were hard to make out and conversation was almost impossible. Words bounced off the walls and mixed in with the music. Someone shouted an introduction to Jason, a guy I hadn't seen before. We tried to chat over the music. He seemed to be an accountant from New Jersey, which amused me, as he looked young enough to be in high school. He had twinkling eyes and curly hair and was wearing a generic gray sweatshirt. When I started to dance, he joined in, leaning back until his hands touched the floor behind him, and pulling off some disco bridge move that had everyone whooping.

He called a couple of weeks later, on a Sunday around noon, and asked if I wanted to meet at the Met. I was not sure about going out with someone so young, but I loved the Met. We wandered around the familiar halls, each of us showing the other our treasures. It turned out he was almost twenty-nine, only a couple of years younger than me. And he wasn't an accountant from New Jersey.

He was a Wall Street lawyer who lived in Brooklyn and had a double black belt in jiujitsu. He had been at the tournament to cheer
on his former students, whom he had taught at Harvard. We left
the museum, not yet ready to say goodbye, and wandered around
the reservoir in Central Park. He had failed to see the beauty of
my favorite Noguchi fountain, and was failing to make the concept of tax structures interesting, and yet sharing the air with him
was strangely pleasant. We ended up walking all the way down to
Chinatown, then up to Little Italy. We said good night sometime
after midnight, a chaste goodbye that left me wanting a kiss.

He was an associate at a Wall Street law firm. What was I doing?
I spent my early childhood in a progressive nook of Cambridge,
Massachusetts, in the seventies, at a Quaker School. I had an aunt
who lived in an old school bus on mountaintops, another who met
her husband when he was busking on the Athens subway. My mom
made a living selling homegrown organic vegetables in Northern
California. I had been warned about the evils of money from the
start. I had probably been warned about the importance of supporting myself, too, but that did not resonate as powerfully. By the time
I had met Jason I had been working for a dozen plus years as a coat
check girl, personal assistant, bicycle messenger, home health care
attendant, researcher, bookstore clerk, photographer's assistant,
sound technician, and waitress. Some of these jobs were better than
others, but they all gave me enough time to work on my writing and
art projects, which is what I really cared about. I could usually afford
to visit my family, have friends over to dinner, and pay my electric-
ity bills, though not always at the same time. Health insurance and
repaying my student loans were beyond me, but they were beyond
most of my friends. Indeed, I was a little suspicious of people who
could afford such things. Just what were they doing, that they were
making so much money? I should mention that there were plenty

of people in my family who were more comfortable with middle class American monetary ideals, and indeed, embodied them—but I didn't identify with them. I identified with those who felt the economy went all wrong when we left the barter system.

And yet, being with Jason made me feel at ease in a way that was rare and remarkable. I figured that I could have a fling. Arizona State had given me a scholarship to their MFA fiction program, and I would soon be leaving for Tempe. Going out with Mr. Wall Street wouldn't mean going over to the dark side. It would just be a form of investigation. I was a writer, after all. Writers have to experience as many worlds as possible.

A few months later, when my old friend Molly picked me up for a road trip out to Arizona, I found myself sobbing as I left Jason's apartment. A week later, Molly and I, rumpled and stiff from our drive, arrived at the door of the friendly graduate student who had agreed to host us. Just then her telephone rang. It was Jason, calling to see if I had arrived safely. He called every day after that. And I, who usually hate the telephone, found myself hurrying back to my Tempe bungalow, so as not to miss him. By the third year of my MFA program, I'd figured out a way to move back to Brooklyn, into his fifth-floor Court Street walk-up, and finish up my degree remotely. I was sitting at his kitchen table, working on my thesis, when the planes hit.

I had this idea to run across the Brooklyn Bridge, find him, and bring him home. My thinking wasn't clear. By the time I had reached Cadman Plaza, where pedestrians access the bridge on the Brooklyn side, the World Trade Center had imploded. The air was an acrid cloud of smoke and dust. I couldn't see twenty feet ahead of me, and realized that the air would be even whiter in Manhattan. I would never be able to find him. I went back to our apartment, where I paced around in circles, gasping for air, yearning for something of his to hold onto, something more than his favorite pebbles. Along with the fear that he might have died was a secondary thought, shocking in its selfishness: He might have died without leaving me anything. I needed something of his, something more palpable, more graspable than memories and emailed haikus, something commensurate with the person he had been to me. It blazed in my mind: We should have had a child. He was too fine a person to die without leaving something of himself. The thought was so jarring and quiet and deep that I could not let it go, even hours later, when Jason returned, white faced, with bits of wallboard coming out of his eyes.

I didn't want him to have a child with someone else. So there I was, a year later, with a brand-new wedding band on my finger, in the midst of my queasy first trimester. Twice a week, I'd take the train to Chelsea Piers to practice Shotokan karate, a style I'd studied when I was at ASU. I was close to my black belt, but wouldn't be able to take the test before I gave birth, as I was barred from side kicks. This annoyed me. I hated being barred from things. I did, however, enjoy the visits to my obstetrician, Dr. Chen, a bicycle-riding triathlete who balanced her traditional Western medical practice with Chinese dragons to ward off evil spirits. She did not have children herself, but she loved delivering them and gleaning anything she could about their embryonic stages. We would listen to the fetal heartbeat together, quietly marveling.

At my three-month visit, the sonogram screen lit up, and instead of the kidney bean that had been there a few weeks before, Dr. Chen, Jason, and I saw a recognizable mammalian form. The creature was so alive, so independent seeming, that I felt voyeuristic watching it. Jason took my hand. I could feel his pulse. Together we watched the embryo gracefully moving about. I finally got it. That's why people were congratulating me. It had nothing to do with what kind of nursing bra I should buy or super-kid I would super-parent.

It was the excitement at a fresh fish swimming in its amniotic sea, a whole new life, beginning again. That's why everyone grinned at babies. After the appointment, I kissed Jason goodbye and walked for blocks, too moved to get onto the subway. In Chinatown, I found myself drawn to a sidewalk table piled high with carrots, the strings of their roots still clumped with earth. Carrots. Carrots had babies, too. Lacy carrot flowers spewing their seeds. Roots funneling into the loamy ground. I was careful not to catch anyone's eye. I realized that I was too happy, would be considered insane, but it felt so good. My little worries about motherhood were just that, tiny. Did carrot seeds tremble, on the verge of blowing in the breeze?

A month or so later, we were celebrating Jason's father's birthday at Artisanal, a fancy French bistro in midtown known for its pungent and gooey cheeses. The sonogram and the carrots had brought me to a sort of peace with my pregnancy, but not with the copious advice directed toward me and my state. When the waiter arrived, my in-laws ordered a cheese plate, then warned me that I should not take any risks, what with listeria lurking in unpasteurized corners. I marched over to the cheese counter. They couldn't stop me from smelling. I leaned over and inhaled. The vapors, apparently, traveled straight down to my womb. The baby kicked. It was the first time I had felt a kick, the first time I perceived the baby without the help of technology. Quite suddenly, I felt as if I knew him. He was a boy, clearly a boy, and not just any boy, but a sweet-tempered boy with a warm nature. The kind of boy who might someday wear a fedora at a jaunty angle. A tap dancer. I was a little embarrassed. I had rolled my eyes at maternal pronouncements. *Not my Johnny, he would never do that.* But here I was, doing just that, without having even met the poor fellow, with only the tiniest of touches to go on. And not only that: I was proud. Proud that he was a boy. Proud that he was sweet natured, proud of the rakish tilt to his someday-to-be-worn fedora. I walked back to our table in a daze, my anger at dietary restrictions forgotten, and announced that the baby liked cheese. A lovely light shone out of my mother-in-law's eyes, a real swell of pleasure.

I judiciously allowed Jason to continue suggesting girl names. He hadn't felt that kick. But I couldn't take any of those Lilies or Madelines seriously. When I hit upon Felix, the first boy name that Jason did not immediately reject, I was delighted. This was our name. But Jason hesitated. Felix means happy in Latin. What if the baby turned out to be a grouch? True enough, I said, trying to be diplomatic, all the while thinking, *but he couldn't be a grouch, not with that jaunty hat.* I told Jason we could wait until he was born to make the final decision, but from that moment on, he was Felix in my mind.

. . .

One morning in the middle of my second trimester, I awoke feeling awful, stumbled to the bathroom, and splashed my face with water. In the mirror, I saw that a couple of worrisome boils had transformed into what I had been telling myself could not happen. The chicken pox. I had been exposed a few weeks earlier. Swollen pustules covered my eyelids, my chin, my swollen belly. More seemed to be popping out as I stared, horrified, at my reflection.

A couple hours later, I pushed myself out of bed, fevered, but with enough energy to move, indeed, having to move, needing to do something, so distraught was I with the itching and the fear of what might happen to the baby. I went down to the lobby of our apartment and checked our mailbox. I found a letter from a literary agent who had read a couple of drafts of my first novel. It is difficult for unpublished writers to get agents to read their manuscripts, particularly to read them twice, and I had been encouraged by his interest. But he was writing to say that he did not wish to represent me. I put his letter down on the table by our doorway, only to discover an envelope from another agent, this one a woman, declining my second novel, my MFA thesis. It turned out that Jason had seen the envelope—thin—and tried to hide it, but I had found it. Both my novels, all I had ever written, rejected on the same day I got the chicken pox? How could this be? I imagined a vindictive fairy cackling at me. My anguish was such that my legs gave way. I curled into a fetal position on Jason and my bed and wept.

Fear for Felix soon superseded the misery caused by those letters. My fever shot up past 105, then plunged down into the freezing regions, then surged back up again. For days it raged. Felix stopped kicking. He stopped scooting around. He would go for hours without any movement at all. Dr. Chen told me not to worry. By the second trimester, the placenta should be able to protect the fetus from the virus. In the unlikely event—a one-in-one-thousand chance—that the placenta is permeated and the virus contacts the fetus, the baby may still be all right. Babies have been born with chicken pox scars and develop normally. I repeated this information to my mother, my father, my in-laws, my friends, everyone who called, but I would have been far more comforted if Felix had kicked like he did before. I wanted to feel his jauntiness. I'd prod him, begging for some movement. He would shift. The feeling was of a tiny, exhausted seal, barely able to roll halfway over.

Sweating in bed, praying that Felix would survive, an image of a golden tent popped into my head. Not a fancy tent—it was a sagging, backpacking tent like the one from my family camping trips in the seventies, but the fabric was constructed of shimmering gold. Perhaps because I do not normally have powers of visualization, and have been highly annoyed over the years by various espousers of meditation urging me to close my eyes and visualize a blue sky or a field of flowers or my colon, I was utterly startled. I could practically measure this tent, it was so clear. I clutched onto the sparkling folds, the tent poles, the sagging fly. It was a product of fever, yes, but it also seemed to be something more, a message, a possibility that Felix might be protected.

After a week, my strength began to return. Felix's did, too, but his movements felt different than they had before. Swishier. One day, my boils assuaged by the Caladryl lotion that Jason had kindly dabbed all over me, I had enough energy to leave the bed and sit, somewhat erect, on the living room couch with a pen in my hand. If he no longer kicked, I thought to myself, well, then, he was great at whooshing. I wrote:

If you were a squid,
We could get rid of the baby clothes
And wooden blocks.
We'd put you in a sea chest
Glassy, sadly square, but filled with the best in pebbles and shells.
We'd watch, noses smushed,
Landlubbing bugs with big eyes and tentacled fingers.
Asking each other: Do you think it's happy?
What would it like to eat?
It wouldn't be that bad,
Except for the neighbors,
The snuffling relatives,
The asinine commentary.
And what, pray tell, is wrong with a squid?
My spittle spotting the sidewalk.
Passersby would shudder or smugly pity.
But when they were gone,
We'd have fun, swirling the water and wondering.

When the scabs dried enough that I was no longer a threat to public health, I left the apartment, and hobbled the length of the Brooklyn promenade. I had only been secluded for ten days, but being outside made me feel like a visitor from another planet. I was astonished at the people who bustled about, jerking their dogs on leashes, shouting into the wind. This is what you people do who are not sick: You wander around as if you own the world. I was exhausted by the time I reached the end of the path and had to rest against the iron fence. Amazing, to be tired out after three blocks. Still, I felt triumphant, as if I'd really accomplished something. I leaned against the fence, treasuring the fresh air and watching the boats in the East River cutting against the white caps. Felix shifted inside me, comfortingly. My fears over the last few days seemed overblown.

I was so sure that he was OK that I looked forward to my mid-term sonogram, excited to see what he would look like at twenty-two weeks. The mid-term appointment is an important one, held at the hospital, instead of the doctor's office, so that they can use a fancy, high-resolution machine and the fetus is checked by a coterie of technicians and neonatal doctors. I set off eagerly, pleased by the fresh air, then the jostle of the subway; I was delighted to be anywhere other than our apartment, which was still resonating with sick-ward vibes. The technician sat me in a reclining chair, smeared my belly with petroleum jelly, then ran the ultrasound wand over the goo. There was my baby, the lovely curve of his nose, the balletic grace of his spine. Feasting upon him, I nodded docilely when the attendant chided me that the amniotic fluid was low, and that I should drink more. I couldn't possibly. I was already drinking what felt like a gallon of water a day and was as taut as an overfilled water balloon. Neither was I particularly disturbed when her brow puckered and she left the room in search of the doctor. That was standard procedure. However, when the doctor leaned over the monitor and puckered his brow too, I began to get nervous. He looked at me. I'd never had a doctor look at me that way before.

"Have you had an amnio?" he asked.

Fuck. Something was definitely wrong. I shook my head, wishing to be back in that unremarked upon mass of people who doctors wave through with a breezy, bluff boredom.

The doctor and technician disappeared for a while. I stared at my chicken pox scars. A nurse came in and told me to get my stuff. Dr. Margono would meet me in another room. I did as I was told and waited in a chair, staring straight ahead, telling myself to calm down. Dr. Margono reappeared, a thin, middle-aged man in a standard white lab coat. His face was narrow, thoughtful, precise. He opened a file and gave me some ultrasound images of a cross section of Felix's brain. "You see the ventricles," he said, indicating two narrow little puddles of black. "This one is slightly larger than the other."

I nodded, hoping to convey that I wasn't upset, that strange brain conditions did not phase me. "What's a ventricle?"

Dr. Margono explained that it was a medical term for an empty space, a pocket of air. That didn't sound too horrible. One pocket of air was slightly bigger than the other, that's all.

"So what's wrong?"

"Not necessarily anything, but asymmetrical ventricles can be associated with a variety of conditions that indicate abnormal development."

Not necessarily anything. *Can* be associated. "Can I get one of these tests?" I asked, thinking that maybe I had asymmetrical brain ventricles, too. Felix probably inherited them from me. My mother's whole family probably had them. That would explain our penchant for living in school buses in far-off meadows on mountaintops. I tried to stare down Dr. Margono, to assure him that Felix was fine, that I was down with asymmetrical ventricles, that in fact I thought that they were a good thing and might help his creative process.

Dr. Margono said that it was possible that my entire family had asymmetrical ventricles, but that he still wanted the fetus to have a heart test.

My heart stopped beating.

"We just want to make sure that the asymmetry isn't a sign of something else. Here, sit down."

"Could this be because of the chicken pox?" I asked.

He said that it was possible, but unlikely. The damage probably would not appear so soon after contact with the virus. He left. He came back with a piece of paper. He had called Dr. Brick, a prenatal heart specialist in a different section of the hospital, and told him that I was coming over. "After you are done, come back," he said. I followed signs to another wing, found the room, talked to Dr. Brick's aide. She said that the doctor would try to slip me in between appointments. There were no free seats in the waiting area, so I sat on the floor in the hallway.

I craved a window, a look at the sun. But there were no windows, just off-white walls, fluorescent lights, and a clock that showed it was 2:30. I'd been in the hospital for four hours. I took out my book, a pink and green hardcover, an example of chick lit. The idea was to broaden my horizons, read stuff that sells. I didn't get very far. The main character was a superwoman type, two healthy kids, great job, decent husband, da da da, complaining about her nanny, her son's haircut, the difficulties of making cookies and getting to work on time. I guess it was supposed to be light and frothy, but how could I feel anything but annoyance for that woman, fretting about problems most of the world would love to have. I wanted to throw the book against the wall, so hard that the spine cracked, but it didn't belong to me. I put it back in my bag and watched the bleary-faced couples stumble past, clutching Kleenexes and trying to reassure each other.

At 4:30, Dr. Brick's aide, a bustling Caribbean woman who looked very neat in her scrubs, tossed me a gown: "Put this on, Mama." She hooked me up to another machine, this one more like the machines you see on TV: an illuminated graph with the heartbeat rising and falling. Dr. Brick came in, shook my hand, asked me questions about how far along I was, my age, whether I'd had an amnio. I watched him monitoring the steady progression of Felix's heartbeat. "Looks good," he said. "No abnormalities here."

I brought Dr. Margono back the report, defiantly. See? Nothing wrong. Dr. Margono looked cautiously pleased. He'd done some research in my absence and said that as long as the asymmetry of the ventricles stayed put, Felix's brain structure still fit into the range of normal. But he wanted to monitor the situation. If the larger ventricle got bigger, it could put too much pressure on the skull and a stent might be necessary. He told me to come back in two weeks. Then he sent me to a genetics counselor.

At 6:30, Dr. Miller was still in her office. A kind-looking woman in her fifties, she sat me down and studied my file. After asking questions about Jason and my families, she drew out a quick family tree: Jason's Ashkenazi roots, my WASPy forebears. In terms of genetic diseases, she said, you are in a good zone, and likely to produce healthy offspring. And since there is nothing irregular with the heart, the baby probably doesn't have Down syndrome.

"What about the chicken pox?" I asked, knowing that she would say what the other doctors had said, but wanting to hear it anyway.

"We can't rule it out, but it's probably not related," she said.

"I had an awfully high fever," I said.

"I wouldn't worry about it. We have done studies of babies born after flu epidemics and we have not been able to find a higher instance of birth defect. We don't see heightened instances of birth defect in Finland, where women routinely take saunas that jet their body temperature way up." She smiled. "We don't have any hard proof that high fevers damage human fetuses, though they do apparently hurt neonatal guinea pigs."

We spoke some more, mainly about the frustration of being inundated with facts about the body, but not knowing how the facts fit together. "It's a problem of technology leapfrogging understanding," as she put it. "We have so much data, but we often are not certain what it means." At the end of our conversation she told me, quietly, that I had the "option of terminating the pregnancy," though only for another week in New York. After that, I could go to Colorado.

"But why would I have an abortion if we don't know for certain that anything is wrong?"

I said the word abortion because I don't like euphemisms, but uttering it felt like treason. I think I was clutching my belly, as if to protect Felix from the concept.

"Some women don't want to take the risk."

But there is always a risk, I wanted to shout, a spurt of rage flaring up. The tests just thrum it into you, force you to linger on the possibility. She nodded sympathetically and admitted that she was glad that she had her children in a time before mothers-to-be had to negotiate so much information. By the time I left the hospital, it was 7:30, totally dark, with a freezing wind whipping down Seventh Avenue. I went straight to the subway, walked to the far end of the platform, and hid behind a beam. Rocking back and forth did not keep the tears at bay. I gave up and entered the subway openly weeping.

Home. Jason listened to my tale. "You should have called me."

"I know."

Jason called his father, as he did any time anything medical entered our sphere. I stood over the sink pretending to do the dishes, listening to his end of the conversation, my frustration rising as Jason's voice became more and more strained. Damn it. Steve is a cardiac pathologist, not a neonatal doctor or a neurologist. He does not know a hell of a lot more about this than we do. Jason hung up and disappeared into the bathroom. He stayed there for a long time. When he came out, his eyes were red rimmed.

"There are some very serious conditions associated with asymmetrical ventricles," he said.

"I know that. I told you that. That's what Dr. Margono said. But at this point, the ventricles are OK. There's just a possibility they might get worse." I marched into my office. "I'm not getting an abortion."

Jason followed me. "I'm not telling you to get an abortion. But we shouldn't rule it out if things get worse. If the baby doesn't have a chance of surviving outside of the womb—" I told him that if we learned that the baby's life would be unremitting sorrow and life-sustaining machinery, then yes, of course I would abort. I am not against abortion on principle, and I have no desire to add more pain to an already pain-filled world. But I would need to be certain. Jason was mollified, although he knew as well as I that certainty was something that we could not get.

Alone, I wondered at myself. I had been so ambivalent about having a baby in the first place, dreading the lack of sleep, spontaneity, writing time, dreading the end of me. Now I hugged my belly fiercely. Nothing is wrong with this baby. No one is even allowed to even question his health. Why? I felt foolish saying that I loved him, this baby I insisted upon calling Felix. I associated love with vision. I could not understand how I could love someone whose body I hadn't seen. As much as I believed that I could feel him, his sweetness, his warm nature, and that I could sense that he was OK, I didn't know if these things were truths, or just desires so firmly held that they feel like truths. I was aware that I might be making an agonizing decision for the baby, for me, for Jason. And yet I couldn't stop.

Later, I would succumb to the magnetic pull of the Internet and tap in "asymmetrical brain ventricles," coating the walls of my uncertainty with lurid facts and descriptions of various possible medical conditions. I recognized this as a form of modern-day prophesizing and chastised myself. There was no way to know the future. Even if I had a genius doctor with great intuition who studied my case twelve hours a day, the best he or she could give me would be a probability based on the confluence of my case and the not-exactly-the-same cases that came before. And though probability has its place, it doesn't accurately predict individual cases. How would I be helped if a future test shows that Felix has a good chance of having brain damage? What would that even mean? Brain damage sounded scary, but conditions as mild as color-blindness were considered brain damage. Epilepsy was another thing that kept popping up on my computer screen. Of course, that is not what you wish for your baby, but it is hardly the end of the world. Prince Myshkin, the main character of *The Idiot*, had epilepsy. I loved him. I had a crush on him when I was nineteen. His creator had epilepsy. You don't abort someone because they're prone to fits and visions.

And his brain might not be damaged at all. Even if we got a 95 percent forecast of damage, there would still be the off chance, the 5 percent possibility. I was supposed to kill him because his numbers weren't good? That was crazy. My first boyfriend, a punk rocker from Chicago, was kidnapped by Colombian guerillas. That wasn't probable. What's more, he came back alive after having been held for almost a year in the Amazon—also improbable. According to the experts, he should have been disposed of after something like 6.2 months, once he became more trouble to keep than to lose. I can't remember the exact number. I just know that I came across a graph that showed the likelihood of a kidnapped person in South America surviving his or her ordeal, and my boyfriend fit squarely into the probable death section.

His name was also Jason. Jason the First, as I refer to him now. Is it probable that my first boyfriend and my husband have the same name? My life hasn't been probable. I dropped out of school, but ended up teaching freshman English. I love Rosa Luxembourg, but married a man who can read *The Economist* without scowling. And chicken pox at thirty-four—that's not probable either. I gave up on the research and wandered around the apartment, resting on different pieces of furniture, squatting on the floor, doing the sort of praying that I do in emergencies. A chant, addressed to any and every force that might be moved: fate, furies, gods, embryonic cells. *Let him be all right. Let him be all right. Let him be all right.* I did this when Jason the First was missing, too, especially during those long months when we didn't even know he was kidnapped. He was just gone. Lost on the continent of South America. *Let him be alive. Let him be alive. Let him be alive.* More than the words, the feeling was the same: the clenched jaw, the denial that anything truly irreversible could have occurred, the scorn and anger toward anyone who proposed or even silently thought of darker possibilities. The sense that as I brushed my teeth, bought groceries, nodded to my neighbors in the elevator, the core of me was spinning around in frantic circles, determined to prop up a life through sheer will.

A follow-up visit with Dr. Margono and a second opinion from an NYU doctor we saw at Jason's parents' request resolved the abortion question to Jason's satisfaction. Felix's big brain ventricle didn't get any bigger, and his small one didn't get any smaller. Slightly mismatched though his ventricles might be, they were within the range of normal. The amniotic fluid, however, remained low. Dr. Chen told me I had to take it easy. No karate. No running. What? I had fully recovered from my sickness and from the travails of my first trimester. I felt myself again, a particularly restless version of myself. I was overflowing with energy. How could the baby be doing badly if I felt so vibrant? I went to the gym where I was taking my prenatal classes and read my *New Yorker* whilst very, very, very slowly pedaling on the exercise bike. I had to do something—I was going crazy with so much enforced stillness. But the next week, during a sonogram, Dr. Chen couldn't find any amniotic fluid at all. She put me on modified bed rest. I could go to the bathroom. I could get myself a drink of water. I could slog through the snow to get to her Tribeca office. That was it. And so, for a couple of months, there I lay, my only exercise making dinner and having sex. I was almost relieved when my water broke early—about six weeks early, according to the doctor's count.

. . .

At St. Vincent's Hospital, the nurses hooked me up to tubes and told me to lie still for another week or two. The longer the baby stayed inside me, the better. After a few days, in spite of their efforts to keep it at bay, labor came—a bone-breaking, surreal pain that had me feeling as if I had entered another dimension. I will spare the reader too many details. Suffice it to say, there was a lot of blood, tearing, and screaming, but in the end, Felix came out the old-fashioned way. Dr. Chen tossed his tiny body into my arms, her movements quick and anxious, and told me that he would have to go to the NICU, which I later learned stood for neonatal intensive care unit. I barely heard her, so consumed was I with him, his wet scalp, his tiny wrinkled face, his limp, purple flesh. A tiny, tender mass of confusion. I kissed him. I rasped "I love you." I only had him for a second before a nurse grabbed him. I watched, bereft, as she raced out of the room, cradling him in her arms. Felix! My Felix. I lay there numb and empty. Well, not completely numb. Dr. Chen was doing something with scissors and a needle and it hurt. But my main feeling was of emptiness and yearning. When my parents and my in-laws came in, their congratulations struck me as absurd. How could they congratulate me when Felix wasn't there? I couldn't concentrate on anything except the memory of his little face, his eyes wrinkled shut, his expression pained and at a loss. His first taste of life outside the womb would be the pulseless plastic tubes of an oxygen machine.

Eventually, the nurses relented and got me a wheelchair. Jason wheeled me down to the NICU. We entered a room filled with the beep beep of medical machinery and dozens of little aquarium boxes perched upon metal carts. On one of these carts, a blue Post-it said, "Factor, Boy. 6 lbs, 4 oz." Oh, the great relief of his skin, his rosy skin, no trace of blueness, no trace of pain. His eyes were closed, his face calm. He was beautiful, simply beautiful. Thank god. He was all right. I hadn't robbed him of all his fluids. A nurse came over and explained that he'd been given oxygen for a couple of hours, but that he didn't need it anymore. He was doing well.

"He got an eight on his Apgar score," she said approvingly. The Apgar test, she explained, is an assessment of a newborn's reflexes, color, respiration, muscle tone, and heart rate that gives a generalized picture of overall health. Anything above seven is considered normal and healthy.

I turned toward Jason, vindicated. My triumph, however, faltered once the nurse sat me down in the wheelchair and placed the bundled-up newborn on my lap. She had not wanted to take him from the crib, but I had insisted, wanting him to know, even through sleep, that I was there, that I had not abandoned him. I'd wanted to hold him in my arms, but the nurse would not allow it. I was too weak. So he lay on my thighs, thickly swaddled in blankets, only his delicate features visible. I had been expecting that the moment I held him, I would experience some sense of reunion, a wholeness after the bloody rupture of delivery. But I could not feel much of anything except my own exhaustion and cluelessness. Who was this tiny baby? And what in the world were we going to do with him? I looked to Jason for comfort, hoping that he was feeling a little more gung ho. But he stared at the wall, pale and worn out. I looked back down at Felix. He was wearing a hat. There was that. A standard-issue hospital cap to correct the head from being cone shaped. Not a fedora, but it had blue stripes and lay at a jaunty angle.

Me and Gino

The nurses at the NICU were a no-nonsense bunch whose business was to keep babies alive. For optimum health and development, a neonate of Felix's weight had to imbibe x many calories in x many hours, x many times a day. Unless Jason and I could do this, they would not release him. Jason and I would go to the NICU every day, listen to the instructions of whichever nurse had charge of us, our arms well-scrubbed with iodine solution, our motives pure. We wanted to feed our baby. Our egos were at stake, as was our desire to take him home. Our initial stunned reaction had given way to a great upwelling of tenderness. We ached to be back at our apartment, all three of us together, no beeps, no rules, no fluorescent lights. So we had to prove to those nurses that we were capable. First, I would try to breastfeed him. Then, when that didn't work, Jason and I would take turns with the easy-suck bottles they have at the NICU, so small they look like accessories for baby dolls. The goal was something like two ounces in a forty-five-minute period. To do this, Felix had to stay awake and alert. The nurses told us not to cuddle him. Otherwise he would fall back asleep. We were supposed to hold him at a distance so that he was somewhat chilly, and scratch his foot if he started to doze. This was difficult. Whoever got to hold him would soon be snuggling him, and he would fall asleep with an ounce left in his bottle. Our nurse would shake her head in ill-disguised disgust.

After ten days, he grew big enough that he could imbibe two ounces of milk in spite of our cuddling. We took him home in a taxi on a cold day in late March. The hospital had released us with a bag full of newborn diapers and formula and instructions to immediately make an appointment with a pediatrician. As I didn't know any pediatricians, I chose the one whose office was nearest to our apartment: Dr. Edna Pytlak on Monroe Place. I have thanked that accident of geography ever since. I am no longer nervous when I call her office, but I was that first time. I have always had a low-grade fear of the telephone, and calling people who I don't know on anything approaching "official business" exacerbates the condition. The receptionist answered. "I need to make an appointment," I said. My voice surged in my throat. I tried to hold back the giggles. "For my son." I had never said those words before. Son? Mine?

Jason and I walked the three blocks to Dr. Pytlak's office, swinging Felix in one of those car seat carriers that a neighbor had given us. It had a white plastic handle and faded blue lining decorated with gold shooting stars. Felix would spend so much time in it during the first year of his life it would come to be known as his La-Z-Boy. But at that point, we were still figuring out how to strap him into it. Dr. Pytlak and her staff showered the delight appropriate to a newborn upon him. Then, Dr. Pytlak informed us that he had jaundice. Jaundice comes about when the liver cannot adequately control the level of bilirubin in the blood, a condition common in preterm babies, as the liver is not yet matured. Jaundice usually goes away on its own accord as the liver develops, so Dr. Pytlak was not worried about it. Now I understood why, when we were taking Felix home from St. Vincent's, a nurse in the elevator had chuckled, "They call him mellow yellow." Jaundice gives babies yellowish skin and tires them out, making for a quiet demeanor. Consequently, those first weeks of Felix at home were dozy and sweet. Dr. Pytlak recommended treating the jaundice by exposing Felix to as much

sunlight as possible, vitamin D being a natural counterweight to
bilirubin. So I'd lay him in front of our sunniest window, in just his
diaper, and watch the rays do their work on his tiny body.

Once the jaundice cleared up, Dr. Pytlak said that it would be a
good time to start breastfeeding. As none of the nurses' recommen-
dations or the DIY breastfeeding lessons I'd watched on YouTube
had been of use, Dr. Pytlak recommended that I hire a lactation con-
sultant. So it was that the tall and stately Stacey, overflowing with a
messianic belief in the powers of breastfeeding, conducted her first
house visit. Under her administrations, our apartment turned into
a web of tubes. Thick, clear breast-pump tubes, and thin, soft feeding tubes, which were attached to elevated milk bottles and then
taped to my finger or my nipple. Theoretically, Felix was supposed
to feed from said finger (easier) or nipple (harder, but more desir-
able) and thus learn to associate my body with nourishment. How
this was supposed to happen when the tubes were continuously
becoming untaped or clogged or caught up on Felix's fingers, and
thus not delivering milk, and instead delivering fury and hunger,
was beyond me.

Yet I felt compelled to follow Stacey's directions. Day after day,
Felix screamed and cried and beat my breasts, his little back arched
in rage. He was hungry. He wanted some milk. Why couldn't I give
it to him? Because only Jason was allowed to give him bottles. I had
to give him my body. When Jason was at work, Felix would lie in
my lap the entire day, sucking at the tube taped to my finger with
angry desperation. When the milk ran out, I would have to detach
him in order to pump more. He would scream as the pump whirred.
I would look at his flailing body, missing the jaundice that had kept
him so quiet, hating the idiocy of the situation: The baby crying on
a blanket on the floor, me unable to hold him as I had to hold suc-
tion cups to my breasts. One day, I called Stacey in tears. "Hang in

there, honey!" she said. "It took me a year to teach my first to nurse, but then it was pure bliss."

A year? That's when I had been planning to wean him from the bottle.

I felt so light, throwing away those tubes and giving in to bottle-feeding. I could ease his hunger. I could hold him without him protesting. Things between us improved drastically.

I wish I could say that that was the beginning of a happy life of motherhood. But shortly after I let Stacey go, Felix developed colic. Apparently 8 to 40 percent of newborns and their parents experience some sort of colic during the first months of life. Friends told me of cases much worse than Felix's, babies who cried twenty-four hours a day, for six months, their parents sleep-deprived and desperate, somehow managing not to throw their offspring out the window, but sorely tempted. Compared with that, we were lucky. Felix's colic came in bouts, a few hours at a time, and he could be consoled. Dance with him, preferably to the soundtrack of *Cabaret*, and his screams would abate and his color would return to normal. On the weekends and late at night, when Jason was home, we'd take turns dancing, passing him back and forth, trying out new moves. Sometimes it was fun. When had we ever danced for so long and so inventively? But when Jason was at work, and I had no one to spell me, my patience and humor could dry right up. I remember one afternoon, desperately whirling and kicking to a Sally Bowles number: *"Don't dab your eye, mein herr, or wonder why, mein herr, I've always said that I was a rover."* I had once been a rover. I had liked being a rover. I liked men who were as big or bigger than me, who didn't scream every time I rested on the couch, who liked my breasts. A deep hole of misery opened up inside me. Made worse because I did not want Felix to sense my unhappiness. I didn't want him to sense anything except gladness that he was alive. But he did not seem to be glad. His life seemed to be an endless cycle of pain, exhaustion, and anger. What kind of life had I given him?

Luckily friends had warned me about how hard the beginning of parenting can be. Even if colic does not come into the picture, the whole business of learning how to take care of a baby can be a shock to those who have until then learned only to take care of themselves. This small, unreasonable, barely decipherable person comes into your life and demands that you bow to their will. It's terrible. You're tired. You want to go to sleep. The situation feels completely unjust. Thanks to these warnings, I knew that I was not alone. I knew that I was part of a shared misery, a soggy cell in an unwashed, bleary-eyed, housebound mass of new parents pumping, jiggling, sterilizing, snapping and unsnapping onesies, wiping and powdering, weighing, worrying, dancing, dancing, dancing, taking deep breaths, wondering if they would ever have a moment to think a thought again. Let alone take a shower.

But there was one area, a wretched area, in which I did feel alone. Felix preferred Jason. It's not that Felix loathed me. He would sometimes cuddle into me. He would sometimes give me a tolerant regard. But his love, his rapture? This he saved for Jason. I could see why: Jason was better at quieting him, better at feeding him, better at burping him, better at getting him to sleep. I enjoyed watching them together. Felix brought a gentleness out in Jason that I had not seen before. He would tote him around the apartment, his patter inspired, his patience apparently infinite. When Jason handed him back to me, all too often Felix's expression changed from quietude to protest. His fists would clench, and a terrible howl would erupt. I would feel like a spike were being driven through my heart. When other mothers crooned to me about the epiphany of their baby's love and how they had never felt so loved before, I wanted to punch them.

I felt like I did at nineteen, that same sense of tailspin, of unan-choredness, of longing and humiliation. By my early twenties, I had learned to conduct my love life on the principle of equality, i.e. pride. If a person did not want to be with me, I did not want to be with him. The moment a boyfriend's interest waned, I'd leave lickety-split. But I was not allowed to leave Felix. I was supposed to love him anyway. And I did. But talk about internal torture. It was E.M. Forster who helped me out here, in particular a passage from his first novel, *Where Angels Fear to Tread*. English Ms. Abbot, on a mission to save a half-English baby from being brought up by Gino, his handsome, disreputable Italian father, undergoes a change of heart when she observes the emotion with which cigar-chomping Gino embraces his baby. His passion is so strong that she must avert her eyes. The scene allows her to see, for the first time, the funda-mental power and asymmetry of parental love:

> For a wonderful physical tie binds the parents to the children;
> and—by some sad, strange irony—it does not bind us children
> to our parents. For if it did, if we could answer their love not with
> gratitude but with equal love, life would lose much of its pathos
> and much of its squalor, and we might be wonderfully happy.

When I first came across this passage, I had been saddened by it, but now it gave me comfort. Me and Gino. We were in the same boat.

Squidish

At three and a half months, Felix smiled. It was a thing to behold, an ebullient comet that obliterated the uncertain pregnancy, the nursing hell, the colic, even the jealousy. It happened on a weekend in early summer. I know because the sun was pouring through the dusty windows, and we were all wearing short sleeves. Jason and I kept handing him back and forth, bedazzled. He kept smiling. This recalled the warm, sweet boy I had felt in my womb. Joy percolated throughout the apartment. I remember taking a shower afterward, elated, grateful. A strange thought shot through me: Were he to die now, his life and all that his life had entailed would have been worth it, for he had known a moment of happiness.

That smile was a watershed, a stroke of healing, the beginning of something new. By the time Felix was four and a half months old, Jason and I could ogle him for hours, admiring the gleam in his eye, the dimple in his cheek. We called him "Felix TV" for his ability to entertain us simply by lying on a quilt, looking cute. He still had bouts of colic, but his smiles afterward built us back up. Life was strenuous, but very, very good. It became even better when I hired a babysitter, Anna, who came two, then three days a week, enabling me to write and run. I was not one of those mothers afraid to leave their baby in someone else's care, particularly not Anna's. She was a supremely nurturing woman, attentive to every bump and burp, and Felix immediately loved her. She would cuddle with him in a rocking chair for hours, singing songs until her voice was hoarse. I would leave the apartment practically skipping, laptop and milk pump bouncing against my hips, and make for a writing center in Gowanus, a neighborhood in Brooklyn named for its murky canal. I was working on a version of *Troilus and Criseyde*, told from Criseyde's point of view.

Now that Felix was smiling, I wanted to take him to my grandparents. I used to visit them once a month, but what with the bed rest and the complications after Felix's birth, I hadn't been able to for a very long time. They lived in New Canaan, Connecticut, a commuter town that did not jibe well with their four daughters, who had all fled to desert arroyos or at least the West Coast, but everybody loved their house, a slant-roofed modern with a wall of windows looking out on a sloping brambly meadow bordered by trees. To get there from New York, you went to Grand Central Terminal and bought a Metro North ticket. Once, during a particularly broke period in my twenties, I got to the front of a long line that snaked around the station, with seven hundred and forty carefully counted pennies in my pocket. When I dumped my change on the counter, and the ticket lady went about counting each individual penny, the people behind me were so frantic with hurry that I almost caused a riot. But I had to see Nancy and Allan. It wasn't just that they'd pay me fifteen dollars an hour to transplant impatiens or help with Allan's photography business or some other agreeable task. Their company and their house was like a balm to me. I loved staying in Heidi's old room, the orange curtains, the faded poster of Snoopy battling the Red Baron, Aunt Hilda's evening gown from the 1920s shedding its beads in the closet. I loved brushing my hair for dinner. I loved it when Nancy and I got tipsy and swapped stories about our respective love lives.

Now, visiting them for the first time with Felix, we lunched on their deck, readjusting. Before Felix, our conversations had been zippy and unpredictable. Now words came more slowly and quietly, and centered around Felix, his appetite, his penchant for not sleeping, his red hair and chubby cheeks. They told me stories of bumbling around after the birth of their firstborn, Pam, my mother. Allan's eyes softened as he described his first glimpse of her, an hour after delivery, cleaned up and beribboned, with a full head of shiny hair. Then they both remembered, with fresh dismay, how this cherished baby had cried and flailed for two frantic months, her yells echoing up the air shaft of the apartment building that they lived in, to the point that they hid from their neighbors in the halls and elevator. Was it colic? I asked. No. She was just hungry. They finally fed her some applesauce, a month or two before the experts recommended, and she stopped crying.

After lunch, Nancy and Allan took a nap. They were both eighty-seven that year, and age, which they had snubbed for so long, was catching up. I walked down to the graveyard with Felix strapped to my chest. Over the years, with and without Nancy and Allan, I'd taken dozens of walks there, wandering around knolls dotted with mossy stones and shady trees, ponds with lily pads. At one of the ponds, Felix and I stopped to watch a family of ducks swimming out from a clump of reeds. The ducklings, newly hatched and downy, bobbed along in an eager line, bracketed by their parents—at the head, the mother, at the tail, the father. Their parents' chests swelled. Their beaks were lifted so high that I laughed in recognition. They looked as proud as the new parents I'd seen in Brooklyn, strolling their babies down the promenade. As proud as Jason and me when Felix was smiling and we thought: He's ours.

· · ·

My chief annoyance those days were those baby books that I would peer into periodically, then stash away, disgusted. According to them, Felix was "failing to thrive." How could they say that about my baby? So what if he didn't like rattles, mobiles, mirrors? He wasn't without his passions. He loved cuddling, he loved yogurt, he loved Cuban lullabies and Emmylou Harris. He was gaining weight, outgrowing his newborn clothes at an alarming rate, and grinning about at the world, charming old Chinese ladies in antique stores and dog walkers on the promenade. He was also beautiful. Many babies are beautiful, but Felix had a kind of beauty that was remarked upon even by those not smitten by infants. I suppose it was his beauty and his increasing pleasure in this world that made me rather cavalier.

Jason, however, had reservations. Imagine us in the narrow little kitchen of our Brooklyn Heights apartment. Felix is asleep. I'm sterilizing baby bottles. Jason's flipping through one of those dreaded baby books, in preparation for Felix's six-month appointment.

"Felix should have turned over by now," he said.

"He has. In California. You just didn't see," I replied.

A couple of months before, we had gone to California for a friend's wedding and stayed at a bed and breakfast with nubby, beige, wall-to-wall carpeting. I remembered the carpeting because I could picture Felix upon it, his diapered bottom rising up, his frantic grunts. He had not only flipped onto his stomach from his back, he had also done a kamikaze crawl for two or three feet.

"Yes, but he hasn't since."

"I told you not to worry about it."

"We should ask Dr. Pytlak about it."

"You ask her if you're so concerned."

I poured the boiling water over the baby bottles and watched the steam coat and disappear from the nipples. I could feel Jason behind me, leaning against the shelf that held our cookbooks. My moral pique was so high that I couldn't even look at him. *It's Harvard,* I thought to myself, *his parents, all that "achieve achieve achieve" business drilled into him over the years, applying such measurements to a baby—my baby. How dare they!*

The next morning, Dr. Pytlak greeted us in her habitual clogs and apron, then puttered about checking Felix's ears and reflexes, all the while asking us questions. What has he been doing lately? How do we play with him? Any concerns? "Oooh!" she said, "Look at that, twenty-seven pounds, twenty-six inches. He's big! Ninety-seventh percentile." I beamed at Jason, not minding the numbers when they appeared to be in Felix's favor.

"Should we be worried that he can't sit yet?" asked Jason.

"He's so heavy," I interrupted. "He's got a lot of weight to hold up, and he's only five months when you consider the prematurity."

"He does have a big head," offered Dr. Pytlak.

"We call him Pumpkin Head," I said, finally getting Jason to smile.

Dr. Pytlak had me lay Felix on her examining table. Disregarding his protests, she lifted him into a sitting position. His head dragged back. His spine slumped. She waved his arms and pushed his palms, all the while emitting a series of mmmm's. Jason and I looked at each other nervously. At length, Dr. Pytlak said, "Hypotonia," then nodded in agreement with herself and said it again. Hypotonia. She explained that hypotonia, or floppiness, to use the old-fashioned term, meant that Felix's muscles were low toned. Muscle tone falls into a continuum—high, normal, low. At the upper end, high-toned muscles are rigid and spastic, while low-toned muscles are relaxed. In extreme cases of low tone, the muscles are so relaxed that they can't make the contractions necessary for movement and bearing weight. Hypotonia, she continued, is not a disease. It's a condition. It may be a symptom of a more serious disorder, or it may be benign. That is, the muscles eventually become more taut as their ability to contract improves. Based on Felix's otherwise good health and appearance, she thought that his hypotonia was likely to be benign. So while he probably wouldn't become a great athlete, he would probably be able to walk to school and climb the jungle gym. His mind wouldn't be affected. In fact, she said cheerfully, kids with physical disabilities often have great memories. Another patient of hers, who was very floppy as a baby, turned into a math genius.

Jason stood under a cardboard mobile of the solar system, growing paler and paler the more Dr. Pytlak spoke. He had played soccer and baseball as a kid. His dad had been a Little League coach. On one of our first trips together, three years earlier, Jason and I had walked down a stretch of deserted beach near my mom's house. He found a well-slobbered-upon tennis ball, left behind by some dog, and a piece of driftwood and insisted that I, who had never before succeeded in hitting a ball with a bat, could be taught. I told him that it was impossible. He showed me how to stand just so. He showed me how to swing just so. He threw the ball. I was dumbstruck when I hit it. Then utterly proud. All of a sudden I understood why people liked this sort of thing. After that, I couldn't get enough of it. We'd go to Prospect Park on the weekends. We didn't have a bat, just a glove and a softball, but it was fun to practice throwing, the immense satisfaction of the thwack when the ball hit the leather.

Meanwhile Dr. Pytlak put her stethoscope to Felix's back. "And just to make sure that we are not missing something, maybe you ought to get his heart checked? Perhaps it would also be a good idea to see a blood specialist and geneticist? If the hypotonia is a symptom of a disorder, we would want to know. It's always better to catch these things sooner." She gathered together a sheaf of telephone numbers as I put Felix's diaper back on and slowly got him dressed. "And physical therapy," said Dr. Pytlak, nodding to herself. "Yes, you should have him enrolled in Early Intervention, too. It's a program that can get you physical therapy." I took the ever-growing list of referrals from her, trying to come off as a capable, pulled-together sort of person who does not shirk from calling strangers on the phone.

On the sidewalk outside, wheeling the stroller over the bumpy flagstones, I told Jason that I would make the appointments with the specialists and get Felix a physical therapist. But for the record: this was Jason's desire, not mine. Yes, Dr. Pytlak had given us the contact numbers, indicating that she did not find Jason's concern far-fetched. But her practice was in Brooklyn Heights, the nub of wealthy Brooklyn. French classes for toddlers were offered at the church. Organic baby food was stockpiled at the Key Foods. She was used to parents fretting about the best day cares, the best nannies, the right schools, the right attitudes. She probably figured that we were constitutionally incapable of taking it easy and waiting to see what happened, that we needed to call in experts to feel good about ourselves. Good grief. Maybe Jason felt that way, but I thought that pushing Felix to develop at a pace faster than he was comfortable with and trotting him about town to test for any possible disorder was wrong. And what if Felix were disabled? I didn't want him to feel pressure to be like everybody else. Kids weren't factory made and that was OK. Better than OK. It was good. You don't want a generation of lockstep automatons; you want quirkiness, diversity. I stopped midbreath when I caught Jason's smile, a slowly unfolding smile that seemed to enter me physically.

"You looked so pale in there," I said.

"I was waiting for her to bring up Stephen Hawking." He was trying to be funny, but his voice caught.

I doubt that I would have spouted off about quirkiness and diversity had I taken seriously the idea that Felix were disabled. My words were too pat and ready-made, an expression of my default way of thinking, rather than a coming to grips with Felix's situation. I was simply not going to consider the idea that he was disabled. I thought that it was too early to assess. Plus, my identity was at stake. I didn't want to be the kind of parent who overthinks and frets. And yet as the weeks went by, I began to see that Jason's methodical respect for timetables and averages had been reasonable. Felix never did the kamikaze crawl again. He did not turn over. He did not sit. His skin was soft and his expressions were a joy. Yet when people would ask what his latest trick was, I never knew what to say.

By October, Felix was eight months old and the slackness of his muscles had become odder and more disturbing. His neck could only hold his head in an upright position for a moment or two. Sometimes, when propped in a sitting position, his head would flop so completely onto his shoulder that he seemed to have no neck at all. One day, observing this, I remembered those words that I had written, when I had the chicken pox and he was a four-and-a-half-month fetus, swooshing, no longer kicking. I had imagined him as a squid. Squids are floppy. Had I known, somehow, even when he was in my womb? Known what? We didn't know anything except that he could barely move. Before Felix came along, I had thought of paralysis in terms of rigidity. But Felix was not stiff. He was a rag doll.

The specialists to whom Dr. Pytlak had referred us examined Felix with furrowed brows. They poked needles into his feet. They strapped him into various monitors. They instructed me to capture his urine in pee bags and bring it back the next day. None of them mentioned the possibility of benign hypotonia. Instead they spoke

of developmental delays, metabolic and spinal defects, genetic disorders that indicated life spans of one or two years. When their tests
yielded negative results, they referred us to other specialists who
could test Felix for other possible lethal and nonlethal disorders. A
visit to one doctor seemed to result in appointments with two others. I would return home numb, fuzzy medical phrases looping in
my mind. My mother would call. My friends would call. Sometimes
I could keep up my end of a conversation, but often I couldn't. I
didn't want to talk about the doctors. The subject was too exhausting. I would hold the phone in the crook of my shoulder, barely listening, feeding Felix as my mind worked out the best subway route
to the next day's appointment. I doubted that Felix was headed for
an abbreviated life span—his chubbiness suggested health, as did his
rosy complexion, his sparkling eyes. But at odd moments the possibility would rear up, and the earth would slip from under my feet.

Most of the time, however, I stood on solid ground, lugging
Felix, stroller, diaper bag up and down subway steps, trying to be
patient when we arrived on time at doctors' offices only to wait
between one and three hours before we were seen. So many waiting
rooms, so many of them dingy, with no clean carpets or pillows for
children to stretch on, stocked with the sorts of chairs you find at
bus terminals, and televisions blaring in the corner. I would remind
myself of all those years I couldn't afford health insurance, tell
myself that I should be grateful. Even if the doctors treated Felix as a
specimen instead of a baby boy, they still might be able to help him.
But it was hard to believe that they would. So far, none of them had
known what was wrong, nor did they seem interested in his case.
They just squeezed his toes, measured his head, stuck a needle in
him, and moved us on, charging hundreds of dollars for the honor.

And those forms. I resented every not-quite-right box I had to
check, every number I had to squinch to fit into a too-small square.

The same old insurance questions, the same old prenatal questions, including the one about drinking alcohol during my pregnancy. Had I given Felix fetal alcohol syndrome? Was his floppiness my fault? I didn't think so. I had been careful during my pregnancy, though I did not adhere to any specific regimen. I was too aware of how medical advice changes from generation to generation, culture to culture. I followed the lead of my mother and grandmother. I took my folate. I ate healthily. I cut out hard liquor, and cut way back on wine. But now I understood those women who abstained from everything. If anything went wrong, they could say: I drank only water. I didn't eat cheese or cold cuts. It's not my fault! And yet even if I hadn't touched a drop of wine, I knew that I would have found other sources of damnation. A number of these were already nagging me. There was that bottle of Nyquil I had before I knew I was pregnant. That slo-mo pedaling of the exercise bike when I was supposed to be taking it easy. Even reading *A Personal Matter*. Could opening myself to Oe's account of his catastrophic baby have allowed my body to work its own version? I would tell myself to stop. Blaming myself or anyone else did not help Felix. What he needed was for me to get up in the morning, or in the middle of the night, and take care of him with a modicum of cheer and hopefulness. I would banish guilt. I would remind myself that guilt could be self-indulgent. But it would sneak back, vile creature that it was.

After the prenatal questions came the developmental questions. Does he stack blocks? No. Does he respond to no? No. Does he look when someone calls his name? No. Can he pick up a pea with a pincer grasp? I didn't know what a pincer grasp was, but I knew that the answer was no. What made those visits bearable was Felix, right there with me. His cupid mouth, his soft "goo" which had turned into "a-goo," his ferocious appetite. He was not the blob the forms made him out to be. He humanized those rooms and he kept me occupied. He needed to be fed, he needed to be changed, he needed to be rocked, he needed to be sung to.

One day, we visited Dr. Deutsch, an ophthalmologist with a practice in a basement office in Brooklyn Heights. The visit started typically, with me jiggling a cranky Felix in the waiting room, trying to keep him quiet while I filled out the forms, annoyed that I wouldn't have time to go to my writing space. I didn't think that there was anything wrong with Felix's eyes. But in order to get Felix physical therapy, which I now wanted as much as Jason, I had to get Felix enrolled in Early Intervention, and in order to get him enrolled in Early Intervention, he needed, among other things, a vision test. Dr. Deutsch eventually introduced himself and led us into his office, an intriguing place with a reclining leather chair and machines resembling robot arms dangling about. He offered Felix a toy. Felix, being Felix, did not respond.

"That's OK," Dr. Deutch said, with a sort of jovial shrug that meant that it really was OK. Something loosened in me. I was not used to joviality in specialists. Dr. Deutsch had me sit in the dentist chair, with Felix propped in my lap. He moved his arm in a large circle around Felix's eyes, snapping his fingers in different places. If the snap occurred in Felix's line of vision, he told me, it would trigger a flinch response. Felix flinched at most of the snaps, but not at all. He had blind spots, as well as a slight strabismus. "Wow," I said. "I'd had no idea." "Why would you?" said Dr. Deutsch. He told me about a pediatric patient who was blind in one eye, but his parents had not known until he was eight or nine. The boy had compensated so well that he could hit a ball with a bat and played on a baseball team. It wasn't until he came in for a routine eye exam that his blindness was discovered. Dr. Deutsch proceeded to flash a combined microscope and flashlight into Felix's eye. His eyebrows popped up in astonishment. "Interesting," he kept saying, with a measure of respect. He hadn't seen an optic nerve quite like Felix's before. It was a strange color, yellowish.

"What does this mean?" I asked, on the edge of my seat. "He can see, can't he?"

"Yes," Dr. Deutsch replied. "But maybe not like you or I." Exactly how he processed sight would be hard to determine until he could talk. Dr. Deutsch wrote down some notes, then explained that the optic nerve is made out of ganglia that carry visual information from the retina directly into the brain. Abnormalities in the optic nerve, therefore, can indicate abnormalities in the brain. He recommended that I take Felix to a neurologist. He also told me that his brother was disabled. He lived in a group home, could play dozens of Irish jigs, and traveled around the country, following his favorite sports team. "He has a good life," Dr. Deutsch said, his Harvard degree framed behind him. "In some ways, it's better than mine."

Finally, a doctor's appointment had led to concrete knowledge: Felix had a weird optic nerve. I was terribly grateful to Dr. Deutsch for not delivering this news in a tragic manner. The acceptance that he radiated had been markedly different from the shrinking inward responses of the other specialists who had examined Felix. I left his office with a spring in my step, eager to tell Jason and Dr. Pytlak the news.

Dr. Pytlak recommended that we take Felix to Dr. Wells, a professor of pediatric neurology at NYU. Dr. Wells's secretary informed me that he didn't have an opening for a couple months, and so an appointment was set for December. Part of me was relieved, another part dismayed at the slippage of time. I had begun to read up on what parents should do for children with "developmental delays." This was the term the doctors most often used in relation to Felix. At first I had taken comfort, thinking that it meant Felix wasn't disabled after all. I associated delays with subways, which in New York often run late. You wait on the platform, fidgeting and anxious, while the train doesn't come and doesn't come, but eventually it does. I soon realized, however, that when doctors used this term, the train sometimes didn't ever arrive. Their delays indicated a divergence from the normal curve of physical, cognitive, emotional, or behavioral development, a divergence that could be the result of an enormous range of conditions, many of which seemed to be permanent and none of which appeared to be good.

Parents whose children had developmental delays were urged to get their children evaluated by professionals who would ascertain the extent of the divergence and try to figure out what was causing it. Once they had a diagnosis, adjustments could be made—diets changed, medications taken—which could help the child. But the timing of these interventions was crucial. There were discrete "windows" when the brain was primed to learn how to crawl, or to develop language. If these windows closed, then the brain might never be able to coordinate these things. What I didn't know at the time is that as there are developmental patterns, there are also exceptions. Windows may open at different times in different brains. And they may open and close, open and close. Each brain contains within it myriad possibilities, as do the environments that influence these brains. A few years ago, Jason's sister sent us a documentary she'd seen at the Sundance Film Festival that featured a girl whose brain could not process language until she was thirteen years old. Language was utterly meaningless to her throughout her childhood, until one day, in early adolescence, it began to make sense. She went on to study history in college. But I didn't know such things were possible then. I knew hardly anything about child development. I only knew what I was reading, which was that we needed to intervene before the windows in Felix's brain closed, but we couldn't effectively intervene before we got a diagnosis, so we had to get a diagnosis quick.

Little mention was made in these articles about the difficulties involved in getting a diagnosis. What if you don't have insurance? What if you do, but none of the specialists who might help your child take it? What if you live far from the sorts of specialists who can help, and can't afford to travel? What if you live near them, but you have four other children, and have to keep your job, and your employer does not allow parents to take off one or two days a week to wait hours in a doctor's office for a ten-minute interview with a harried doctor who might or might not be able to help? The frantic directives to do it now, the admonitions, the implicit message that you can "save" your child or "fail" your child were pervasive. The writers did not mean to be cruel, of course. They probably imagined themselves to be imparting useful information, and perhaps some of it was, but their lack of compassion and understanding of the complicated nature of most parents' lives was striking. Even I, in New York City, with a good insurance plan, extra money when our insurance plan refused to cooperate, and a flexible schedule, could not perform up to par. How, for instance, do you convince a doctor's secretary to give you an appointment next week, instead of in two months, for a nonemergency visit? Scream? Squeak? A bribe, perhaps? Alas, there is an art to bribing that neither Jason nor I had been taught. Jason tried, once, though not in the field of medicine. He was trying to get the garbage men to take an extra load of garbage after we moved, but the lack of finesse with which he waved his bill was such that the garbage man he offered it to flicked it away with an "I'm shocked, shocked!" expression on his face.

For most of us, the wheels of business and bureaucracy move slowly. Four months passed, for instance, between my first visit to the shabby offices where Early Intervention was administered to

Felix's first physical therapy session. These months were filled with paperwork and visits to our home by a coterie of evaluators, but the outcome was well worth it. In early December, Fred Mahon knocked on our door with a sack full of rainsticks, an inflatable therapy ball, and other squishy and intriguing tools of his trade. He was one of the roving pediatric therapists that I soon learned inhabit our city, popping in and out of brownstones, housing projects, day care centers, fancy condos, and slipshod apartments, massaging, stretching, bouncing, and otherwise trying to engage the muscles of thousands and thousands of young children who cannot move like their peers.

By the time that Fred came to us, I was eager to begin therapy. I had not, however, considered Felix's feelings on the matter—feelings that were made clear that first session. As Fred calmly and assuredly cupped his hands around Felix's plump hips, manipulating him into a slumped sitting position, Felix's screams rang through the apartment. The screaming would continue for the next thirty minutes, and into the next session, and the next. For the first year of physical therapy, Felix screamed almost continually whenever he was being therapeutically handled. Thank goodness that Fred was so likable. I couldn't help but trust him, even when he appeared to be torturing my son. Still, there were moments when I balked. Not long after therapy began, I wrote this diary entry:

> I don't know if PT is going to do any good, but I do know that I am glad to see Fred. Not just because he's cute and appreciates books by Saramago, but because he is remarkably kind and forbearing. He is genuinely fond of and amused by Felix, even though all Felix does in his presence is scream in protest. He hates, hates, hates therapy. He does not want to lie on a ball, lie on his stomach, try and grasp stupid toys. He does not care about toys. Why should he be made to hold them? He wails and cries, his face red, his fists

balled. Fred says that he has seen this before and that Felix will come around, eventually. For now we should appreciate his robust self-defense. He has a low-key sense of humor that keeps me from bawling along with Felix. But the intensity of Felix's misery is emotionally exhausting, as is comforting him at the same time as I aid and abet his tormenter.

In the aftermath of yesterday's session, my hesitation returned. What if we're trying to push Felix to be something he isn't? What if he is supposed to be a squid? We're being Nazis, trying to force everyone into the same mold. But Fred is so clearly not a Nazi. I admitted to him my concerns, in a little more nuanced language. He nodded, hearing me. All we're trying to do, he said, is to help Felix gain some control over his own body.

• • •

This unease about therapy would periodically clutch at me over the months. We still did not know why Felix was hypotonic. If he did have a degenerative disorder and would die in childhood, then why were we forcing him to acquire life skills that he wouldn't need? Wouldn't it be better to feed him ice cream, sing him songs, and cuddle him, letting him be exactly the baby that he was? Yet I was always glad to see Fred. I loved talking with him, after the torment was over. I'd cuddle Felix, or Fred would swoop him in gleeful arcs, and we'd chat. Maybe about muscle tone and the mysteries of the body, maybe about books, maybe about how hard it was to find parking in Brooklyn Heights. The subject was of little concern: It was the pleasure of exchanging words and feelings with another adult with whom I felt comfortable. Aside from Jason, Fred was the person I most enjoyed being with those days. Seeing or talking with my family and friends had become hard. Their concern exhausted me. Their cheer angered me. Their questions about doctors, tests, prognoses made me gasp for air. Even their silence bugged me, their pauses, our pauses, heavy with hesitation and awkwardness. Partly it was manners. We did not have satisfactory phrases for handling the experience of uncertainty. Plans, results, explanations, expectations, positions, opinions, achievements—we were all good at tossing that stuff back and forth. But chatting about ignorance and worn-out care? Shoots of joy regardless? The words just didn't come.

There was none of this hesitation or awkwardness with Fred. He spent his days with all sorts of babies who were developing according to their own odd, untrodden pattern. To him, Felix was normal: a funny, fierce-willed kid. He didn't need to spell this out. His appreciation of Felix, of the fullness of the pleasure and the pain that Felix caused, was present, in the room, as palpable as Felix's plump cheeks. When he left, I'd feel an emptiness. Jason didn't get home from work until nine or ten at night. I remember wishing that I could hide in Fred's pocket and travel with him as he did his rounds. I wanted to see the other kids, hidden away in their homes. Were they floppy, too? I never saw anyone who looked like Felix on the street. And what of the parents of the children Fred saw? I longed to meet them.

I knew that I should make some parent friends, but my conversations with new mothers in the neighborhood left me bruised. One would talk about music classes that I couldn't go to because of Felix's therapy schedule. Another of the toys her child loved, when Felix loved none. Another of the heartbreak of sleep training. Her baby had cried for a whole hour before falling asleep!

I had tried sleep training, too. Jason and I lay bolt awake in bed, staring at the ceiling until the sun came out. In the next room, Felix screamed with the conviction of someone who had just started screaming fifteen minutes ago, even though he had been screaming for eight hours straight. On night two, we made it four hours before Jason growled at my stubbornness and marched into Felix's room. Silence. Beautiful silence. Jason snuggled with Felix for two hours, as I slept. Then I snuggled with him for two hours, as Jason slept. That's how most nights went. Sometimes Felix would sleep until five or six in the morning, and we would hop out of bed, giddy with rest, astounded at the energy coursing through our bodies. But more often Felix would wake at midnight and remain awake until four or five in the morning. As long as someone was holding him, he was fine. He just wanted to be held. How could we deny him that? Babies with developmental delays, I had read, often have irregular sleep patterns. There's little you can do except wait until they regularize. By the time they are two, they usually learn how to sleep. Jason and I just had to hang in there. But I couldn't share this with another mother, traumatized because her baby had cried for an hour before falling asleep. So I would excuse myself and retreat to our apartment.

I realized that I was getting lonely, and was relieved to get a call from Molly, my old friend who had driven out to Phoenix with me. We had been roommates in our teens, the two of us making movies and writing silly songs in a succession of low-rent apartments in Hoboken, New Jersey, Sunset Park, Brooklyn, and the Mission in San Francisco. She now lived in Western Massachusetts with her husband Sean and their six-month daughter, Adelaide. Jason and I had visited them over the summer. They were both easy around Felix, loving and thoughtful, not distant at all. So when Molly said that she and Sean had a bunch of friends they wanted to visit in New York, and wondered if they could use our apartment as a home base, I happily agreed.

When I learned that Molly and Sean's New York friends had all had babies at practically the same time, I suggested inviting them over. It would be easier than Molly and Sean trucking Adelaide all over New York, and besides, Felix hardly knew any other babies. Maybe he'd enjoy it. And so they came: five couples with their newly sprouted offspring, a young, friendly, bleary-eyed crowd, chatting about diaper rash and the difficulty of getting back to work. The adults settled in a circle on the living room floor, their babies perky in their laps, or bouncing on nubby legs, or scootching out of their parents' grasps, wriggling into the middle. I could not speak. I could only stare. All those strong spines, all those necks effortlessly holding those heads, all those hands easily grasping, pulling, tugging. They were younger than Felix and yet they could sit, they could wiggle across the floor. I had known, of course, that Felix's muscle tone was lower than that of most babies his age. But the reality of what these other babies had was almost unbearable. Why could they just do this, without having to suffer as therapists manipulated their muscles? They looked back at me, eyes gleaming with delight—*look at me! love me! here I am, splendid!*

Felix sprawled in my lap. He was very chubby at that point. When he lay on his side, as he was doing now, his features got lost in his flesh. I tried to shift him into a more erect position. I wanted to show him off, to demonstrate to these people that he, too, was splendid. I wanted them to see the compelling sparkle in his eyes, to hear his tipsy samurai laughter: Hee-hee-hee! Ha-Ha-Aka! But Felix did not want to show off. None of my nudging or bossy kissing did any good. His eyes were glazed over, his expression slack, his head so heavy that my arm ached from supporting it. What is the opposite of revelation? A feeling that plunges you into despair. A sinking emptiness followed by a hot well of shame. I could no longer see his beauty. I was embarrassed at his lumpy, strange body. The parents in our living room kept chatting and laughing, their babies kept grabbing and gooing, unaware of the turmoil in my heart. Felix, however, wailed the loneliest wail I'd ever heard.

All of those people I had wanted to meet? Now I wanted them out. Even Molly and Sean. When we were alone, Felix was perfect, my creaky Mr. Pumpkin Head. I had to have that feeling back. I was almost breathless with the need for it. When our living room finally did clear, Jason and I shut the door together, then faced each other, exhausted.

"That was hard," Jason said.

Both of us had been hit. Jason, with the thudding realization of how different Felix was. Me, with the unexpected and horrid taste of shame. We had also been struck by the tone of Felix's wail. He had been hit by something, too.

A few days later, my friend Jenny Breznay brought her baby over. I hadn't seen them in a while, and in the interim Josie had grown into a beautiful, plump, bright-eyed sprite who could sit straight as a ballerina and hit her jar of baby food with a plastic-coated spoon. Jenny asked if she could feed Josie in our high chair, an old-fashioned wooden high chair that I had bought before I knew that Felix was hypotonic. Now it was uselessly cluttering our living room. The backrest was too straight. If I put him in it, Felix would slip right down and get tangled in the straps. I cradled him in my lap and tried to be happy with him just as he was. The sight of Josie, however, sitting in the chair once meant for Felix, kicking her booted feet in delight, made me curdle with bitter longing. Jenny asked me what was wrong.

I started to cry. I ended up telling her about all those perfect babies who had come over and that terrible onrush of shame. What if Felix had sensed it? What if that was what had provoked his lonely wail? Not his body, but his mother's betrayal. Who cared if he could sit? Had I filled out so many forms regarding his gross motor delays that I was starting to measure him that way, too? I felt like I had betrayed myself. Not since junior high school had I cared about popularity, fitting in, being at the center. I was happy on the periphery, so why was I desperate for Felix to act and look like all the other babies? I couldn't have spilled to a better person. Jenny was not only compassionate, she was also a family doctor, and so had far more of an understanding of what Felix, Jason, and I were going through than most people. She shook her head kindly and firmly.

"Of course you want Felix to be able to sit," she said. "You're his mother." She hugged me, wiping away a tear herself. "Sitting is good. It's an important skill. You sit. You want your baby to be able to sit, also. It's nice to sit." I started to laugh. Of course it was. As she was leaving, she reflected that she and her husband and their friends who had just started families were, in spite of sleeplessness and diaper rash, all of them in a sweet spot. "A honeymoon period," I believe was her phrase. "But you guys, you are getting the full brunt of parenthood all at once."

I was grateful to her for shrugging off my shame, although in retrospect I can see that even this would be covered in her "full brunt of parenthood" comment. For if almost all children are at some point ashamed of their parents, perhaps it is inevitable that almost all parents are also at some point ashamed of their offspring. At the time, however, I treasured her comment because it interwove Jason's and my experience with everyone else's. We were not that different. We were just getting it all at once. It was the first time a friend said something that helped.

Scary Elders

The day before the appointment with Dr. Wells, I tried to quell my nerves with a walk. It was a cold, gray December day, but Felix, strapped to my chest in a stained Babybjörn, kept me warm. We traipsed down the cobblestone streets in Dumbo, past old factories in the midst of renovation, under the Manhattan Bridge, the cars rumbling on the metal above. I stopped for a pastry at Almondine, then headed back home. Felix's bootied feet dangled by my thighs, his good smelling head bumped against my chest. I was panting up the hill on Columbia Heights, by the Jehovah's Witness compound, when I got caught up in a daydream in which I was a Yoruba woman, who had just given birth to twins. It was a strange kind of daydream, as vivid as the sorts of dreams that overtake you at night. I was no longer in the present. I was in the past, when the Yoruba believed that twins brought bad luck and so cast them out of the tribe. An implacable elder, with grave unwavering eyes stood outside my hut. I held my twins to my chest, protecting them. The elder firmly shook his head. I had to give them up. They were to be exposed in the forest. I froze, clutching their warm bodies to my chest. The vision paused there.

I had reached the top of the hill, and was walking by the playground. Children whooped merrily. A month before, I had taken Felix there, only to leave in dismay, for there was nothing he could do. He was too floppy even to sit in the bucket swings. I wondered if there were Yoruba women who had escaped with their twins, if they had formed a sort of Amazonian tribe of mothers and twins, hidden away in the forest depths. The dream returned. We were no longer in Africa. Now I stood before a present-day Anglo judge. His office was dark with enormously high ceilings, so high you couldn't see them. The feeling was half cathedral, half elevator shaft. From over the ledge of a towering desk, he peered down, your prototypical old white man in a white wig. I stood tiny beneath, lifting Felix toward him, an offering to be inspected. Every cell in my body trembled with fear.

• • •

In real life, Dr. Wells presided over a ground-floor medical office decorated with illustrations from *Babar* and *Curious George*. He had neither staff nor wig; his desk was of the normal size. The only trait he bore in common with the shifting man in my dream was gravity. His face was kind, but graven with lines, the result, I imagine, of delivering difficult news to parents of the neurologically impaired. Jason and I observed him like skittish birds, alert to every move and expression. He examined Felix. He listened stoically as we answered his questions about pregnancy, delivery, and development. He interwove his fingers on his desk and recommended an MRI of Felix's brain. My heart sank. We walked into the cold December wind, the little blue prescription note tucked carefully in Jason's backpack. "At least he agrees he's cute," Jason said. "He's been clinically proven to be cute."

As this was not an emergency procedure, we had to wait five months for the MRI. The daffodils were out, and Felix had turned one by the time that Jason and I checked him into the subterranean depths of the MRI unit at NYU hospital. In the air conditioned antechamber, we took turns singing "Wheels on the Bus," Felix's favorite song at the time, and trying to distract him from his hunger, for he was not allowed to eat or drink anything due to the anesthesia. He giggled at all the attention, delighted at the presence of Jason, who he didn't usually see on the weekdays. A sticker of a blue Gumby-like character had been pasted to one of the lockers for storing the clothes, shoes, and metallic objects of patients headed for an MRI. A scrappy reminder of other kids who had been here before.

I stepped back as Felix was strapped to the gurney, howling in protest as the anesthesiologist sought to give him a shot. Jason murmured soothingly to him. I could not speak. I could barely look at Felix. A few months before, he had been scheduled for a surgery to remove a testicle that hadn't descended, but the procedure had been cancelled when the anesthesiologist learned of Felix's hypotonia. If the hypotonia extended to his organs, he had explained, the anesthesia could be dangerous. Dr. Wells had assured us that Felix's organs were working fine and would not be adversely affected. He had written a clearance. Still, how could he know beyond a doubt? His guess was simply better than ours. I couldn't understand how Jason could be so trusting, calmly teasing Felix as he succumbed to the drug. Felix became still and the doctors pushed his little body into the big white magnetic tube. We were told to wait outside. It was May 11, our second wedding anniversary.

. . .

Weeks later, on an evening in early summer as I was making dinner, Dr. Wells called. The MRI had revealed a significant loss of white matter and lesions around the ventricles of Felix's brain. The findings were consistent with a disease known as periventricular leukomalacia, a serious disorder that affected children throughout their entire lives. I held the phone to my ear, nodding numbly. Felix had had a good day that day. He had not cried all the way through Fred's PT session. He had chortled with Terra, his new occupational therapist. Now he lay in his La-Z-Boy car seat, his skin glowing in the evening sun, his eyes sparkling, happy, funny sounds issuing from his lips. Dr. Wells continued to talk. There was no prognosis. He could not say exactly how the periventricular leukomalacia would shape Felix's development, only that it would, and its marks would be moderate to severe.

"What about the plasticity of the brain?" I asked.

"These types of cells don't grow back."

• • •

At Dr. Pytlak's suggestion, we had another neurologist, reportedly a genius at diagnosis, look at Felix and his MRI. Dr. DeVivo's genius cost $600 a half hour, and he didn't accept insurance. He was one of those New York doctors with a big reputation with whom you had to schedule an appointment six months in advance, instead of two or three. When we finally met him, he confirmed Dr. Wells's findings, but grumbled about the resolution of the MRI and ordered us to get another one at his hospital. So poor Felix had to go through anesthesia again. On our second visit to Dr. DeVivo, he told us that the second MRI showed the same as the first. Felix had periventricular leukomalacia. He shrugged his shoulders. There was nothing more he could do for us. But then, he did. Almost as an aside, he told us that periventricular leukomalacia was associated with the varicella virus, that is, the chicken pox. That's most likely what did it, he said.

I had feared for Felix during the chicken pox. I had prayed for him during the chicken pox. It was during the chicken pox that he had stopped his athletic kicking and begun his swooshing. It was during the chicken pox that I had written the squid poem. When my pregnancy went awry, I had thought that the chicken pox was to blame, but as our doctors did not seem to agree, I had given up on the idea. Having this idea brought back to life by a white-jacketed "diagnostic genius" had an immediate calming effect. Gone were those pangs of guilt that periodically beset me. I understood that I would never know for sure. Felix's condition still might have been brought on by my openness to Oe, my downing of Nyquil, that wine at Laura's party, my sins, my skepticism, my irreverent behavior. We are very much blind men poking at the elephant in this regard. But just as likely, it was the chicken pox. I suspect that Dr. DeVivo may be considered a diagnostic genius because he is adept at suggesting useful diagnoses. His words could not bring back Felix's white matter, but they allowed me to move on. That was good medicine, well worth $1,200.

His words worked magic for our extended family, also. We now had tangible news to share with them. The chicken pox. Double-checked MRI results. Solid information. When I told my dad about Felix's white matter, his voice cracked. "Poor kid." It was the first time anyone had said that. Up until then, our family's concern had been centered on Jason and me, then Felix. My father's immediate apprehension of Felix's plight still brings tears to my eyes. And gratitude. He had pierced through that isolation that I'd felt whenever the subject of Felix came up. He identified with him. He got it.

Therapy

None of our doctors knew, or could know, how Felix's dearth of white matter would affect his growth. The only thing of which we could be reasonably certain was that his condition was not a developmental blip. He would not be racing around the playground in a few years' time. He seemed to be smart. When he was engaged, the light in his eyes was sharp and twinkling. But his language was as strange as his movement. He'd say a word once, but not ever, it seemed, again, leaving me unsure as to whether he'd said it, or if I'd dreamed it. Nothing was clear, but there was a sense, growing ever stronger, that we would be responsible for him, most likely, forever.

A sobering thought. Thank heavens Jason hadn't adopted my political beliefs and quit his job! The strain of disability is usually compounded by the staggering costs of medical and home care. But, barring a major war, comets, the end of the reign of the dollar, we would most likely be able to feed, clothe, and house Felix throughout his life, as well as pay for his aides and the therapies that were not covered by insurance. The pain and stress of not being able to take care of our child was lifted from us, which is certainly not the case for most parents in our position. Jason's job also gave him paternity leave and the sort of flexibility that is necessary for any sort of parental life, but which few jobs give. Yes, he worked twelve to sixteen hours a day, but he could leave the office when necessary.

He could meet me at hospitals and doctor's waiting rooms around the city. He had been there, and would be there for every surgery, MRI, and important consultation. His colleagues supported him. We were lucky.

So lucky. I was so lucky. I would run down the street (while money from Jason's job paid for Anna to snuggle with Felix) marveling at my legs, my arms, my lungs. My muscular structure was an amazement, connecting so nicely with the axons of my brain. I could sit. I could slip keys into locks. I could boil water for tea. I had never understood how precious this was. I'd get teary seeing little boys with skateboards and baseball bats, understanding how lucky they were, too. A lump would rise in my throat. Why couldn't Felix share our luck?

The diagnosis had eradicated any last shred of ambivalence I had about therapy. According to Dr. Wells, therapy was the only thing we could do to help him. So, I, who had scoffed at mothers who overscheduled their children's lives, found myself organizing Felix's weeks into tight blocks of doctor's appointments and therapy sessions, four sessions of physical therapy (PT) a week, three of occupational therapy (OT), and two of speech therapy and special education. Judging whether this therapy was effective was another matter. If you did not know what Felix was capable of, how could you tell whether he was reaching his limits or not? I learned to rely on Felix's body language and his level of engagement to guide me. If he interacted with a therapist, if he smiled, if he brightened when that person was in the room, pursuing that treatment seemed worthwhile. For Felix often did not interact with people. He would gaze past them as if they did not exist. I figured that anyone who could interest him in the outer world was of great value.

Judging by Felix's level of enjoyment, determination, frustration, and attachment to his therapists, OT and PT worked. We also saw tangible results. He learned how to sit. He learned how to hold his head erect. Terra, his OT, could do wonders with Veggie Booty, a snack food consisting of rice and cornmeal puffs, dusted with a green powder said to be nutritious. She would come over and discuss the intricacies of her art projects, her kiln, her house in Ohio while stabilizing Felix's hips with one hand and judiciously holding the little green puffs above and before Felix, making him cross over midline, making him stretch his rib cage. She'd burst into laughter when he made like he couldn't stretch far enough. "You faker!" Her laughter often startled him and caused him to cry, but her workouts helped him gain enough control over the muscles of his arms and hands that he began to grasp and ponder objects on his own. His favorite objects were keys. Not toy keys. Jason's and my keys. He would dangle and jangle them for hours, the light glinting off the brass, a contented percussive accompaniment to my daily chores.

A couple months shy of his second birthday, PT Fred firmly held his hips and showed him how to walk. Felix walked six paces, screaming at what must have been terrible pain, but after Fred gave him a rest, he wanted to do it again. Crawling or standing without support were feats that never came to him, but walking with assistance, that he could do. That spring we bought him a bright blue Gator walker, a four-wheeled device equipped with handlebars that he could grab for support and balance. Almost every day he would scoot around on this, cheerfully clattering down the flagstones.

Speech and special education were harder to gauge. A variety of special ed teachers came through our home, their task to make Felix play in an age appropriate manner, i.e., stack blocks, vroom cars around, decipher picture books, play patty cake. Much of their curricula demanded physical movements that were impossible or very difficult for Felix. He would dim. Gone were his bright eyes, his irrepressible giggles. His speech sessions followed a similar pattern until we hit upon Fran Warren, an energetic, tenacious single mother from Gowanus who simply would not let Felix drift off. She'd strap him into his Rifton chair and force him to deal with her grubby Fisher Price toys, her ideas, her patter. And Felix responded.

He was not a silent child. He was replete with whoops, giggles, cries, sighs, covetous grunts, vowelish songs, and words of his own making. Bah, for no. Mmm-bah for absolute negation. He had even spoken a couple of conventional words around his first birthday: "book" and "kiss." Lovely words that accorded with typical speech development—first words are usually spoken around the first birthday—but they had not been repeated. I had begun to think of "book" and "kiss" as his kamikaze crawl, puzzling manifestations of ability that he did not, or could not, pursue. Fran was not intimidated by his irregularity. Kids are weird, she'd say. Each one is different. And she'd get to work. She went at Felix from two directions. Modified sign language that didn't rely on intricate finger control, and exercises to jump-start and improve the muscular coordination involved in moving his tongue. She had many exercises to do this, one of which was the lollipop trick. She would give him a taste of a lollipop, then hold the lollipop away from his mouth and firmly grip his chin, thus forcing him to extend his tongue in order to regain the sweetness. The movement was very difficult for him, and it would take a great amount of struggle and coaxing before the tip of his tongue would pass over the border of his lips. But it was a satisfyingly measurable exercise. One afternoon, after much labor, and building on weeks of practice, Felix managed to poke his tongue a half inch out of his mouth. I was amazed. "Yay! Felix!" I cheered. His eyes shone with pride. His tongue was orange from candy.

Here was a clear, quantifiable accomplishment, but it also caused a jag of pain. I remembered a friend coming to our apartment when Felix was a little baby, maybe four months old. She had leaned over him and cheerfully clicked her tongue in greeting. He had clicked right back. How? That motion, a tongue curl followed by a sharp, decisive flick off the roof of the mouth was far more difficult than the simple lollipop touch for which he'd worked so hard. He'd done other things as a little baby that he couldn't do at two. Once, taking him out of his crib, I said "good morning," and he'd tried to mimic me: "guh maw." He no longer mimicked. And he'd gooed. How he'd gooed! His first "goo" was the sweetest sound Jason and I had ever heard. We adopted "goo" for ourselves, using it to express unmitigated delight. But Felix couldn't goo anymore. He couldn't make a hard /g/ sound.

Why? Why could he not do what he once could? None of the doctors or therapists could tell me. I couldn't help but wonder: If he had lost what he could do before, who was to say that he wouldn't lose the skills he was working on right now? Would this half-inch tongue extension go the way of goo? A discrete stunt that caused applause one sunny afternoon in Brooklyn, only to fade away? What if he never figured out language, what if he would forever be left outside of it? My mourning over Felix's physical difficulties had lifted as Felix became able to use his body in a way that worked for him. He could grab at keys. He could sit on a swing. He could move his walker in the direction that he wanted to go. A body dependent on a wheelchair or walker no longer seemed so terrible, that is, as long as he could talk, or sign, or read, or write, as long as he could travel through the huge realms of human thought and language. But what if he couldn't?

Jason and I would struggle with these questions, usually after dinner, in our kitchen, with the sink half full of dishes and second and third glasses of wine within easy reach. We reminded each other that everyone's brain eventually goes. If it doesn't go by way of depression, boredom, drugs, car accidents, guns, grenades, dementia, there's always death: All that is learned will one day be lost. We imagined the pain of having a child with a magnificently working brain, a poet and a scholar and an athlete, all set to go off to college when he gets smacked by a bus and loses great chunks of his mind. We spent a lot of time feeling badly for other parents, imaginary parents or parents we'd read about in the papers in sadder situations than ours. We piled up huge mountains of potential woes and misfortunes, then appreciated the fact that we weren't afflicted with that. We eventually dissolved into laughter when we realized what we were doing. We told ourselves to stop. A week later, we were back in the kitchen, groaning over the plight of a single father who killed his violent autistic son in a fit of despair, then turned himself over to the police. That poor father. That poor boy. At least Felix did not have autism. We'd return to the dishes, the bottle of wine empty. Felix would cry from his crib. Jason would bring him into the kitchen. The moment he was in his father's arms, Felix would settle down, his red hair silky against Jason's shirt, his green eyes lit with delight, his loosely cupped palm stroking Jason's stubble. When we held him, all was well. His warmth comforted us. It was the thinking about him that was hard.

Fort Greene

One Sunday, not long after Felix's second birthday, Jason and I decided to wander over to Fort Greene and check out a few houses listed for sale. The weather was nice. Felix loved long walks in his stroller. And who knew? Our apartment was small and we were starting to listen to Dr. Pytlak. Immediately upon hearing the results of Felix's MRI, she had confounded me by joyfully raising her arms. "Great news!" As relieved as I'd been that Felix wasn't dying, periventricular leukomalacia did not strike me as great news. "You can have another child," she explained. "It's not genetic." Our following visits were peppered with seemingly off the cuff comments about various children she knew with disabilities, and how those from big families were happier, and their parents, also, seemed to be happier. I could see how the funnel of parental concern, focused on a single child, particularly a child who needed and would probably always need a great amount of specialized help and care, could get stifling. But yikes. How to take care of two kids if one of them was Felix? And what if we had another disabled child? Even if Felix's condition wasn't genetic, there were always viruses, falls, malevolent fairies.

I kept thinking about a woman I'd seen at the Transit Museum. I'd been pleased with myself for having hauled Felix, his stroller, and his walker down the stairs to get there, only to find myself completely outclassed by a trim Hasidic woman guiding six spotless children, two of them visibly disabled, through the exhibit. The mother pushed one wheelchair. Her daughter pushed the other. Her other ambulatory children held on to the wheelchairs, as if the wheelchairs were an extension of their mother's hands. When the younger children saw Felix darting about on his walker, they burst into excited chatter and raced over to greet us. I shook my head in wonder and congratulated that woman on her brood. She grinned back, justly proud. If she could do six, I figured I really ought to be able to do two. Though I'd never be able to keep my children that clean.

We found our house that very first sunny Sunday. An old brick federal on Cumberland Street, with grapevines in the backyard and bright red floorboards in the kitchen. There was a warm friendliness to it that seemed to extend beyond its walls and encompass the whole neighborhood. We were astonished at the way people caught our eyes and said hello, the way they smiled at Felix and did not turn away. This was not our experience walking around the tonier streets of Brooklyn Heights. There were exceptions. I'd met Davide, an Italian artist caring for his son Orlando, on Columbia Heights, when he challenged Felix and I to a stroller race. And there was an older panhandler, whose name I do not know, stationed outside a pricey health food store on Remsen, who made my day when he insisted on giving Felix five dollars, tucking it into his stroller, and sending us off with a cheerful blessing. But these are the only encounters like that that I can recall. In one day of house hunting in Fort Greene, we came across more people who were not afraid of interacting with Felix, who seemed to enjoy him as he was, than we ever had in Brooklyn Heights.

In the summer of 2005, when we moved in, this friendliness only continued. We soon realized that it was almost de rigueur. Fort Greene was a more rough-and-tumble neighborhood back then, inhabited by more classes and colors than it is today, and guided, for the most part, by a small town, courtly politeness. You did not pass people on the sidewalk without offering a good morning, good afternoon, or hello. If it took five minutes to run out for a bottle of milk in Brooklyn Heights, then it took ten in Fort Greene, because of all this helloing.

Our new neighbors went out of their way to integrate Felix into the neighborhood. He was, I see now, in some ways our ticket into the neighborhood. There was the man in the flowing African clothes who used to sell copper and brass necklaces in front of Madiba, a South African restaurant across the street from Camel Park. Felix could now sit in a bucket swing, so we were often at Camel Park, as he loved nothing as much as swinging high in the air, hour after hour. When the necklace seller saw us, he would run across Dekalb, leaving his wares behind, to give Felix a free chain and show us pictures of his family on his phone. He missed his relatives deeply, and would talk to them many times a day. He was drawn to Felix because Felix reminded him of one of the kids in his village who had been struck by polio. And there was soft-spoken Mrs. Miller, down the street, who walked with a cane herself, and was caring for her mother. She always stopped when she saw Felix, her face radiant and smiling. She'd compliment him on his growth and bless me casually. Even teenage boys, who in my experience don't usually pay attention to babies and toddlers, sometimes went out of their way to be friendly. I remember one boy in particular, gorgeously muscled and dressed gangster style, who loped alongside us shouting "Go! Go! Go!" as Felix ran his walker down the slope at Fort Greene Park.

Not long after we moved, I explained to a neighbor who had not yet met Felix that my son was disabled. My voice did not catch. It was the first time I had been able to say the word "disabled" smoothly. Perhaps I'd simply had enough practice. But I suspect it also had to do with Fort Greene, the ease with which Felix was accepted, even celebrated, here. It was all right that he was disabled. There were plenty of people with diabetes scooting around on their electric wheelchairs. It was just another thing.

Pride

Our first winter in Fort Greene, Nancy and Allan visited. They had become rather wobbly on their feet, and Jason hurried to help them along the sidewalk and up the stoop to our front door. Allan's face lit up as he entered. For a moment, he couldn't say a thing, he just beamed. Then he told us that the post that accented the bottom of our front hall staircase was of the same design as the post that had grounded the banister in his boyhood home in Fayette, Missouri. It might have been manufactured at the same factory, for the house that he grew up in and our new home on Cumberland Street were both built in the 1860s. I had admired our banister post before. It was a handsome detail—a thick chunk of wood, carved into a tapering octagon, with a flattened disk on top, worn smooth by generations of hands. But I had no clue that I had seen one just like it before. I must have when I was a little girl, on those long car rides out west with my mom and brother. We used to spend a night in Fayette, and my great-grandmother's house had fascinated me. Mushy canned peas in fancy silver serving dishes, a grim old grandfather clock ticking in the hallway, glass-paned cabinets lined with moldering books from centuries past. The place was stuffy and vaguely terrifying, yet mysterious, too. "Holy cats," said Nancy. She had been consigned to Fayette during World War II, a difficult time for her as well as Allan, a northerner stranded in the south with a teetotaling mother-in-law and a new baby. Her memory, she told me, was opening and closing in odd new ways. Scenes from her past would burble up to her consciousness with startling vividness. She could, for instance, recall word by word an ordinary conversation she had with her mother when she was seven years old. But she would forget what she did an hour ago. And names, never her forte, well ... she had stopped even pretending that she could remember Jason's name, as fond as she was of him. Instead she would shoot him a conspiratorial grin and say, "Oh you, husband!"

The next time we saw Nancy and Allan may have been in the southern Canyonlands of Utah, where my aunts live, at a big family reunion on the occasion of Nancy's ninetieth birthday. Jason put Felix in a blue Kelty backpack carrier and we took glorious hikes along the slick rock, Jason stooping down every minute to pick up another intriguing bit of stone, me flapping my arms in abandon at the enormity of the sky and the play of light and shadow on the cliffs. Jude the Dude, a cousin from Canada, who I met for the first time, brought his daughter and a red rover wagon, which was a great treat for Felix. We'd plop him on the bed and wheel him around and he'd giggle at the bumps. We must have brought his walker too, but it would have been hard for him to use. There are no sidewalks where my aunts live, and the ground is uneven. On the night of the party, I read a poem I had written to Nancy, and danced a dance with Allan, then excused myself early to crawl into bed. I was a bit sad to miss out on a Mitchell night of dancing, but I was pregnant with Miranda, and being careful.

A fine, uncomplicated pregnancy it turned out to be, although I worried about my lack of sleep. Felix's irregular sleep patterns had persisted beyond his second birthday. The baby books, those maddening compendiums of averages, tell you that a toddler will sleep from ten to twelve hours a day. But Felix could get by on two or three hours of sleep in a twenty-four-hour period, and occasionally none. Usually, he'd fall asleep at ten at night, wake up at midnight, then stay awake until four or five in the morning. Aside from sleep training, I had experimented with holistic sleep serums, melatonin, Benedryl, other medications prescribed by Dr. Pytlak, cutting out sugar (which worked for a while, then stopped), and not letting him nap, but nothing had much effect. So Jason and I continued doing what we'd done from the beginning: taking turns cuddling him in two-hour shifts. In this way, we'd usually get four to five hours pieced together, sometimes six.

My mother, concerned about my and the baby-to-be's health, made the mistake of calling one day and telling me that chronic sleep deprivation was a torture device practiced by the CIA and various despots in Latin America. "How is that supposed to help?" I screamed into the phone. Also unhelpful: newspaper articles that report on how lack of sleep not only renders you crabby and pasty, but permanently kills off your brain cells. Or pregnancy books, urging pregnant mothers to pamper themselves and get plenty of rest. How many mothers of toddlers, disabled or not, can get plenty of rest? Being told that you need more sleep when you can't get it is the torture, taunting you with how much smarter and prettier and kinder you'd be if your circumstances were different. I recall a morning that I could barely move, so paralyzed with resentment was I at all of those people out there with their frigging beauty sleeps.

I learned to con my body into thinking that I had slept. How did I do this? I sternly banished the memory of the prior night and pretended that I was waking up from a six-hour sleep. For such a simple technique, it was remarkably effective. Often I could feel fresh energy welling up. I also meditated at odd minutes of the day. And stood on my head. The yogis say that standing on your head for four minutes equals a sleep cycle. I don't know about that, but it does shake things up and makes you feel young. It is hard to feel sorry for yourself when you are upside down.

On those days when I was too tired to meditate or stand on
my head and too crabby to get past my self-pity, Fort Greene again
came to my rescue in the guise of Mrs. Munoz, our next door neighbor, a formidable woman with a stern forehead and dyed hair neatly
tucked under a rayon scarf. I don't know if any of her children were
as sleepless as Felix, but she'd had fourteen of them, one of them epileptic. I reasoned that even if every single one of her children slept
through the night by the end of their first year, she'd still have had
fourteen years of drastically interrupted sleep. And there she was,
still standing, and strong as an ox. Once, I had come across her resting at the corner of our block, two big bags from Target at her feet.
I offered to carry the bags back to her house. She nodded. I grabbed
her bags. Sweat popped from my forehead. They seemed to be filled
with stones. By the time I got to her stoop, my knuckles were white
and aching from the strain. How had she lugged those bags all the
way from the Target, ten blocks away? I was in my thirties at the
time, honed from hauling Felix and punching at a heavy bag, a gift I
had given to Jason for his thirty-sixth birthday, and soon took over
myself. I was not used to being out-powered by other women, especially those who had thirty years on me. But there she was, with
her rayon scarf and her strong jaw, hauling one hundred pounds of
goods, at once putting me to shame and giving me strength. If Mrs.
Munoz could do it, then so could I.

• • •

Aside from the lack of sleep, I remember those days with great tenderness. Felix had started going to a therapeutic preschool. Most
mornings, a little yellow school bus would roll up to our house and
his face would shine with happiness. He had turned into a great
lover of public transportation. We could not push his stroller by
the globed MTA poles that marked the subway stations unless we

intended to carry his stroller into the subway depths and board a train. If we walked past the poles without going into the station, he would protest with Olympian fits. Buses, which he rode with Anna, held the same magic. One morning, Jason returned from having put him on the school bus, and told me that he had felt pride bubbling up in him as he handed Felix off to the attendant. It was a new feeling. He'd felt plenty of Felix-inspired love, care, and joy, but not pride. I knew what he meant—I'd had similar experiences myself. A pride in Felix as Felix really was, not the jaunty tap dancer I'd once imagined him to be.

I'd known this pride early on, somewhere in between the end of the colic and Dr. Pytlak's identification of Felix's hypotonia. I had identified with those ducks and their glorious puffed chests as they showed off their ducklings in the cemetery near my grandparents' house. But that simple pleasure had given way to more complicated feelings as Felix's disability became apparent. I could still remember the pain and shock of that afternoon when those spry, toned babies had come over to our apartment in Brooklyn Heights, and Felix had slumped in my lap, an unresponsive lump. The shame that had risen up in me. The embarrassment that I could be ashamed of a baby for something completely out of his control. The pride that held me together afterward had been of a brittle sort: Felix is fine. Don't pity him. Don't pity me. Go away.

But now in Felix's third year, somehow and quite wonderfully, this brittleness gave way, or returned, to that softer, sweeter feeling that Jason and I had known when Felix was a smiling four-month old: Look at our boy. Isn't he fine? We found this pride, this simple, duckish pride interesting because it had little to do with Felix's accomplishments. We loved his accomplishments, but they were fleeting. There was that time on our summer vacation when he walked, supported by Jason and my hands, from the restaurant where we ate dinner to the border of the town, which must have been a good quarter of a mile away. There was the time on his walker, when he ran a third of a mile from our house to Brooklyn Hospital. There was the time when I lifted him out of the bath and he said, "I love daddy." The three-month stretch when he sang out "Eeee-liiiii-zaaaah" for no particular reason except, presumably, that he liked the sound of my name. All amazing achievements. All one-time feats. He could not usually walk more than a block or so on his walker. He has not, to my knowledge, said "Eelee-liiii-zaaaah" in the past eight years. His seeming inability to build upon his accomplishments, to repeat them, and progress along conventional lines had once caused us pain. They no longer did. We had learned to admire the determination and creativity that lay below these accomplishments. He might lose what he could do now, but he would come up with new tricks that would delight both him and us. This is what we were proud of, this energetic, undaunted spirit.

And perhaps also there was a tendril of pride that stemmed straight from his difference. His strange relationship with language, for instance, his essentially nonverbal nature, which I had once found terrifyingly bleak, now seemed more interesting than terrible. Because of him, I was beginning to see how much of human communication occurs outside of language, before language. I saw that hunger pales the skin and makes it look as if it is sucking in on itself. I saw desirous fingers, resentful nostrils, unforgiving jaws. I was continuously reminded, in a visceral way, of the clunky after-the-factness of words, the way that we use them, sometimes beautifully, often redundantly, to explain or justify our experience. The way that they so often mislead us. There were times when I thought, almost smugly, that our extended nonverbal communication with Felix was taking us places where language never could, that we were exploring new worlds, enlarging our consciousness.

I had started to make friends in the neighborhood who had boys Felix's age: cute mischievous boys, who said funny things and whizzed around on scooters. Sometimes, after hanging out with them, I'd go home, secretly pleased that Felix was the way he was. Enigmatic, gleeful, not hitting other kids with sticks, not stealing their toys. I loved that he could wipe away my crankiest mood with a smile. I loved how his laughter traveled, infecting passersby on the streets, restaurants, buses. I loved how he left me so perplexed so much of the time. I remember watching him standing by the back door, supported by his walker. A cool light came in through the window, illuminating his face, which at that moment was pale and thoughtful. His hand was on the doorknob. He was into doorknobs in those days. He may have been opening and closing the door. He may have been fondling the doorknob. In any case he was absorbed and I was absorbed watching him, wondering what he was thinking, and how he was thinking. If he did not think in words, how did his thoughts form? Were they mathematical, pattern making, musical? Music he responded to immediately; it was as dear to him as the wind on his face.

Maya Angelou famously said, "I've learned that people will forget what you said, people will forget what you did, but people will never forget how you made them feel." I was beginning to realize that Felix had a genius for making people feel. His ability to intrigue, attract, encourage, and trouble went well beyond our little family. He had become famous in the neighborhood. He was welcomed as a VIP at Rice, the restaurant on our corner that served deep fried spinach rice balls, which he loved to smush and scatter on to the floor. Strangers would stop me on the street to ask if I was Felix's mom. They would tell me that they saw him in the park with Anna, laughing in a swing, or watching Anna as she sang, and how happy it made them. They would pause, their eyes shining, like they wanted to say more, but didn't have the words.

The Downside of Body Language

In the summer of 2006, midway through my pregnancy with Miranda, I got a call from Felix's preschool. Mina, his speech therapist, who had been working with him for the better part of a year, wanted me to come in for a conference with her and his special ed teacher, Marie. When I arrived, Mina, with a rather disconcerting intensity, asked how Felix was doing at home. I said fine. She looked like she wanted more. I fished around, trying to think of something that would be of interest to one of her profession. I had already told her, on another occasion, about the "I love dada" sentence, and there were no new words to report.

"Well . . ." I said at length, "I'm trying to teach Felix the concept of "inside voice" and "outside voice." Felix's happiness was marvelous, but loud. Doing things like taking him to Rice for spinach balls could lead to eruptions of ground-shaking glee. I often thought of him as my punk rock soul, still with me in these days of graying hair and modest skirts, just in another body. I loved his exuberance and disregard for convention, but there were times when a little quiet, a little modulation would be good. But how could I teach him this? How to teach a boy who does not imitate and does not follow directions?

Mina and Marie exchanged baffled looks.

"Inside voice? Outside voice?" Mina repeated. "I wish we were having that problem. We don't hear any voice here. He won't make a sound." She dated his silence from an adenoidectomy he had had in the spring. She had speculated that maybe he had had a bad reaction to the anesthesia. "You really haven't seen any change in his behavior?"

I shook my head in bewilderment.

Words spilled out of Mina and Marie's mouths. The Felix that they had seen this summer was a totally different character than the friendly little boy they had known in the fall and spring. He was retracted into himself, uninterested in his therapy sessions, and steeped in a mood best described as "pissy."

My Felix? Pissy? The idea was so contrary to his nature at home that I could only stare at the women. They sat side by side, in the diminutive seats they have at preschools, leaning toward me, their faces earnest and concerned.

"Perhaps," Mina suggested, "you should have him checked for absence seizures." She and Marie had observed that at times Felix blanked out. For several seconds, once half a minute, he had stared ahead and not responded to stimuli. Perhaps these blank outs were absence seizures, also known as petit mal seizures. Such seizures can go unremarked as those affected by them are not aware of experiencing them. From the outside, they simply look like episodes of staring. They are not dangerous. However, if they occur frequently (it is possible to get hundreds of such seizures a day), concentration and learning become almost impossible, as the person afflicted is continuously flickering in and out of consciousness. Absence seizures could, therefore, explain Felix's difficulty in acquiring language and participating to the best of his abilities in school.

"Your neurologist could find out if he's getting them," Mina suggested. "You can see them on an EEG."

I stammered a thank you. I had been warned that Felix might start developing seizures. Kids with low white matter often get them around three to four years of age, but we had noticed nothing strange at home. Yes, he zoned out sometimes, but he always had, and Jason and I zone out sometimes, too. The women kept talking, emitting unsettling waves of sympathy. My throat twisted up. I wanted them to adjourn the meeting. They would not stop talking. I stood and said I would go to the neurologist and apologized for Felix's behavior. "Don't apologize," they said in unison, standing to usher me out.

I made it to the car relatively intact, got into the driver's seat, and collapsed. What followed was one of those fits of crying so intense that they remove themselves from the ordinary flow of life. They do not feel like reactions. They feel like shearing, scarring events in themselves. I can remember crying like that only three other times: when I learned that Jason the First was missing in South America, when I ended an affair with a man I was passionately in love with, and on 9/11 when I realized that I might never see Jason the Second again. But I had not broken up with anyone or lost my beloved. Felix was OK. Even if he had absence seizures, and I doubted that he did, he was basically OK. I gulped in draughts of air, trying to stabilize myself, only to collapse again. The thought that kept throwing me back into chaos was that I hadn't had a clue about Felix's unhappiness. He was usually so happy when I took him off the bus, his face glowing with excitement, his body squirmy with affection. I wanted so much to be able to hear his side of the story. To be able to ask him about school, to have him be able to answer.

I knew that even if he had been able to speak, he might not have been able to express what was wrong. I had hated school when I was a kid, and although as an adult I can enumerate many reasons for this, I couldn't at the time. I remembered my mother, an enthusiastic student in her day, standing in the kitchen door, wincing in incomprehension as I blew off the entire educational system as an exercise in stupidity. Still. I wanted to hear what Felix's explanation would have been. I wanted a wedge into his mind, a clue, however fragmentary, into his experience.

All of a sudden, his body language, which I had relied on, which I had treasured, was useless. It could not speak in the past tense. It could not relate details, thoughts, impressions. His speechlessness, which I had before viewed as a mystery, a puzzle, a frustration, reared up as something far more cruel: a barrier that separated him from everybody, including me. What if something awful happened to him? He wouldn't be able to tell me, or anyone. He would be trapped in an isolation we were helpless to penetrate.

He already was.

Over the following weeks, Jason and I studied Felix's every look and gesture, searching for clues as to his state of mind. We fished through our own memories of school, trying to explain his experience through ours. To no one's surprise, my spoken queries: "Felix, are you bored at school? Do you want to stay home?" were met with no outward signs of comprehension, merely a friendly face, gazing at me.

I remembered Todd, a friend of a friend who was studying music therapy. Music therapy sometimes helps people with aphasia. I hired him to come to our house and see what he could do. On the first day, when Todd took out his guitar and strummed a chord, Felix's face lit up and he burst into a wonderful peal of laughter. At the end of the session, Felix looked at me as if to say, finally, you bring me someone who can talk my language. For the next year, Todd visited about once a week, toting guitar, tripod, and video camera. The sessions were taped so that Todd could review Felix's expressions and determine the techniques that generated the best responses. As much of music therapy has to do with relationship building, I was not supposed to be present during these sessions, which suited me fine, as I was always looking for time to write. My office bordered the hall where Todd worked with Felix; it became a particularly cherished half hour, stretching and playing with my words, while Todd and Felix constructed a musical language of their own.

If only schools were conducted in song, I thought, then Felix might listen.

In August, Jason helped to check Felix and me into the NYU Pediatric Epilepsy Ward. We had decided to go ahead with the EEG although both of us suspected that rather than having seizures, Felix was zoning out at school because he couldn't follow what was going on. The class was a special ed class, but his classmates were far better equipped to deal with the world than he. They could walk. They could talk. They could sit in a circle, listening to the teacher, sometimes acquiescing to do as she said. What would it be like to be Felix in that situation? Awash in noise that made little sense, unable to rip the Velcro stripped picture of the sun from the felt board and put it in the weather box, or get up and hide in the corner to show his discontent. He had neither the words nor the muscular contractions to do any of it.

Jason and I, pleading and cajoling, held Felix while an attendant tried to glue a sensor to his scalp. Felix did have the muscular contractions to dodge, scream, struggle. Jason and I gripped him, paid attention to our breath, pretended to be calm. The attendant finally got a sensor on. "Only 35 more to go." As interminable as the procedure seemed, it did eventually end. Each sensor was then attached to a long electric wire that hooked up to a portable EEG machine. The EEG machine was then stowed in a backpack that could be hung from Felix's walker or his bed. The wires, loose enough to enable movement, hung down like thick cords of hair, giving Felix a vaguely Rastafarian air. He shook his head from side to side, no longer miserable, a white kid with multicolored electronic dreads. Jason helped us into our room and kissed us goodbye.

Our roommates were another mom and son. She was on her phone in sweats (you learn to pack sweats when you spend a lot of time in the hospital) and her son was in pajamas, reading a book, the same sorts of EEG wires as Felix's glued to his scalp.

As we settled diaper bags and applesauce on our side, their quietness made me feel preemptively guilty, aware of the chaos likely to break out in the middle of the night. Sure enough, Felix woke up around two. I moved from the armchair and squeezed myself into his bed, which was difficult as my pregnancy had reached the seven-month mark. I was hoping that by cuddling with him I could keep him quiet. But he was in one of his great, euphoric moods. He hooted. He whooped. He clutched me with amorous conviction. He got up on his knees and twisted his torso to and fro, whipping the wires that sprang from his head, giggling maniacally. By four thirty, he had reached such heights of hilarity that he set off the EEG monitor and a couple of night observers rushed in to see if he was all right. "Oh, he's fine," I said. "He does this all the time." I realized that I was, if not bragging, then pleased that his sleeplessness had been scientifically established.

Around 7:30 a.m., Felix finally closed his eyes. I watched enviously as he slept through the parade of doctors, the clipboards and questions, the aides coming in with breakfast trays. The head doctor told me that they had not seen any epileptic seizures, but the EEG readout showed irregular activity at night. She wanted to keep us in the hospital a night or two longer for further observation. I nodded, too crushed to speak. I hated hospitals. I wanted to be home with Jason, swapping off night shifts, with at least the potential of sleeping in a real bed. The curtain drew back, and there were our roommates, dressed and combed. "Good morning," said the mother.

"Good morning," I said. "I'm sorry about last night."

She smiled, shrugging. "I didn't hear a thing."

"They're going to keep us here another couple nights." My voice broke.

"We've been here for four weeks." She wasn't trying to one up me. She was patient, calm. Her son's epilepsy had gotten worse and his doctors could not prescribe a new medication until they had observed what the new seizures looked like. The new seizures however were playing hide and seek. They would not discharge the mother and son until they captured one on their recording devices. "What can you do?" she said simply. She had five other children at home and a job that she was in danger of losing.

Felix and I were released three days later with a prescription for Trileptal. This was an antiseizure medication that the lead doctor thought might regularize Felix's EEG readouts, and in the process, help him to retain language. Though the language retention did not happen, and later EEG readouts remained irregular, Jason and I loved the Trileptal. For six months, after taking a teaspoon of the stuff (it tasted like melted vanilla ice cream), Felix fell asleep at a reasonable hour and remained asleep throughout the night. Every night! The effect would eventually wear off, but those six months seemed like a gift from the gods.

A Bigger World

Around four in the morning on November 18, 2006, I awoke. Miranda was coming. I woke Jason and we entered that intense spell when all you seem to be doing is counting the intervals between the internal stabs and clutches known as labor. At some point we realized that we had to take a picture. We had tons of pictures of me pregnant with Felix, but had forgotten to document the particular bump caused by Miranda. So now I have this image of me, standing erect in between spasms, in front of my bookshelves. My belly is straining through an old white satin nightie, and I'm looking at Jason, with an urgent, do-it-now-before-I-double-over-again expression. My friend Diane took a taxi over from the Lower East Side in order to look after Felix, and Jason and I headed to Long Island University Hospital. The sun was just rising. It felt like all the world was just the two of us, speeding down Atlantic Avenue, wondering how it would go this time.

In a word, it went loudly. It would have been a quieter delivery if the doctors had given me an epidural, but according to my dilations, and their calculations, the baby could be entering the birth canal at any minute. This meant no pain relief, as I had to be alert to push. I was assigned a remarkable nurse named Noreen, who managed to coach me through breathing techniques better than anyone else has ever been able to. It wasn't so much that she explained what to do, it was more that she emanated a calmness that made her directions possible. When she held my shoulder and murmured to exhale a little more gently, I found that I could. But the moment she left the room, for she had other patients to attend to, my pain became so unbearable that I was back to howling like a mad wolf. Poor Jason tried his best to emulate Noreen, but he only enraged me more. I bit him. Hard. He showed me the tooth marks afterward. Right before noon, however, all that pain, effort, and tamped-down worry lifted. Miranda entered the world. A beautiful, full-term baby girl with a dark fringe of hair, a pink face, and a lovely firmness to her muscles.

The next morning, Anna and Felix visited, Felix in a striped sweater and combed hair, emanating a cleanliness that he only seemed to attain when Anna was attending to him. I was desperate to see him, worried that he might have been feeling abandoned. I had been joking with my friends over how atrocious the whole second child business could be to the first. Imagine a wife whose husband comes home one day with a huge grin across his face. Darling, you know I love you very much, but I also love this other lady, Priscilla. I've invited her to come live with us. You guys can keep each other company. But Felix did not seem to have minded my temporary absence. His face lit up when he saw me, and we hugged. He didn't seem interested in the baby, but the hospital room caught his attention, and he was soon scooting around on his walker, investigating. He didn't seem unduly upset when it was time for him to go. He was stable.

I, on the other hand, was not.

Perhaps it was hormones. Perhaps it was lack of sleep or plain old worry. First I was worried because Miranda wouldn't poo, and the doctors had discharged me from the hospital under stern orders to bring her back if she didn't poo within four days. Jason and Anna and soon my mother, flown in from California, did most of the Felix duties while I tried to get Miranda's intestinal tract working. My main tactic was singing, off tune, but with feeling: Miranda, on the veranda, my little panda; Poo! Poo! Poo! It worked. On the fourth day, a little smear colored her diaper and we rejoiced. But soon I was fretting about her feeding and her weight and a million other things. I remember bawling in the guest bed, Miranda asleep beside me, certain that Jason didn't love me anymore and that my mother was trying to poison me by putting sweetened yogurt on my chili.

My moods had settled down by the new year. I started keeping a notebook for Miranda to read when she got older. It began with this entry:

January 3, 2009.

You have weathered jaundice, bleeding nipples (not yours, mine—you my poor dear, had your moment as a vampire baby, pulling away from my right breast, your mouth red, drops of blood dribbling down your chin. I'm happy to say that we are well past that—you are a happy and enthusiastic feeder, your father calls you the lamprey, but enough with this overlong parens). As I was saying, you have weathered your fair share of viruses—an abnormally warm fall and winter has gotten the whole city sniffling, hacking, vomiting. Our house has not yet hosted the stomach bug, but the way things are going, we are sure to. The most dramatic thing you've gotten was RSV, which came as an unsettling wheeze the midnight after Christmas, and entailed an overnight at the hospital, a chest X-ray to make sure that you didn't have pneumonia, and the use of your brother's nebulizer.

But enough of sicknesses.

You are not sickly. You are a toughie, as my mother put it, batting them off. Right now you are lying on the living room floor, making sweet noises—"eh, ah, eh" at a plastic batting machine (Felix's) that seems to entrance you. You are zipped into a ridiculous pink velour bag, one of the dozens of pink gifts you've been presented with—in the optimistic hope that you might be on the verge of sleep, it being 11 p.m., and me being sleepy. But indeed you look more animated than you have been all day, cheerfully batting your arms about and kicking your legs and panting and ahhing. It is intoxicating watching you. If you have babies, you'll understand this mad flood of love and admiration. Everything you do is sublime.

Your first real smile happened a few days ago, last Friday I think, the day before you were officially six weeks old. A hilarious, full-mouthed, slightly lopsided smile that had an element of conspiracy to it—like you were somehow winking at me, besides giving me this wonderfully joyous thing. Your father finally saw it, your smile that is, in its full glory yesterday, an event that prompted him to get after me to start this book to record these marvels.

Around this time, I remember dressing Miranda on the diaper table in Felix's room, a hand me down from Ikea, a rickety old thing that hinted at collapse but never quite did. The radiators were cozily sputtering, and she was sweet smelling and warm from her bath. I was getting her into a cotton jersey, and as I pulled her fingers through the sleeve, I was struck by a memory of my own hand as a child, emerging from a cuff. Pulling at her hand felt as if I were pulling at mine. I'd never had this myself-doubled experience with Felix. It's possible that this is because Felix is a boy. But I have often identified with boys. More likely it was the shape of Miranda's fingers, long and strong, and their tone, the way that they moved, stretching out, already exploring on their own.

In some ways, Miranda was like another first child. Our astonishment at typical baby development was brand new. We would watch in delight and quite a bit of relief as she rolled around on her plump bottom, batting at stuffed elephants and shiny butterflies that hung from a plastic hooped baby gym I'd bought in a fit of baby product glee. She liked toys! We loved that she liked toys, that she grabbed onto necklaces and napkins with an iron grip, that she breastfed, that she pulled herself to stand, that she would eventually prefer a three-legged crabwalk to a crawl, as my mother's sister Molly had also done.

By this time, Felix had developed an appreciation of toys, too, at least those that dangled and jangled. He would grab Miranda's stuffed zebras and caterpillars, designed to stimulate the senses with shiny parts and crinkly parts, elasticated parts, floppy parts. He'd wave them around, studying their movement with rapt attention. As to what he thought of Miranda herself—that was less clear. He did not glow with brotherly pride. Nor did he glower with jealousy. He was aware of her presence and on the whole, he seemed to be OK with it. He bit her once, when I was getting dressed and left them in close proximity on my bed. But I believe this was more of an investigative procedure than an act of aggression. Felix did a lot of investigating with his mouth. He was continuously tasting the playground equipment and licking the subway poles.

What with Miranda's naps and nursing, and Felix's accumulation of mobility gear, it took Jason and I months before we figured out how to take them both out of the house at the same time. It was on one of our first neighborhood ventures with both children that I met Jamila. Jamila worked at Choice, a cafe we frequented as it had spectacularly good French fries (Felix's favorite food), only one step to navigate, and was close to Underhill Playground. Underhill Playground was important because it had a disability swing. Felix was now too big for the baby bucket swings. He could balance on the regular playground swings, but it was hard work and we couldn't swing him that high for fear that he'd fall off. On the disability swing, a wide sheath of molded plastic with straps to contain him, we could swing him as rambunctiously as he wanted. He loved it. He'd wheel his walker over to it and yell angrily if other kids were playing on it. He was not yelling because the other kids showed no outward sign of disability. He was yelling because turn-taking and waiting in line were not concepts that he grasped. Or if he did grasp them, he did not like them, and voiced his discontent with all his soul.

On the day that we met, Jamila was working the register. As I waited for the French fries, she cooed over Miranda, hanging from my chest in the Babybjörn. She remembered how tiny her son had been when she first put him in the Babybjörn. Too small, really, she said with a laugh. She had been so desperate to get out of the house. She gazed at Felix, who sat at the common table with Jason, his mouth open with desire, his hands reaching toward other people's food. How old was he? He just turned four, I said. Jamila's son was five. Maybe they could have a play date? I wanted to say yes, but I felt that I should warn her that "play date" was not an accurate description. Felix would play with adults. That is, if they swung him, tickled him, played music for him, he would whoop with happiness. Children, on the other hand, made little impression on him. We were hoping that as Miranda got older, they would become friends and she'd be able to awaken in him an ability to play with other kids. For now, he mainly seemed to acknowledge other kids when they were taking his spot on the disability swing.

That's all right, Jamila laughed. Bashir is special needs, too.

They came over on a spring day, Jamila looking fabulously unmotherly in a seventies-era dress and heels. Felix lay on the floor as Bashir, tall and skinny, a nonstop runner, ricocheted around him. They both seemed to be enjoying themselves. Bashir didn't talk,

either. Just as I had, Jamila had tried communication tools like pictures and signs and hadn't found them very effective. Their primary
means of communication was familiar: the telepathy and body
language that develop when words are not useful. Jamila cuddled
Miranda and admired me for having two. I admired her for taking
care of Bashir alone. Bashir's father was a musician who was often
on the road. Though he cared for his son and helped with child support, Jamila had no one at two in the morning, and Bashir's sleep
habits were as erratic as Felix's. I could not imagine pulling off those
nights alone. I relied on Jason taking the 2 a.m. to 4 a.m. shift. Now
that I was nursing Miranda, he often took on more than that, sometimes going an entire night without sleep, with no hope for recoup-
ing on the weekends. I didn't ask him to do this. Felix did. He had
only to peep and Jason would jump. The connection between them,
which had been so strong from the start, had grown even stronger.

Jamila admitted that one time, she needed rest so badly that she
checked Bashir in to the pediatric psychiatric ward of St. Vincent's
and herself into the regular hospital. Anyone who has spent a night
in a New York City hospital knows that they are not conducive to
sleep, with lights continually flicking on and off, nurses coming
in to check your vitals every three hours and people fighting and
shouting and laughing in the halls. But when you are that tired,
they can seem like a luxury hotel, and they cost even more. It was
an expensive nap, and Jamila did not feel good about it. But she did
not know what else to do.

The boys got restless. I suggested the backyard, where there was
more room for Bashir to run, and fresh air for Felix, who almost
always enjoyed the breeze on his face. There was also a large, three-
tier fountain, which Bashir promptly jumped into, jeans and all.
"No, Bashir!" Jamila yelled as he tried to climb onto the narrower,
not as sturdy, second tier. She kicked off her heels and climbed into

the cold water after him. That was seven years ago, but I can still see her, in her long yellow dress, with her slim arms, grappling with Bashir. Partly this is because Jamila is a remarkably beautiful woman and the sun was shining down on her, but even without her looks, I imagine the scene would have remained etched in my mind. It was in that moment that I understood that I had made a friend whose child was as disabled as Felix, and who needed a level of care that could be even more intense.

Bashir could toilet himself, dress himself, eat without assistance, but his mind was as unpredictable, mysterious, and inconsistently accessible as Felix's. He had to be blocked from climbing out the window, running in front of cars, turning on the stove. The physical toll of blocking him from these things was surely as exhausting as the shifting, feeding, wiping, dressing, transitioning, hoisting, stretching, and exercising of Felix. His looks, too, created difficulties for Jamila that I did not have to face. He looked like an ordinary boy. Had he climbed into the fountain in front of the historic Borough Hall building in downtown Brooklyn, Jamila would not only have had to get him out, she would have to do this while passersby clucked at her parenting skills and yelled suggestions as to how she might do better. Because any sighted person could see that Felix's body was different, he and I were judged differently. When he grabbed French fries off a stranger's plate, licked the subway pole, or bellowed at the child on the disability swing, his behavior was attributed to his disability, not my parenting. Indeed, I was often told by people who barely knew me that I was a "good mother" because they happened to have caught me tousling Felix's hair or helping him to walk.

The other thing about that scene in the fountain was Jamila's smile. It was not a saintly smile. Her feet were cold and she was trying to get Bashir out of there without hurting him or herself or the fountain of her newly made friend. But she was also aware that fountains are there to be climbed into, especially on an early spring day, after a winter spent indoors. How could she not get a kick out of her son, showing off his love of climbing, adventure, mischief? She was proud of him. I recognized this pride. It felt similar to the pride I had for Felix, a pride distinctly different from the pride I had in Miranda, who was turning into an achiever.

Here's a portrait of her, from that notebook Jason had gotten me to keep:

> You are almost seven months old, an expert sitter and banger on
> whatever you can get your hands on. You are extremely sociable,
> more so, I think, than either Jason or I, and I am sometimes almost
> jealous of the way you fearlessly engage everyone in the vicinity
> with your friendly eyes. When you particularly like someone—
> for example, Kevin, the dreadlocked house painter who is doing
> a masterful job on our stairway—you lock eyes with him and
> stick out your tongue and wiggle it. When he laughs and comes
> closer, you burrow into me, pretending to be shy. You like having
> conversations that consist of humming. You love being tickled
> and flying through the air. I lie down and zoom you about with my
> upstretched arms and you giggle and giggle. It is a joy for Jason
> and me to watch you explore and experiment with whatever is at
> hand—my boxing wraps, a colander, your lamby—apparently your
> favorite stuffed animal. It is almost like being new parents—all
> this typical baby behavior is new for us . . . at seven months you
> already can do things that Felix can't—get the spoon into your
> mouth with the food still on it, for instance. And you love to do this.
> You bat the spoon out of my hand when I try to feed you. You and
> Felix don't interact much. Occasionally, you pull his hair and he
> paws at your face, and then I pull you apart, and that's that.

The Warped Synthesizer

Felix's preschool called. This was a new school. His former preschool, that of Mina and Marie and the pissy moods, had not asked him back. Much of the previous spring had revolved around faxing forms back and forth and meeting with social workers and officials from Felix's new bureaucratic overlords at the NYC Department of Education, the Committee on Preschool Special Education (CPSE). After Miranda and I had visited the handful of therapeutic preschools that might accept Felix, I had settled on one that was designed for children with cerebral palsy.

Cerebral palsy refers to brain damage incurred in utero or immediately afterward that affects movement and control, coordination, and tone of the muscles. It does not affect cognition; many people with cerebral palsy score high on intelligence tests. I learned that Felix had cerebral palsy inadvertently, in Dr. Pytlak's office. She was filling out a form on Felix's behalf, thinking out loud. Cerebral palsy might be good, she said. There had been a lot of advocacy centered around cerebral palsy; as a result, Felix might get better services than if he were diagnosed simply with periventricular leukomalacia. "You mean he has cerebral palsy?" I asked. Sure, she said, as if surprised that I hadn't figured that out.

I had had high hopes for the cerebral palsy preschool after having observed the class to which Felix would be assigned. The children did not have to sit at desks, which Felix could barely do, but were allowed to exercise their muscles by rolling, crawling, and/or otherwise propelling themselves across the carpeted floor. Presiding over this was a lovely teacher who, on the day we visited, sang a lesson to her students in a rich, warm voice that entranced Felix. I thought that Felix might identify more with these children, so many of whom, like him, were wearing leg braces. Felix's were meant to address his toe-walking. They were made out of plastic, molded specifically to each foot, shoved on over his protests and fastened with velcro each morning in the hopes of someday getting his heels to touch the ground. Some of the kids had walkers like his. Some had wheelchairs. Some could walk independently and could move quite smoothly, their palsy, perhaps, limited to a tremor. But Felix did not seem to strike up any friendships. As the school year progressed, and the teacher became aware of how little verbal skill Felix had, he was transferred into the nonverbal class. This class was conducted according to a different philosophy, if you can call it that. Hence the telephone call.

The administrator on the line was sharp voiced and angry. Felix was screaming, slapping his face, biting his hand. He had seemed so happy before. "What's wrong with him?" she demanded. My Felix, screaming? Slapping his face? And how dare she use such an accusatory tone. If Felix were slapping his face, clearly something was wrong. Why wasn't she sympathetic? I drove over there as fast as I could, which wasn't that fast, as it took some time to get Miranda ready. I found Felix strapped into a therapeutic chair (picture a dentist's chair zigzagged with buckles and belts and harnesses) his face turned up toward the pockmarked ceiling tiles, his voice hoarse from yelling, half-moons of tooth marks still visible on his hands. Five other children, less loud, were also strapped to chairs, all of them facing the ceiling. The chairs were designed to straighten out the children's spines and stretch their hips and shoulders, but they looked like torture devices.

The scene made me feel as if the school had given up on the children's minds and was just trying to fix their bodies. This was not their official policy, or course. The teacher, a thin, weary woman hammering away at the keys of a Fisher Price synthesizer, most likely wanted to reach her students' minds. Perhaps she hoped to approach them through music. But her synthesizer was warped. The notes stretched and curdled, the result of a dying battery. She sang, regardless. Her voice was high and squeaky, veering toward hysteria. I wanted to rip Felix out of that chair. How could anyone expect Felix, who loved music and movement, to be tied down and forced to listen to that? Didn't it hurt the other children's ears as well? It hurt mine, and I am no tonal snob.

I called CPSE and asked for a list of alternative schools. I did online research. Most of the schools I visited did not look much different from general education programs. The teachers were trained to be more flexible and aware that each mind learns differently, but the set up in time and space, the teacher in front, the children before her, the teacher's requests followed by the children's responses were more or less the same. Based on Felix's experience at his two previous schools, I couldn't see this setup working. I was lost until I came across a website for a school that featured a photograph of a young woman making a funny face at a boy who was lying, belly down, on a platform swing. The boy gazed back at the woman, smiling with his whole face.

That's what I wanted: a school with interesting indoor swings, young therapists, and grinning children. The schools that had these things, it turned out, were geared toward children with autism. They emphasized one-on-one learning, small groups, and tailoring education to the child, instead of tailoring the child to the school. I didn't know anything about autism except for what I'd read in the papers: alarming stories about how autistic people didn't know how to love and didn't like to be touched. As loving and snuggling were two of Felix's great attributes, I figured that he couldn't have autism. But I'd also read that autism was being overdiagnosed, and so I began the process of getting him evaluated, hoping that we could get him placed somewhere on the spectrum, and so open the doors to an education that might work for him.

Our evaluator, the kindly Dr. Wenderoff, came to our house on a weekend in May, not long after Jamila and Bashir had come over. He sat with us on our stoop, and tried to engage four-year-old Felix, who stood a few feet away, in his walker, shaking a set of keys. Jason and I answered Dr. Wenderoff's questions, which were nuanced and conversational. Miranda was in my lap, the sun shone down through the leaves, and Dr. Wenderoff's manner was such that I felt more like I was talking to an intelligent neighbor than a doctor. The informality of the interview, the doctor told me, was by design. Autistic people tend to be particularly sensitive to their environment. The doctor therefore wanted to see Felix, and us, in a place where we were comfortable. Our front stoop was perfect. At the end of this interview, Dr. Wenderoff assigned Felix four on a scale of zero to twelve, where zero was as autistic as you can get, and twelve was the "most normal" end of the autistic spectrum. Jason and I were surprised. "But he's so loving!" we said. Dr. Wenderoff explained that what tied the very wide population of autistic people together was not an inability to love, but a lack of the sort of innate social intelligence that governs things such as smiling when you are smiled at, detecting boredom and frustration in others, being aware of social hierarchies. Autistic people could become socially intelligent, but they had to learn social cues from the outside. They weren't born with this knowledge neatly stored and accessible within them.

An autism diagnosis is often devastating for parents. Many autistic children seem "normal" at birth, and thus parents feel as if autism has "taken" their child. They are torn between terror at what the future will bring, and grief at the loss of the child that they thought that they had. Jason and I, who had known for years that Felix was a most unusual character, were spared this particular torment. Indeed, I remember us laughing, perhaps in shock, after Dr. Wenderoff left. The latest Felix trick! We'd always felt sympathy for parents of autistic children, while apparently all along we'd been among them. As the diagnosis settled, though, a sadness crept in. Now we knew why Felix didn't wave to people when they waved to him, why he barely acknowledged other children, even when they said hi.

But Felix didn't have time for this sadness. He was, after all, the same adventurous, sweet-tempered four-year-old he'd been before the diagnosis. And Miranda had to be celebrated. She had started to talk. "Nose" was her first word. As you would expect, but what we were not quite prepared for: She retained "nose" even when her vocabulary grew to include "mom," "no," and "Fegit" (her word for Felix).

I began to research autism, and the more I read, the more I saw it to be an enormous grab bag of traits and uncertain knowledge. Any clear idea of how it might affect Felix faded. Indeed, the term was so fuzzy that Dr. Wells seemed annoyed that we were using it. Felix's behavior, he argued, could be explained by periventricular leukomalacia. Why bother invoking autism, also? Because it was useful. It helped us and others to understand Felix better, or at least to frame him in a way that seemed to answer questions. His irregular language processing became easier to digest. If someone asked, "Why can't he speak?" we could say, "He's autistic," and our interlocutor's mind would be put to rest. Most importantly, after a Byzantine bureaucratic odyssey, the diagnosis allowed him to get into a decent school. I later learned that the diagnosis had been expanded for precisely this reason. Steve Silberman's book *Neurotribes* charts out how parent advocates like Lorna Wing worked to widen the definition of autism. In a numbers-dominated world, the greater amount of people affected by a disease or a condition, the more likely governments and foundations are to fund research initiatives and educational and therapeutic programs designed to help them. So rather than divide "developmental delays" into discrete units characterized by particular traits, some of which would be too small to garner attention, advocates combined them into a large mass that has become known as the Autism Spectrum.

Red Tape

By this time, most of the time, I felt we had beat disability. It was a nonissue, an illusion that causes fear then recedes. The things that didn't work in Felix's body and brain were legion and real, but they hadn't ruined his life. He might not walk independently, but he could do parallel bar tricks on his walker. He might not speak, but he could laugh. He might have autism, but he was loving and affectionate. In terms of how his disabilities would affect him in the future, he would probably never have a job that made money, but that had eluded me, too. He, at least, would generate jobs for others, jobs in health care, in therapy, in research, in education. His life was intriguing and full, most of his days spent contentedly pursuing his own peculiar tricks and talents. I began to think that the crux of his disability did not reside in his mind or body, but in the world that we lived in: the stairs that blocked his stroller, the graphs and grids that labeled him this and that, the fear of difference that made certain pedestrians nervously look away.

When Felix was happy, I could forgive the varicella virus for eating away at his white matter; it was harder to make peace with the bureaucracy that fed upon his disabilities. I sometimes felt as if he were on parole, his crime his inconvenience, his bulky refusal to fit into the existing world. I had bridled against this bureaucracy early on, when Felix was six months old, and I had submitted the layers of paperwork and attended the appointments necessary to enroll him in Early Intervention (EI), a federal program that is administered through the states. But once that program began, my grumbling was replaced with gratitude. On the receiving end, EI, as it was then, was efficient, helpful, and simple. Talented, intuitive therapists visited our home, showed Felix how to get the most out of his body, taught me techniques to continue this work in their absence, and developed a caring relationship with both of us. Until Fred, Terra, and Fran came into our lives, I had not experienced this level of kindness from people I did not know well. Through them I saw how Felix's disability could open up new worlds, more compassionate and altruistic worlds than I had been aware of when immersed in writing and art. I stopped complaining about the forms and letters and not-really-necessary quarterly meetings, as I had begun to understand the reasoning behind the hoop jumping. EI's advocates had to prove that their program was working, or else budget slashers in Albany would cut their funding. The accepted way of proving this was through quantifications and goal making (goal: Felix will grab for a veggie puff 70 percent of the time; he will sit at a ninety-degree angle on a therapy ball for sixty seconds, and so on). I was excused from the brunt of this quantifying, but poor Fred's eyes were giving out as he stayed up past midnight filling out progress reports. Alas, even with these efforts, Albany would eventually gash EI's funds, more or less eviscerating the program. But that is another story, and luckily for us, it happened after Felix aged out.

• • •

After Early Intervention, the connection between the bureaucracy Felix engendered and the care that he received became more vague. I began to think of my bureaucratic duties as pots of gruel that I had to keep simmering on the stove for an unwanted guest (the parole officer). One pot contained the forms and obligations due to the NYC Department of Education (DOE); another the telephone calls and reimbursement forms for United Healthcare, the private insurance company that we were enrolled in through Jason's work; another the questionnaires and meetings at our social service agency; another the appointments and interviews necessary to obtain Felix various sorts of transportation. If I left any of these pots alone too long, they might dry out and the bottom of the pan would burn through. The house might catch on fire, though more likely the damage would be contained to the ear-splitting shriek of the fire alarm and fire trucks surrounding the house, all-a-frenzy for a kitchen full of smoke.

. . .

The swirl of acronyms, forms, telephone calls, appointments, interviews, lawyers, and paper trails involved in transferring Felix out of the preschool that strapped him into the chair a la *Clockwork Orange* provides an illustration. After talking with an official at the NYC DOE's Center for Preschool Special Education (CPSE), I faxed CPSE Dr. Wenderoff's evaluation, establishing that Felix was autistic as well as physically disabled. As it was agreed that the school for cerebral palsy could not handle both of his disabilities, CPSE sent me a list of new schools to investigate. Most of these schools were housed in buildings that did not have wheelchair ramps or elevators. This didn't bother me as Felix was still light enough to pick up, but the admissions officers would take a look at Felix's braced feet, his pediatric stroller, his walker, and collectively shake their apologetic heads. One school, named after a saint, and located on a ground floor, agreed to do an intake interview with him. Afterward, the admissions official met me in the hall. "He didn't do a thing I asked," she said. "He doesn't respond to verbal directions," I explained. She seemed both offended and puzzled. Apparently that school's children with autism were those who liked directions. Only one of the admissions officers at the schools on the CPSE list appreciated Felix's spirit, but she said that they could not consider his application as he did not have an IFSP (individual family service plan). An IFSP? I'd vaguely heard of an IFSP—I believed I'd even signed my name to one, but maybe that was an ISP (individual support plan)? How could anyone keep these forms straight and why in the world were they necessary? "How do I go about getting an IFSP?" I asked the woman. She shook her head sadly. It was too late. No IFSP could be generated without the DOE, and the DOE was closed for summer break.

I looked into other schools, not on the CPSE list, hoping that they would not ask me about this IFSP business. But Felix's physical disability, his inability to use the toilet, his lack of language, and his imperviousness to directions cut out all but one, the Rebecca School in midtown Manhattan. As it turned out, the Rebecca School was the school that had first sparked my interest in getting Felix diagnosed for autism. It was their website that featured the grinning boy on the carpeted swing. On the tour, I learned that the Rebecca School followed the Floortime method of instruction, a method well suited to Felix as it emphasized relationship building and following the child's lead. The students spanned in age from four to twenty, which meant that if Felix got in at preschool, he could stay on, instead of having to be switched to a new elementary school—where would I ever find one?—the following year. The classrooms were comfy, with carpets and beanbags; the teachers and aides were young and encouraging; there was a padded sensory gym, with an array of carpeted and foam-covered swings, where Felix could get occupational and physical therapy. There was even a music therapist, a respectable one, who had studied the Nordoff

Robbins method and played a tuned piano. The admissions officer and the director enthused over Felix. They were not bothered
that he could only walk with a walker and was not toilet trained.
Directions? Language? Pah! This was a school for kids who had no
other place to go. They would work with him.

We applied. Felix was accepted. Jason and I should have been
elated. But our relief was weighted with dread. Up until that point,
we had been innocent of how the schools that Felix had attended
were funded. Felix's first school and the cerebral palsy preschool
were privately run, but they were state-approved, which meant
that the government paid the tuition directly. This arrangement
had been worked out in the aftermath of the Individuals with
Disabilities Education Act (IDEA), a federal law first passed in
1975 as the Education for All Handicapped Children Act. IDEA
was a major piece of civil rights legislation that established that children with disabilities should not be warehoused in institutions or
confined in their homes. Instead, they should be integrated into the
larger society through the public school system. Thus, since 1975,
children with disabilities have been entitled to a free and appropriate public education (a laudable entitlement often reduced to the
acronym FAPE). As the public schools cannot always provide the
necessary support and educational environment for every child
with every sort of disability, the government will pay for private
schools that can.

The Rebecca School was not on the list of schools approved by
the state. While this freed up teachers and therapists to be more
creative and independent in their work, it also meant that the DOE
did not have a financial arrangement with the school. To obtain the
funds for tuition, parents had to sue the DOE and demonstrate that
the public schools could not provide an appropriate education for
their children. If they were successful, the DOE would pay all or

some of the Rebecca School's tuition. A new suit had to be lodged for each year the child attended. I would have liked to have paid the bill privately. Our lives were hectic enough without having to sue the DOE every year, and Jason made good money. But the Rebecca School cost $80,000. A year. And that was in 2007. It costs more now.

Because Felix's earlier schools were approved privates, I had not thought about their costs. I had simply signed the forms, and Felix went. Their tuitions must have been steep, too, though not as high as the Rebecca School. The Rebecca School's mind-boggling tuition was a product of Manhattan real estate prices and the one-to-one or one-to-two staff to student ratios designed to engage an entire school populated by children who could not follow group instruction. The Autism Charter School, which was DOE-approved and saved money by being housed in a public school building, still cost an average of $65,000 per student. Meaningful education for children with autism is expensive, but the money is well spent. The benefit is not only limited to the child and the child's family. Aides, teachers, and therapists get jobs, jobs that—given the right sort of environment and administration—are intellectually stimulating and emotionally rewarding. In a better world, this kind of intensive education would be even more expensive, and the aides would be paid a living wage.

There were two ways to sue the DOE. Parents with modest household incomes could sue for direct tuition payment. Parents with immodest household incomes had to come up with $80,000 to pay to the Rebecca School, then sue the DOE for reimbursement. All parents, regardless of income, had to hire a lawyer or find a good pro bono one. We hired a lawyer. These lawsuits did not delve into the wisdom of trying to make a nonverbal child sit quietly through lessons that he could not understand. They did not consider how

Applied Behavioral Analysis (ABA), the prevalent means of training and treating children with autism, would work with children
like Felix who were also hampered by significant physical disabilities. They focused on bureaucracy. We were advised to keep track
of each letter we received from the DOE and to make copies of
the envelopes, as the DOE sometimes sent letters out long after
they had been written, lapses that could be used against them in
court. We successfully settled our first suit because of that IFSP that
DOE's CPSE had neglected to initiate.

. . .

Rebecca School's funding strategy was clearly tilted in favor of
the wealthy, and so when Felix started attending the school, I was
moved to see how few of his classmates came from money. It was a
testament to the passion of their parents, all of whom had fought
enormous bureaucratic battles to get their children to a place where
they might learn and grow. The place itself was warm and friendly,
the antithesis of all the legal jockeying it took to get there. When we
pushed Felix's stroller through the glass doors of the building, we'd
be met with a cheerful chorus of "Hi Felix's." Everyone knew his
name, the janitors, the receptionists, the staff of other classrooms.
There were six other children in his class—the bubble room, conve-
niently located on the first floor—all of whom could walk, and many
of whom could talk. But they were more like Felix than the children
in the other schools he'd attended. Something about the brightness
of their eyes and the unguardedness of their movements struck
me as familiar. Felix fit right in. When we went to parent-teacher
conferences, the Felix the teachers and therapists described was the
Felix I knew at home. He was not pissy. He was not screaming and
biting his hand. There was none of the disconnect I'd felt when he
was at his previous schools.

But we did not want to keep suing the DOE year after year. I kept looking for a public school program or a state-approved private that might work. I found only one. The Autism Charter School did not offer the physical, occupational, and speech therapies that Felix needed, but their instruction was one-on-one and their teachers were young, with the right sort of energy, conviction, and flexibility. I applied, figuring we could schedule Felix's therapies after school. Admissions were determined through a lottery, as hundreds of other children also needed a spot. Our number did not come up. Jason and I resigned ourselves to annual swamps of litigation.

To keep Felix at the Rebecca School, Jason and I would annually meet with officials from the DOE's Committee for Special Education (CSE) in order to hash out an Individualized Education Plan (IEP) for Felix. In theory, the purpose of these meetings, held in cheerless conference rooms at the DOE offices on Seventh Avenue, was to convene a team of experts and family members to collaborate on an educational strategy specifically geared toward Felix's abilities and disabilities. The CSE's side of the IEP team consisted of a DOE special ed teacher, a school psychiatrist, and a parent representative, the latter being a mysterious participant who sat in a chair and nodded hello or sometimes just gruffly sat there. However opaque her function might be, her presence was noted, for if she were not there, as she sometimes was not, we could use this lapse in protocol in our lawsuit. Felix's side of the IEP team was Jason and me, a social worker from the Rebecca School, and—via phone—Felix's Rebecca School teachers and therapists. Felix was not present at these meetings, and so few people on the CSE side of his IEP team ever met him face to face. Together, we would carve out goals for him, determine how much therapy he could realistically be allotted, as well as special supports, such as a one-on-one aide to help with his transitions and diapering. A thick document would emerge, ten or twelve pages filled with goals, quantifications, recommended student-to-teacher ratios, and so on.

The Rebecca School, being a nonapproved private, did not have to follow Felix's IEP. Nor did it. His Rebecca School team fashioned their own program based on their pedagogy. But we had to create this IEP so Jason and I could demonstrate that we would send Felix to a public school if a public school existed that could provide Felix with the sort of education that his IEP laid out.

Several months after the IEP meeting, we would receive a letter from the DOE with the name and address of the public school deemed appropriate for Felix. I would then visit this school. Most years, it was on the fourth floor of a Fort Greene public school with no elevator, although sometimes it was on the second floor of a Coney Island school with a broken elevator. As it was against DOE regulations for aides to carry him up the stairs or onto a school bus, he was physically barred from these buildings. Jason and I do not know if one of our CSE IEP team members kindly intervened to garner us these placements. Or if it was simply the bungling of bureaucracy. The CSE IEP members denied that they had anything to do with it. But then they had to, rather than admit to tangling in the affairs of a different department.

Our lawyer would write up the requisite letter pointing out the difficulty of getting Felix's wheelchair up four flights of stairs. There would be a hearing. Faulty DOE procedure would be established. We would usually settle. The DOE would usually pay a great chunk of the tuition, and we would pay the rest. And so it would go, year after year, the outsized Rebecca School tuition further ballooning with legal fees that both we and the state incurred. A wise use of money? We didn't feel that we had a choice. Apparently the state didn't either.

Over time, I grew fond of the CSE special education teacher and psychologist most often assigned to Felix's IEP team, and the meetings took on a homey feel. The document we were dusting off and renewing each year was a formality, a legal tool that allowed the DOE to show that it was complying with IDEA and allowed us to show that we were complying with the DOE. But our conversation was informal and our team's desire to help was real. That the help was strategic—that is, that a teacher and a psychologist, presumably best at directly interacting with students, were instead trying to help us figure out the most effective boxes to tick (Should Felix be classified as "autistic" or "multiply disabled?" Can we call him "nonambulatory" even though he can walk with a walker"?)—spoke to the tangle of regulations and red tape in which we were all trapped.

Other DOE requirements arrived out of the blue. When Felix was five, for instance, I opened an envelope to learn that he had to be evaluated by a psychiatrist the following week at an obscure address in Queens. To blow off the request would be to give the DOE ammunition in our tuition battle. So I took Felix out of school, drove an hour and a half to a residential nook of Queens, and arrived at a house with a basement office—the sort of place that Felix would not be able to get into were I not physically fit. I carried him down a flight of steep steps, and asked the evaluator to look after him while I retrieved his walker and stroller. She declined. It was not her responsibility.

We sat on either side of a card table while Felix sat in the next room, half-heartedly pawing at a Fisher Price phone. Does Felix play with blocks? Does he toilet himself? Does he know A) 0 words, B) between 1–25 words C) between 25–100 words D) between 100–250 words E) over 250 words? I was so sick of these questions. This last one in particular bugged me. Felix's phrase of the moment was: "Whassup" which we interpreted at "What's up?"

Did this count as one word or two? Did he still remember the words he had spoken earlier in his life? I could remember some, but not all: Eliza, Allan, sky, gate, water, I love daddy, all the animal sounds of Old MacDonald, book, kiss. And then there were Felixisms, the sublimely dismissive "Mm ... Bah," and multisyllabic constructions like "Eh-zoy-ee," a favorite of his that might have had a meaning. And what of his receptive language? He had not to my knowledge ever said, "ice cream," but he understood the word very well. Jason and I had learned not to say it while compiling a shopping list. If we did, Felix would emphatically pound his chest to indicate that he wanted ice cream and was expecting us to give it to him NOW.

I wonder if it's possible to accurately quantify anyone's vocabulary. Sometimes I know the name of my grocer, sometimes all I know is his steady gaze and careworn face. Sometimes I can remember to say *mort aux vaches* in French. Sometimes *je ne peux pas*. If the extent of my vocabulary is in flux, wouldn't the extent of Felix's also be? I had been asked how many words Felix knew a dozen times a year, by a dozen different officials, for the past five years. Why the hell did they keep asking me these questions? "E," I said. Over 250. At the very least, I would screw up their numbers.

I was not being held in jail; my interrogator was not slapping me around. It was one afternoon of my life, forty-five minutes of nonsense in a moldy basement in Queens. Afterward I would carry Felix up and out of that basement and we would both see the light of day. Yet the memory still rankles. Had I been allowed to reply in a thoughtful manner, I might have felt differently. Felix's language acquisition, after all, fascinates me. But the answers I was made to choose from never felt right.

We are all swept down this path. The other day, in the stairwell of a fancy private school in Brooklyn, I watched a teenage boy tromping down the steps, hairy and fleshy, smelly and clumsy. His

ungainliness touched me. He could walk and talk and would probably go to one of those colleges considered good, but he was not
that far from Felix. None of us are. We all have parts that are messy
and indeterminate. We can be articulate in one environment; we
helplessly roar in another. We do not fit into the lines, boxes, and
categories we must scrunch ourselves into when filling out forms,
taking tests, and attempting to comply with the layers of government, business, education, and so on that play such a large role in
modern life.

. . .

The DOE bureaucracy was humane and downright neighborly
compared with United Healthcare, our private health insurance
company. Three-hour telephone calls. Double talk. Muzac. Passive-
aggressive computer-generated voices designed to make you slam
down the phone and pay the frigging bill yourself. Someone at one
of Felix's schools advised me to get Felix Medicaid on top of our private insurance, because private insurance did not cover all the procedures that children like Felix might need, and because it would be
very difficult to get him Medicaid once he became an adult. Based
on my failure to get United Healthcare to reimburse us even for
things that were on our plan—his $2,000 disability strollers, for
instance—this seemed like a good idea.

Felix could get Medicaid through a program called Medicaid
Waiver, designed to protect children with severe disabilities regardless of family income. Applying for this involved gathering about
fifty pages' worth of reports, evaluations, doctor letters, financial
papers, and notarized documents, and sending them around to
various social service agencies that administered the waiver. After
sending in the packets, I called the agencies to make sure they had
arrived, then waited. Slots are scarce and don't open that often. I had

been told the typical wait time is between six months and two years.

Eventually, I got a call from SKIP, a nonprofit that helps parents navigate the medical, health, and welfare programs intended to help children with chronic medical conditions and disabilities. Felix could get the Medicaid waiver, provided that I sign up for SKIP's Family Education and Training program (FET). This meant either Jason or I had to go to SKIP's offices and learn about such things as emergency preparedness, future-needs planning, and the healing power of the drum. I signed up. Felix got his Medicaid card. To keep it active, once a year, I get a babysitter and take the subway to West Twenty-Sixth Street for an evening drum workshop. SKIP social workers also visit our house. These meetings are short, maybe ten minutes, and take place four times a year. Young women arrive with clipboards and earnestly ask: What does Felix like to do? What food does he like? In some file cabinet somewhere, perhaps in triplicate, is a record of Felix's culinary tastes. These women did not go into the social services with the hopes of tracking a young disabled boy's taste for bacon. They want to help. Sometimes they get a chance to. One of them, for instance, enrolled us into a program that delivers free adult diapers to our door. This was very useful, as by the time that Felix was six, he had outgrown children's diapers. Our current social worker is helping us get a wheelchair accessible van, also very handy. Just imagine how much more they could do if less money went to record keeping and more to direct services. Why should anyone care whether Felix likes cucumbers or not? Wouldn't it make more sense if the money spent collecting and filing information like this was instead spent on creating jobs for people who could help Felix and people like him eat cucumbers?

Logistics

Right after Felix turned four, I made a movie that I posted on YouTube. If you search for Felix the Fab, you can see him, a skinny little boy whose hair had by now turned blond, clad in a shiny green raincoat maneuvering his walker down Fort Greene Place. You can't see the braces, hidden beneath his brown corduroys, but they were there, helping to stabilize him. With his walker and braces, he could scoot about, investigating stoops, pizza parlors, laundromats. Anna or I would follow behind, wheeling his stroller, ready to scoop him up when his legs failed. He could not walk for too long before he sank to the pavement, exhausted. Terra once explained that the energy that it took for him to hold his body up and move his legs to walk was immense, roughly equivalent to me walking on the bottom of the sea.

The morning of the day that I shot the movie had been stormy, raindrops hitting the windows, Felix howling and whining. He liked the elements. He insisted on the elements. He stared meaningfully at the chipped blue paint of our front door and made his noise. Once the rain settled into a drizzle, I strapped him into his stroller, strapped Miranda into her Babybjörn, folded up the walker, and balanced it on the handlebars. We always took the walker with us. It was bulky and it pinched our fingers, but the more walking Felix did, the better for his muscles, the better the chance that he might someday walk unassisted.

It was too wet to play in the playground, so we wandered. On the block where the enormous Brooklyn Tech High School is, the flagstones give way to a wide, smooth, expanse of concrete, the perfect terrain for Felix's walker. I detached it from the stroller and helped Felix into it. He grabbed the handlebars and took off. I hurried after him, pushing his stroller, Miranda bobbing along under my chin. He stopped at the entrance of Brooklyn Tech and tried to lift the front wheels of his walker onto the stoop. I began filming him. I usually forgot to bring my camera along, and was pleased that I had, and that I was getting such good footage. When he took off again, down the sidewalk, I ran in front of him, wanting to get a shot of his face. He had a ton of endurance that day and kept right on walking, and I kept right on walking backward. On the original audio you could hear Miranda's baby breath and her baby grunts and me shouting "Go Felix! Go! Go! Go!" as he hurtled down the street, stopped for breath, steered around a street lamp, and continued his march onward.

I didn't want to stop him, and I didn't want to stop filming, but as we got farther from his stroller, I began to worry. Would he have the stamina to make it back? I couldn't carry him more than a foot or two with Miranda bound to my chest. By the time we'd reached the end of the block, the stroller was fifty yards away. I pocketed my camera and turned his walker around. *Come on, sweetheart. Let's see if you can walk back there.* He repositioned his walker and started in the opposite direction. I blocked him off. The stroller was now out of sight, around the corner. It wasn't just any stroller—it was a disability stroller, which meant that it was expensive, and United Healthcare had declined to reimburse us for it. What to do? I couldn't say, wait here, Felix, don't move. I'll go get your stroller. He'd never followed my directions before, why would he start now? Miranda started to cry. The sweet smell of her scalp had been replaced by the smell of poo. She squirmed and kicked. The cars whizzed by.

I usually relied on the kindness of strangers to get me out of these fixes. But perhaps due to the rain, there were hardly any people out, and those who I did see did not seem approachable. They might have been. When you don't get much sleep, figuring out how to form a simple, but unusual request can be strangely difficult. The words don't fit together. A woman in a gray overcoat walked by. She seemed friendly enough. I could have said: Excuse me, ma'am, would you mind going around the corner and retrieving our stroller for us? But I did not seem to be able to open my mouth. Miranda's cries grew more insistent, her smell worse. Felix lowered himself down on the wet pavement.

This was good. He could not pull himself up into the walker without my help. If I ran for his stroller, he would not be able to walk into the traffic. But what if he bunny hopped? Bunny hopping was our name for his version of crawling. He moved forward on his arms, then hopped both knees to meet them. After all that walking, I doubted that he'd have the energy to bunny hop anywhere, but I arranged the walker around his body in a cage-like manner, just in case. I sprinted around the corner, the fifty yards to his stroller, the fifty yards back. My heart pounded. My legs were gelid with fear. What if a pedestrian came by and found him alone on the sidewalk? What if a car pulled up? What if he got past the walker-cage and bunny hopped into Dekalb? I returned, the stroller clattering, me panting. There were no other pedestrians to be seen. Felix was quietly munching on a wet leaf. He was relaxed, content. I couldn't stop shaking.

It's funny the nostalgia and pride that rises up in me when I see that movie. Felix's sweetness and courage are so apparent, and he is so mobile, more mobile than he is now. I forget the terror and confusion that arrived so quickly afterward. I suppose parenting most all young children is like this, glory so quickly morphing into chaos.

Jason had similar logistical troubles. Thanks to those IEP

meetings, the DOE's Office of Pupil Transportation (OPT) paid for a school bus to pick up Felix from the house every morning and deliver him back every afternoon. When the system worked, it was an enormous help, but every year, there would be a month or two when a bus strike stopped all city service, or someone at OPT lost our paperwork, or new regulations decreed that we were no longer allowed to carry Felix on the bus, and there were no buses available with wheelchair lifts. Luckily we lived near a wheelchair accessible subway station (not the norm in New York) and there was another wheelchair accessible station, Herald Square, not far from Felix's school in Manhattan.

The elevator at Herald Square, however, was not reliable. When the elevator was out of order, Jason had to figure out how to get Felix, his stroller, his folded up walker, his diaper bag, and Jason's briefcase/backpack, up a crowded, grubby, midtown flight of subway stairs. Sometimes people offered to help, but not always, and there was too much gear, too loosely connected, to lift all at once. Jason could have taken the walker and diaper bag up first, and left Felix in his stroller down below, but what if a malevolent or lonely person mired in confusion wheeled Felix away? Jason's solution was to take Felix out of the stroller and prop him on the bottom step of the subway stairs. Someone could still pick him up, but it would take more effort, and therefore seemed less likely. Jason would then sprint up the stairs with the walker and stroller, leaving Felix behind, a floppy blond boy, slumping on the filthy steps, as adults rushed by in their heels and business shoes. He'd deposit the gear at the top of the steps, curse OPT, and run back for Felix. No one ever stepped on Felix. No one tried to whisk him away. Nothing bad ever happened except for the thumping in Jason's heart, that feeling that he was doing something wrong, but he didn't know what else to do.

• • •

Felix had a one-on-one aide at school. As Miranda got more mobile, it became clear that Felix needed someone like this at home. I didn't have the eyes and the arms to take care of both of them at once. I asked one of SKIP's visiting social workers if there were any programs that provided children with disabilities one-on-ones at home. Not exactly, she said, but there was a program that allowed me to hire a health aide and get partially reimbursed. Just don't call the health aide a babysitter! she warned. She sent over a five-page form, which had to be submitted within thirty days, and a doctor form, which also had to be submitted within thirty days. Both forms MUST arrive within thirty days, she urged me, or you'll have to start all over again. One morning a few months later, the doorbell rang. A frowning woman with a very straight back stood on our doorstep. "Is this Felix Factor's home?" She was from an entity I'd never heard of: CASA. Apparently, it was a city agency that administers home care services for its residents. I told her that Felix was at school. "How am I supposed to evaluate him?" she snapped, and left without saying goodbye.

Dr. Pytlak and I filled out the forms again. The next year, when our paperwork reached the appropriate desk, an agent from CASA called and I kept Felix home from school. Two ladies arrived. Their disapproving looks softened when they saw Felix. We sat around the dining room table, talking, as Felix lay on the floor, jingling a jangle. In response to their questions, I told them that Felix needed someone to help him eat, drink, dress, change his diapers, bathe. They asked about his medical history. In the midst of reciting the litany, I mentioned his unusual EEG readouts. They shook their heads. They doubted that he would be approved by their program and they couldn't think who might take him. As they made their way out, they blessed Felix and wished me good luck. We were formally rejected a few months later on the grounds that Felix was "medically fragile."

An Idyll

We couldn't get help from the government or private insurance, but thanks to Jason's salary and our big house, we could get an au pair. On a weekend morning in June 2007, I put Miranda in her car seat and headed over the Manhattan Bridge to New Jersey's tangle of turnpikes, where we swerved around, looking for the Fairfield Marriott in East Rutherford. Somewhere in the hotel, Bruna, a twenty-year-old journalism student from Indaiatuba, a town outside of Sao Paulo, Brazil, was waiting. She had spent the last week at the Marriott, getting "oriented" to American family mores. As per the au pair company's instructions, we had been emailing pictures back and forth, and I had conducted a phone interview. She had seemed friendly and happy on the phone, though she only seemed to understand about half of what I was saying. This didn't worry me too much. In high school, I had been an exchange student in France. When I first arrived, I had been so shocked by the experience of real French that I had promptly lost whatever speaking ability I had, and had to learn everything from scratch. I figured she'd learn English eventually, and besides, I was used to communicating nonverbally. What worried me was the "click." My first French family and I had not clicked, a painful experience for all parties concerned, and I didn't see how you could judge click from an application essay and a ten-minute telephone conversation.

The Starbucks in the hotel lobby was crowded with young women in blue jeans. One of them, with glossy long hair and big droopy eyelids, stepped forward, her face lit with recognition. "Hi, Mom!" she said, her voice sunny and warm. Mom? I couldn't help but grin.

Many times, during that happy year with Bruna, Jason and I remarked that Bruna's forte, long-distance swimming, might be the ideal sort of training for taking care of children like Felix. I had not hired her for Felix. She was twenty years old. Away from her country. Learning a new language. Expecting her to tackle all that Felix needed on top of that would have been asking too much. I had hired her to look after Miranda three days a week, when Felix was at school, and to pinch hit those afternoons and evenings when Anna couldn't come, and to babysit with Anna every now and then, so Jason and I could have a date. But the very first day that Bruna spent with us, she asked if she could give Felix a bath, and I realized that separating the babysitting duties made more sense on paper than in person. She was unintimidated by Felix's strangeness. Perhaps his nonverbal nature and her spotty English were a good match. Certainly the extra physical work that Felix entailed didn't faze her. She was an athlete. She could swim twelve-mile races through the ocean. Pushing Felix, his stroller, and his walker over a couple of miles of bumpy bluestone was nothing.

With Bruna, my life expanded. I could write *and* run. I had time to do things like research after-school activities for Felix. In doing so, I found SNACK, a privately run after-school program for kids on the autism spectrum, which ran a swimming program in the basement of St. Bart's Church in Manhattan. I'd leave Miranda with Bruna, pick Felix up from school, push him and his dangling walker up Park Avenue, around Grand Central Terminal, past the Waldorf Astoria, into the modest side-door entrance of St. Bart's. There was a rickety elevator that took us down to a subterranean gym, locker room, and warm water pool. Felix was light in the water, able to move in ways he could never dream of on land. He would whoop and splash, kicking up a gleeful chlorine spume, and that feeling that sometimes burdened me—that we should be doing more, that we should experiment with this therapy, or that diet, or that behavioral technique—would disperse.

This feeling of relief didn't come cheap. When you combined the one-on-one swimming lesson ($70) with the babysitting Miranda needed ($45), Felix's new passion was the equivalent of going to a Broadway play once a week. Bashir would not have been able to do such a thing, though he surely would have loved it as much as Felix, and seeing her son in the water would have lightened Jamila's heart as much as mine. I had read an article in *Exceptional Parenting* magazine about the extra stressors involved in raising children with disabilities, with tips on how parents could alleviate some of this stress and enjoy their children more. The number one tip had been: Make more money. Families with higher income reported more family happiness and less stress. Maddening advice. If Jamila managed to get a job that paid above the poverty level, Bashir would lose his Supplemental Security Income benefits. But the likelihood is that she wouldn't be able to break the poverty line anyway. Jamila is an artist. Some artists manage a decent salary, but most juggle many jobs and end up in the same income range as adjunct professors, nonunionized motel clerks, and security guards. Even for professional parents, there aren't that many great paying, flexible jobs out there. Statistically, special-needs families make 20 percent less than nonspecial-needs families led by parents of the same educational level. It is not because they wouldn't like to make more money. It is because they have to take time off from work to camp out at the hospital while their children's brains are hooked up to EEG machines, or take off half a day to answer questionnaires in a moldy basement in Queens, or spend a week working to get reimbursed for a disability wheelchair.

But Jason had a one-in-a-million job and what's more, he enjoyed it. We were lucky. Thanks to his money, and Bruna's help, and Felix's happiness, and Miranda's first wobbling, fat-bottomed steps, I remember family life that year as being particularly sweet, a memory given ballast by the entries I wrote in Miranda's notebook:

Mid-October, 2007. Not sure of the exact date as I am so very domestic these days. I look at the calendar only to plot doctor's visits and half the time I don't even do that, but jot appointments down on backs of envelopes and hope that I will find them when necessary. I'm having a glass of wine, waiting for Jason to arrive home, so dinner can finally be eaten. Felix, who pretended to be asleep for Bruna, is upstairs, clapping, yodeling, giggling, and kneeling. I can tell because of the resounding thumps that occur when, after rising to his knees, he lets himself fall forward, catching himself with outthrust arms. He has not yet hurt himself, though I wince when watching.

This kneeling thing is a new ability of his. No longer will he walk a block in his walker. Instead we're lucky to get five steps out of him before he remembers that he can kneel! Down he goes, and once down, he can rarely get up without assistance. Our progress is slow, but horizontally, we're going places.

I mention this kneeling of Felix's because you have been an avid walker-and-runner-with-assistance. That is, you cannot yet balance yourself for more than a few seconds, but you can trot down six midtown blocks as long as you can grip my fingers as you go. It is wonderful and amazing to watch the glee with which you run, your movements punctuated by panting grunts, your whole

body quivering with excitement. A little heart-wrenching, too, as
you easily outpace Felix, who's been working at this for four and a
half years.

But today, at the Museum of Natural History, where you and I
and Bruna and Felix went to see an exhibit featuring mermaids and
dragons, as well as the ever-pleasing dinosaur bones, you squirmed
out of my arms as if you wanted to run. But instead of running, you
wanted to do what Felix does—that is, take a few steps, then kneel.
It is the first time I've seen you so obviously imitating him.

Miranda Doodle—it is November 1. You took your first steps two
days ago. On October 30—a Tuesday afternoon. I was writing,
you were in your room, naked from the waist down—we are in the
process of trying to heal a very bad case of diaper rash—playing
with Bruna. All of a sudden, I heard Bruna shouting Miranda! Little!
(pronounced Leetle—her name for all sweet things smaller than
herself) Bruna shouted for me to spy on you through the rarely
used closet passage way. If I had opened the main door, you would
have seen me and you are in an extreme mommy mood these
days—the sight of me and you betray all other loves to scramble
toward me with the most heart-melting enthusiasm on your face.

So I spied on you. Watched Bruna help you stand then let
go—and march, march, march—three paces you made to her,
your sweet fat thighs and meaty bottom bursting with confidence
and sublime disregard for the falls and sploshes that inevitably
occurred as we repeated the trick over and over. For of course I
could not stay spying for long and rushed headlong in and gave you
a hug and you laughed with pleasure and pride and didn't want to
stop showing off your new trick.

Today you walked five paces.

Tomorrow, who knows?

Jason and I had both come from two-child families, so a third seemed extravagant, but Dr. Pytlak's advice to have a large family had not been forgotten. There had been other people, too. Strangers seeing Miranda and her older brother had excused themselves, then passionately blurted out: please, if you can, have another. They were cognizant of their presumption. But their own histories bubbled up, insisting on being told. One woman stands out, a thin blond in scrubs, bearing a clipboard with a form that I had to sign. She had grown up in New Jersey with an autistic older brother and a younger sister. Her sister was the only one who got it, she said. No one at school even knew what autism was. No one else understood the strangeness of her life. She told me a story about getting straight A's on her report card and her parents patting her on the head. But when her brother said "Hi," they leaped up in a standing ovation, their chairs clattering to the floor behind them. I identified with the parents, and silently cheered along with them, but I could see the frustration that the incident still caused their less-applauded daughter. I wanted to say: What if we had a third child who was disabled—how would that help Miranda? And even if this theoretical third child were not disabled, siblings are not always compatible. They sometimes hate each other's guts. But she was looking at me with such an open, pleading expression that it would have been cruel to share these thoughts. Besides, she understood that life is a gamble. She worked in medicine.

I went off birth control.

• • •

Around Miranda's first birthday, the commute from New Jersey to our home and back again finally caught up to Anna. She had cared for, doted on, and cuddled Felix for four years. She had driven me nuts by spending half of her paychecks buying him new clothes. She had not been in it for the money. Her husband had a good job. She had been working because she loved Felix as if he were her own. Her love for him was such that neighbors would often report to me, beaming, on the experience of seeing them together, her face shining with tenderness, his eyes sparkling in return. We had never been able to talk about Felix's disability directly. That first year, when I was shuttling him from doctor to doctor, trying to find out why he was so floppy, I would tell her what the doctors said, and she would nod cheerfully. The realization of how difficult his life would be must have caused her as much pain as it did us. But she wouldn't acknowledge it, at least not to me. A picture of her, holding Felix at the fountain in Central Park still has pride of place in his room.

Only a day or two after Anna's departure, a poet from my MFA program emailed. She had just been at an artists' colony where she met a painter who lived in Brooklyn and was looking for part-time babysitting work. Did I need anyone? Enter Emily Church, who was so tall, she almost grazed the ceiling of our ground floor kitchen, a room where she would spend much time, for she was a great brewer of teas and baker of cookies. Once a week, she and I would take Felix and Miranda to Fairway to stock up on groceries, each of us pushing a cart with one child inside. Felix could still somehow be stuffed into the front of a grocery cart, his long legs dangling down, his trunk twisting back and forth, his arms flapping in a Felix dance. He loved the aisles of Fairway, the music on the speakers, the intriguing, colorful boxes on the shelves, the bags of chips to be grabbed at and crinkled. We would discuss the week's menu and the merits of different sorts of ingredients, along with art, books, the missteps of our friends and selves.

The only real pain I can recall from that year arose from writing. What was I doing struggling over sentences that no one, it seemed, would ever read? Every now and then, I'd send out a slew of query letters—letters to agents or independent publishing houses that didn't require agents, touting revisions of those novels that had been rejected on the day Felix and I got the chicken pox. Rarely would our mail carrier bring back a reply. Though I did receive a faded copy of a rejection letter, and some flattering missives applauding my talent, but bemoaning the state of the market, the impossibility of publishing work such as mine, and so on. I couldn't tell if I was being self-indulgent or self-deluded, or both, a rather gruesome psychic spot to be in, and here Bruna and Emily helped again. Bruna, fresh from the university, would say: Mom! You have to write! It's your voice! And Emily, intimately acquainted with the loneliness and humiliation of art making, read my first novel, gave it to her friends, and insisted that it not be abandoned.

Oscar

A picture from Easter 2008: Miranda is one and Felix is five. They sit side by side on a step, Miranda in pigtails, Felix in his orange elf jacket. They both look deliriously happy, with chocolate smeared all over their cheeks. Their faces, however, are pointed in opposite directions. They barely seem aware of one another. I had hoped as Miranda grew older that she and Felix might develop their own sorts of games, that Miranda might be able to decipher his utterances, that they might be able to create a language all their own. This wasn't happening, though a relationship was forming. Felix would affectionately paw at Miranda, and one of Miranda's first sentences was, "Fegit funny." But they lived in separate spheres. Part of this was spatial. Not wanting Miranda to feel like the neglected "normal" sister, I had taken to doing her bath-books-bed routine almost every night in her bedroom on the top floor of our house while Bruna stayed on the floor below with Felix. But even if we lived in a one-room apartment, and they were continuously in each other's company, I doubt things would have been much different. Felix was an expert at being alone in the most crowded of settings.

Miranda would have more company soon—I had become pregnant in February with a baby who had a strong, energetic presence from the very start. A sonogram taken soon after Easter showed that she was a girl. We decided to call her Penelope. If Miranda

was getting a sister, maybe Felix would like a dog? I had heard that
therapy dogs could do wonders for kids on the spectrum. But when
I looked into acquiring one, I found that we would have to put
ourselves on a wait-list that might take anywhere from two years
to never. Should our number come up, the cost of the dog and the
training—the entire family had to be trained—ran about $12,000.
The wife of one of Jason's colleagues, who had seen the transformative effects of untrained dogs, cats, and horses on older people and
people with disabilities at a program she worked at in Long Island,
suggested adopting a regular old dog.

I grew up with Charlie, a big galumphing mutt with black fur
and a dashing splash of white on his chest. He had been there for all
my angst and loneliness, consoling me with his soulful eyes. He had
been there for my younger brother, dyslexic and indomitable, who
would lure him into his bed, in spite of his asthma. He had held our
family together, at least three quarters of it. As the story goes, when
my parents' marriage was coming to an end, my father asked if it
would be him or the dog, and my mother had opted for Charlie.

My mother, my brother, and I had found Charlie when he
was a wee puppy at the pound, but it turned out that you cannot
just go to the pound and pick up a dog anymore. At least not in
New York. I called pounds in several boroughs only to be told that
there were no dogs available for a family with young children. So I
went online. Jason had grown up with a beloved dog, too, and was
more or less on board, although he was hesitant about whether we
should take on the responsibility, what with the new baby coming.
I couldn't understand his hesitation. What was there to a dog? You
took them on walks. You picked up their poo. Poo didn't bother me.
Sometimes I felt like all I ever did was pick up poo. What was one
more crapper?

I inquired about a black lab that reminded me of Charlie on
a site called All About Labs. A few days later, a nice lady with a

Southern accent called. She lived in Little Rock, Arkansas. The South, she told me, has a glut of stray and abandoned dogs, the North, plenty of families willing to adopt them. This meant that her rescue operation had become adept at transporting animals across state lines. It also meant that adoptees rarely met the dog they intended to take in, but her organization had a good track record matching dogs to families based on telephone interviews and deep knowledge of their canines. It was a strange way to get a dog, but then again, Bruna had come to us through a similar sort of telephone and Internet vetting. I answered the woman's questions. What with Miranda and the baby on the way, she did not think that the dog that had caught my eye would be a good match. But she did have a four-year-old dog who was gentle as could be, and proven to be good with children. His name was Chris. She referred me to his online file. He had the beige and black coloring of a German Shepherd, and Chris was a strange name for a dog. But he looked appropriately kind and canine, and the woman sounded so sure.

Jason and I decided that we would rename him Oscar, in reference to the *Odd Couple*. Felix would have his Oscar, and we would have a friendly furry creature around the house. Bruna was very excited. A dog! A new baby! Life! The way the program worked, I had to promise to take Oscar to the vet and to training school, and I had to purchase a crate, for the dogs were all trained to go into crates in the home. As I recalled, life with a dog in the eighties had been a more casual affair, but what can you do? I went about finding a crate and a vet and writing a check for $250 to cover the cost of shots and transportation. The woman told me that Chris would be on the next dog caravan, due to arrive in a couple of weeks. The nearest drop off point was in New Jersey. In the parking lot of a Dunkin' Donuts. At 5:30 in the morning. I couldn't help but wonder, as I put the check in the mail, if I were sending it off to a cheerful swindler in Little Rock. A couple weeks later, I drove across the George

Washington Bridge through darkened hills to an exit that led to a
Dunkin' Donuts. The sign was wanly illuminated against the night
sky. There were other cars in the lot. Couples and parents with children huddled in the chill, looking as doubtful as I felt. The sky grew
lighter. A mass sigh and cheer arose as the caravan appeared. The
dogs were let out, one at a time, shaking and anxious from the drive.
Toward the end came Chris/Oscar, who had to pee.

We set up the crate, food, and water in Felix's room, but Oscar
would not enter the crate, no matter how many treats we lured him
with, nor would he stay in Felix's room if I wasn't there. He was not
interested in Felix. Nor was Felix interested in him. What Oscar
liked to do was follow me around, his nose in the crook of my knee.
This was also Miranda's favorite activity. Once she started walking,
she liked to be a step or two behind me, usually with her pudgy
hand gripping my skirt or my pants. The two of them trailed me
everywhere, including the bathroom. They would gather round the
toilet, watching. I had to pee often, as the baby was growing inside
me, pushing down on my bladder.

Oscar never snapped at Miranda, even when she sat on his back,
which must have hurt, for he had dysplasia in his hips, a condition
that made it difficult for him to run and climb up stairs. His hips
made playing with the other dogs at Fort Greene Park difficult, too.
He couldn't chase after them, though he could bonk them with his
strong and bony head. Most of the other dogs didn't like this. They
would snarl. They declined to sniff him back when he sniffed them.
I would walk him around the tennis courts, a little embarrassed,
wishing he knew how to socialize better. He was a strange dog. He
would not find balls that I threw for him, even if I only threw them
ten feet away. Sometimes he circled the room frantically, looking
for me, even though I was right there. I'd have to shout, "Oscar!
I'm here!" and grab him before he would calm down. I wondered if

rather than getting a companion for an autistic child, I had acquired an autistic dog.

Bruna volunteered to walk him at night. In the long evenings of late spring and early summer, she would yank him, reluctant to leave his post behind my knees, get him on the leash and pull him out of the house. Once they had gotten a block away, he would relax and she would walk him and Felix around the park, circling the field where the soccer players kicked up dust, trying to get Felix to hold Oscar's leash, urging them both along. A half an hour later, she would return, rolling her eyes with magnificent Brazilian disdain at the soccer techniques of New Yorkers. Oscar eventually made friends with a couple skinny Vizslas who didn't mind his bonking. After that, the other dogs started to sniff him back, even though he couldn't jump and chase them.

Bruna also volunteered herself for Felix's nightly stretching. Together, she and Fred had developed a routine to lengthen Felix's hamstrings and calf muscles, which were continuously shrinking due to his bent-knee, heel-up way of walking. Over the years, I had tried to administer these types of exercises myself. But as I had little time, and Felix resisted strenuously, my efforts were inconsistent. Bruna, on the other hand, attacked this duty with fabulous regularity. Every night before bed she would force Felix into a squatting position, then hold down his hips with one arm, and lift his leg with the other, counting steadily up to ten, up to twenty, undeterred by Felix's protest. Her father had coached her throughout her swimming career. She was used to a degree of familial rigor that neither Jason nor I had managed to achieve.

I was much better at overseeing the exercises that Felix enjoyed. The stair exercise was a favorite of both of ours. If I helped Felix place one hand on the stair rail and the other on the banister, then stabilized his hips, he could lift one foot, and then another, onto the step. Over time, he learned how to position his hands himself, and could even manage a step or two all on his own, without any spotting. All of us loved watching him do this. The amount of determination and muscle that it took left us with the sense of elation and wonder you can get from watching the Olympics. We would cheer and cheer and cheer, and Felix would, too.

. . .

At the end of Bruna's year with us, driving her to the airport, I missed the turnoff for JFK and somehow ended up on the Tappan Zee Bridge. Some childish spark in me, perhaps, hoping that if she missed her plane, she might stay. But she had to get back to Brazil. She had a fiancé, a big family, a journalism job waiting for her. There is something that she said toward the end of her stay with us that has lingered in my mind ever since. We were all flopped around the living room, in that state of exhaustion that young children can cause. Felix lay on a blanket on the floor. Miranda toddled about. Oscar was at my feet, Penelope in my belly. Bruna studied Felix through half closed eyes, "You know, Mom," she said slowly, and I thought she was going to say something about how incredibly tired she was. Instead, she said, "We all think that we do so much for Felix, but he does even more for us."

The Devil Screech

When the au pair that we had hired to replace Bruna did not work out, a neighbor suggested Svetlana, who had just graduated from college and was interested in physical therapy. On the day I interviewed her, we met at the Rebecca School. Observing the warmth of the staff and the intrigue of the students, she promptly got herself hired as an aide, and so it came to be that she worked at the Rebecca School during the day, learning the tools of Floortime, and two or three evenings a week, she helped out with Felix. Bruna had been a swimmer. Emily had been a basketball player. Svetlana had a black belt in Tae Kwon Do. I was learning to appreciate athletes. I was also beginning to wonder if Felix had a magnetic power that attracted good people right when we needed it. For we sure did need it.

On a Sunday, in the autumn of Felix's fifth year, Jason and I brought the kids back from a typical visit to the playground. We had spun Felix belly-down on the rubber swing. His feet, clunky in their braces, had scrabbled against the pavement, and though you couldn't see his face that well, for his trunk dangled toward the ground, his whoops were cheerful and loud. We had bounced on the squeaky bridge with Miranda, who was now almost two. We had chatted with other parents. Now I rested on the couch, exhausted from my pregnancy, summoning the energy to get up and make dinner. Felix sprawled companionably beside me. Then, out of the blue, he began to scream. Not an ordinary scream. It sounded as if he had been shot, or as if someone were yanking the hair out of his scalp. But no one was attacking him. We had a set routine when Felix was upset: first, see if he was hungry or thirsty by offering him food and drink. Then check his diaper. Then pick him up by the trunk and swing him around. Turn him upside down. Tickle him. Sing, too. If your voice was too strained, put on a CD. Jason and I tried all of these things. Felix kept screaming. We were beside ourselves. We had no idea what was going on. Then as suddenly as it started, it stopped. Poof! Felix was back to himself, calm and sweet.

I started making dinner. But we never got a chance to eat it. A half hour later, and just as abruptly, he began screaming again. Felix? What's wrong? His hand swung through the air in a swift, angry arc. He slapped himself on his cheek. Hard. He tried to hit himself again. I grabbed his wrist. I had never seen anything like this. I knew that he had hit himself before, at the preschool where they strapped him into that torture device chair. But I had neither witnessed those slaps, nor had I been puzzled by them. I had assumed that they were a form of protest. But what could he be protesting? There was no warped music assaulting him, no harnesses, no flickering fluorescent lights. He was well fed, clean diapered, in a comfortable, well-known room, surrounded by people he knew and loved. I released him, talking to him gently, telling him he would be OK. He grabbed one cheek and slapped the other with merciless fury. We struggled. He slipped away and slapped again. Over and over, the sickening sound of flesh hitting flesh. I shouted, "Are you in pain? Are you scared? Are you angry?" His only answer was more slapping, more screaming. Jason called our neighbors, Ward and Siyon, and asked if they could look after Miranda while we took Felix to the hospital.

We drove up to Columbia Presbyterian on 168th in Manhattan, as that hospital had treated Felix particularly nicely during one of the devil screech   143

his MRI's. Felix calmed down in the car, and I worried that the doctors were going to think that we were crazy. But once we got to the
emergency room, his screaming and slapping came back. The staff
whisked him to the front of the line. Jason restrained him as doctors
examined his eyes, ears, nose, mouth. They searched his insides with
a CAT scan. Jason, prone to stomach aches himself, thought maybe
his intestine had been crimped. Or maybe this was a simple case of
gas? We were given a suppository to push up his anus and clear out
whatever might be stuck up there. We were given diazepam, a type
of valium. For him, the doctors joked, not for us. We were told to
come back if his "irritability" continued.

The suppository cleared Felix's intestines, but his woefully
understated irritability continued, in intermittent bursts. The next
night or the night after, one of those cold dark October nights with
the wind whipping, we awoke, taut with alarm. The noise Felix was
making set our hair on end. It was a noise we would soon come to
know all too well. We would dub it the tritone devil screech, awful
for both its aural quality and the spate of violence it presaged.

The Columbia Presbyterian doctors had told us to come back
if the irritability continued. We packed his diaper bag. I took him,
alone this time, as we didn't want to wake Miranda, asleep in her
crib. Felix was happy by the time that we arrived at the hospital,
and darted his walker around on the smooth marble floor. He loved
smooth marble floors. When his legs gave out, I bought him a pack
of Wise potato chips, and held out each chip for him to grab, a trick
I'd been taught by Terra. It helped with his fine muscle coordination and it conserved the goods. Otherwise he'd paw into the bag,
obtaining a couple of chips and spilling the rest to the floor. He
looked so cute, so pleased with his treat. Maybe it was over? Could
it, please god, be done? He started screaming again. Again we were
admitted, again the doctors knitted their brows. They asked me
questions that I couldn't answer. I asked them questions that they

couldn't answer. We confirmed each other in our inability to understand how to help him. The valium hadn't helped. They gave him a
painkiller. That didn't help either. They told me to take him to the
neurologist.

We were discharged at three in the morning. Our car was parked
a few blocks away, in a lot on 165th and Amsterdam. I was nervous
to be out so late, alone, but I wasn't alone. I had Felix, quiet now.
I walked through the dark, the wind whipping down Broadway,
remembering when I lived on West 122nd, and used to come home
late from shows, walking with a swagger and my keys balled up in
my fists. I felt safer with Felix than I had with my swagger. There
wasn't anyone on the streets anyway, it was so late and cold. The
man at the car park, who I woke up, was a gentlemanly sort in a
tweed hat. He helped pack the stroller and walker in the trunk and
sent me off with a wave.

I drove toward Riverside Drive, checking the rearview mirror.
Felix seemed to be asleep. Please let it last. The other night, when
Jason and I had driven back from the emergency room, Felix had
started out calmly only to erupt into a terrible frenzy when we hit
Canal Street. I had wanted to unstrap myself and crawl through the
front seats. Though I might not have been able to quiet him, I could
have grabbed his hand and stopped him from hitting himself. But
my pregnancy made such a squeeze impossible. We had driven over
the Manhattan Bridge, the sound of his slapping filling up the car
and extending beyond it, taking possession of the night. At the red
light at Flatbush and Tillary, Jason braked, rigid and exhausted. He
had a classic profile, like you'd see on a Roman coin. I imagined him
driving a rickety Red Cross ambulance through a minefield, and me
a soldier at his side, strained and numb, but grateful, so grateful for
his company.

Now I was alone, without my comrade in arms. The memory of
the previous night's ride scared me. I did not want to be at the wheel

if Felix started screaming and slapping. I felt I might lose control of the car, run us into a wall, run someone over. I got to Riverside Drive and turned south. The lanes stretched out before me, empty, blissfully empty. Street lamps shone down on pavement occupied only by a scattering of brown leaves. I had never been on Riverside Drive without another shining headlight or taillight, some taxi, some pedestrian, someone. Block after block, green light after green light, the stately limestones to my left, the park to my right, the stillness inside our car, the stillness outside our car. No cat, no dog, no homeless person, no policeman, Felix continuing to sleep. Gone were my fears. I felt like a kid, a grandiose wonder blooming in me: I'm the only one awake in the whole city! Broadway. The Manhattan Bridge. All quiet. All empty. I arrived home safely and got into bed with Jason, reverberating with the feeling of that drive, a strange gift out of nowhere to see the city like that, and Felix still quiet, at peace for the moment.

A fragile peace. Fits would burst upon him, multiple times a day. We took him to the neurologist, the pediatrician, the dentist. Dr. Wells agreed that his behavior could be neurological, a pain receptor firing off for no good reason? A migraine? Perhaps, Dr. Pytlak offered, abdominal migraines? Those were supposed to be excruciating. She prescribed Cyproheptadine, a medication known to ease the pain of this sort of ailment and which had the added benefit of helping kids to sleep. How hopefully I clutched that prescription, how dashed I was when it didn't work.

After a week of this, I hardly recognized Felix. He had howled and screamed so hard and long that his voice was a ragged whisper, a mix of Darth Vader and a hissing snake. His face was red and swollen from hitting. His hands and knees bloody from where he'd bit himself. How to explain the staggering amount of energy that went into these fits? Boxers box for three-minute rounds, and anyone who has ever boxed knows how much a single round can take out of you. Felix's fits, as brutal as a boxing match, usually lasted from twenty to forty minutes, and he could manage multiple bouts in a day.

I was afraid he was dying, being eaten up by an excruciating, unknown, unforgivable disease. But twelve days after that first scream, he woke with a glowing complexion and a twinkle in his eye. The day passed without a fit. Then two days. Then three. Jason and I were elated, euphoric. It was as if Felix had been kidnapped and given back to us. Here was our boy, now dubbed Bug Bug, with his smile and his laugh! Jason and I kept nuzzling into each other, laughing helplessly. Normal life was the sweetest thing in the whole world.

But it was not to last. A week later, the tritone devil screech returned. Sometimes the motion of the stroller or the feel of the wind on his face could calm him, so if it was possible, we'd strap him into his stroller at the first sign of a fit. One time, hoping to soothe him with a walk around Fort Greene Park, his slaps became so savage that I had to turn back, not wanting to traumatize the children playing there. Ozge, a neighborhood babysitter who'd always been fond of Felix, ran toward us. She leaned over Felix and hugged him, managing to kiss him through his rage. For a moment he was calm. I was too upset, too moved to speak. Tears ran down my cheeks. Ozge hugged me, too. She began working for us soon after that.

A zigzag pattern emerged. On the zigs, Felix would be riven by self-annihilating eruptions. On the zags, he was "himself" again. The face slaps, alas, continued even during these "himself" periods. They seemed to be a gesture that, once developed, could not be discarded. The "himself" slaps were different, however. They were less fierce, shorter lived, and had a purpose that we could decipher. They became his way of signaling frustration, anger, impatience, hunger. He needed something done, and once we had figured out what it was—a new diaper, a snack, a walk outside—he would laugh and we would laugh, all of us grooving in the aha! of mutual understanding. But after a week or ten days of relatively normal life with Felix, something would switch. His skin tone would dull and gray, the terrible screech would break forth, and he—we—were back in the midst of chaos.

We racked our brains trying to figure out what was going on. Mainly we demonstrated how our own minds worked. Emily and Jason, who had stomach issues of their own, remained convinced that Felix was suffering from unbearable intestinal cramps. On bad days, they would rub his belly, make him drink prune juice, and cheer optimistically after each bowel movement. My mother, whose teeth have tortured her over the years, kept thinking the cause was dental. I, who have been lucky to have a strong stomach and good teeth, had no idea, and just kept driving him from doctor to psychologist to therapist to dentist and back to doctor, hoping for a clue.

A friend who was studying Chinese medicine suggested that I take Felix to Jackie Luna-Knapp, a pediatric acupuncturist who had impressed her when Jackie taught a course at her school. So one slushy afternoon, I drove Felix to the East 90s, where Jackie and her husband had an office on the ground floor of a sixties-era apartment building. There were three steps to get Felix's stroller down, which was awkward, but inside, the doorknobs were decorated with dangling bells and red dragons and a stone fountain tinkled. A far better set up, as far as Felix was concerned, than a regular doctor's waiting room. He was so charmed by his surroundings that I wondered if I'd be able to explain to Jackie the intensity of his troubles, so I did not mind when he started hitting himself. Jackie appeared. She was about my age, with a handsome face and a gentle, somewhat amused, demeanor. Seeing the state of my belly, she took charge of Felix and helped him into the examining room. She felt his head, which he did not like. She held his feet, which he allowed. She listened with her hands. She did not use needles on one so young and squirmy. She practiced acupressure, and she did a remarkable job, for soon Felix was quiet and calm. The color came back into his face.

I drove home with a sheet of seeds attached to a sticky, Band-Aid-like paper. They had a special vibration, Jackie said, that could activate pressure points. I was to put them in Felix's ears and at places on his feet. I laughed: magic seeds. Felix giggled in the back seat. A few days later, in spite of the seeds, the tritone devil screech broke out and he started hitting again. I wondered if the transformation I'd seen in Jackie's office was a fluke of timing. I brought him back to her. Again she calmed him. Her effect seemed real, if short-lived.

Slaps and Nonces

Penelope was a breech baby. This meant that I had to have a C-section. After the physical struggle of Miranda and Felix's birth, the process seemed unreal: I went into labor. Jason drove me to Methodist Hospital. Drugs were administered. My obstetrician cut me open. Barely a couple of hours after the first pangs of pain, I held in my arms a beautiful new baby, beguiling and, for the moment, serene. I was in heaven, but a couple of nights later, my incision became infected. I awoke in a cold sweat, my teeth chattering, and spent the next six weeks on the couch in the living room, with Jason, my mother, Emily, Ozge, and Svetlana taking turns dousing my wound with hydrogen peroxide. I was not allowed to get up. All I could do was boss people around and nurse Penelope, which ended up being OK. Bed rest no longer tormented me. I was forty, on the cusp of forty-one, aware that Penelope would probably be my last child. I held her. I nursed her. And this, this was lovely. All I wanted to do. Miranda helped, passing me wipies. She had just turned two and couldn't manage the syllables of Penelope. Instead she said "oppey," which morphed into Happy, a nickname that we all adopted.

• • •

And Felix? Felix was peaceful. He was back, our boy. Week after week, he was fine. He would arrive home from school, bang his walker around the ever-messy living room and eat his snacks with abandon. His cheeks were pink; his eyes sparkled. After Christmas, by my forty-first birthday, I was strong enough to get off the couch and make dinner again. I resolved to take a year off from writing—I knew that I wouldn't have the time to carve out even an hour a day, and I didn't want to go bitter with the effort of trying. I'd start again at forty-two. In the meantime, I would take in Happy's tiny feet, Miranda's pudgy, two-year-old tummy, Felix's delightfully expressive five-year-old body. Tending to them, nuzzling them, puzzling over their movements and desires, along with the house and the dog was more than enough. I was so taken with the increased bustle of our home life that I frightened Jason one day by wondering if we might have a fourth. He shot me a baleful look.

The devil screech faded into an eerie memory. An inexplicable thing that seemed to have been resolved, that perhaps hadn't been as bad as all that—for it was hard to conceive of such madness when it was spring and the children were healthy and the magnolia in the backyard was blossoming in pink abandon. I started guitar lessons. Even if Felix someday used words or signs in a conventional manner, I figured that music would always be his first language, and I wanted to be able to converse with him. I loved practicing chords with him sitting next to me on the couch, reaching out his hand to feel the vibrations of the strings. In the mornings, when Felix was at school, I'd take the girls to Camel Park and get to know the parents and nannies who likewise frequented the place. They had been friendly when it was just me and Felix, but our conversations had rarely led to any sort of deeper friendship, as Felix and their children seemed to have so little in common. But now that I had Miranda toddling about and Happy poking her not quite bald head out from the baby carrier, I could swap anecdotes about teething or teddy bears with the best of them, and social interactions became much easier.

After school, when Felix was home, he and a babysitter would come along, too. Emily or Svetlana and I would take turns, one of us swinging the girls, the other trailing Felix as he clattered along in his walker, making his rounds to the gate and water fountain. Maybe he'd stop at the bottom of the baby slide, lower himself onto its lip, and try to bunny hop up. He had become ingenious at figuring out how to make that equipment, not designed for bodies like his, enjoyable nevertheless. He also had his walker trick—swinging himself up and sitting on his handlebars, a precarious perch that gave him great pleasure while it terrified the adults. Once, at Rice, a woman asked where she could purchase a walker for her son who had Down syndrome and did not seem to be picking up walking so easily. It turns out that Frank wouldn't need a walker and would indeed develop into a remarkably good basketball player, but the question led to a friendship, and the welcome discovery that we were not the only family in our immediate neighborhood dealing with disability. Indeed, over the next couple of years, I would find in the blocks surrounding our house a handful of other parents whose children had disabilities as significant as Felix's. We couldn't see each other often, as we were all entangled in complicated therapy schedules, but I would find that a simple conversation with one of them could lighten my mood for a week.

. . .

In the midst of this happy stretch, Jason and I were jolted awake by the unmistakable sound of the devil screech. We raced into Felix's room. On his red polka-dotted sheets, he assaulted himself with a fury that beggars description. Those terrible fits that I'd begun to think I'd imagined, or at least exaggerated, were back.

I resolved to beat this thing, somehow. For starters, I took Felix to Jackie as often as possible, and her acupressure usually brought on a couple days of increased peace. Also, Svetlana had recommended a new sensory gym called the Smile Center. Her friend Marcus, an occupational therapist at the Rebecca School, had opened it with another occupational therapist named Huck. I had been hearing about sensory this and sensory that ever since Fred and Terra entered our lives, but I still wasn't clear on what sensory meant. A sensory gym, I would soon discover, is a place where you work on your sensory integration.

As any bright kindergartener knows, our understanding of the world comes through the senses—but the way that the senses work, the way that the information enters the brain, is processed and synthesized, gets complicated. There are two senses that we don't learn about in kindergarten that are equally important to sight, smell, touch, hearing and vision. There is the sense of motion (the vestibular sense) and the sense of the body's placement in space (the proprioceptive sense). For a coherent understanding of ourselves in the world, these senses need to work together in harmony. When their input is ill-coordinated, the brain becomes agitated or "disregulated." Environments and conditions that are benign to a well-regulated brain can be torturous to a disregulated one. An example, all too common among autistic children, is when their sense of touch becomes so amplified that a cotton T-shirt feels like a vest of thorns. Any sense, or part of a sense, can go awry, its signals becoming too strong, or not strong enough, or lost, or overly found. To help with sensory-integration problems, therapists create exercises intended to give controlled practice with the senses that are presenting difficulties. A sensory gym, therefore, is equipped with all sorts of interesting means of experiencing speed, dizziness, pressure, and so on.

I figured I might as well give the Smile Center a shot. When I took Felix there, I was delighted by the look of the place: a series of big, beautiful, sunlit rooms filled with equipment that made me want to move. There was a slide to go down, a ball pit to lounge in, and piles of foofs to be climbed on. Foofs look like huge beanbag chairs, but they are filled with foam scraps, which press more firmly against the body than styrofoam beads, and are therefore more useful for those who are not always aware where their body is in space.

Huck broke through one of Felix's fits on our very first meeting. It might have been with his hands. Sometimes his hugs were enough to calm him. It might have been the motion of rolling Felix over a half-filled waterbed mattress, then spinning him on a rotating swing. The specifics don't come back. I only know that Felix's response to Huck was bright and clear. Thank goodness for Huck and Jackie. Perhaps because neither of their practices were overly concerned with diagnoses, they saw Felix less as a compendium of lacks, a broken kid who would never be cured, and more as a unique young boy whose suffering called out for their attention. They could not wave a wand and relieve him of his fits, but they could hold him, touch him, rock him when he was pale and bruised and hoarse from screaming. They could apply their arts; they could be there with him and me; they could make him feel better, us feel better. If not for a week, then at least for a day or two, they could provide an easing, a break in intensity.

Still, I wanted more. I had been leery of psychiatric drugs, shaking my head over the overuse of Ritalin and Paxil, suspicious of some of the motives that lay behind pharmaceutical tinkering. But now I was desperate for something, anything to calm him when his furies spiraled into madness, as they continued to do, with grueling regularity. There had to be a way to sedate him when he was at his most violent. Felix and I ricocheted from doctor to doctor. I delivered to our pharmacist an abundance of prescriptions, among them, oxycodone, codeine, Xanax, clonazepam, diazepam, lorazepam, clonazepam, and Haldol. It was as if we were feeding him sugar pills.

None of them worked. I was astonished. I had grown up with *Get Smart* and assumed that you could always slip a mickey in someone's drink, causing your victim to slump over, quiet and harmless, for a few hours. Turns out that's just television. Jackie suggested that the antiseizure drug we'd been giving him might be causing harm, so we took him off Trileptal, which no longer helped him sleep, and could cause delusions. No change.

I thought perhaps I should not to be so dismissive about the stomach business. What if it was his digestive tract? Many people asked me if he ate gluten, a mixture of proteins found in wheat, spelt, rye, and barley that seemed to be irritating an ever-increasing number of the population's intestines. He did, but because Jason sometimes experienced gluten intolerance, I had been careful about introducing it into Felix's diet, limiting his carbs to rice-based products until he was two or three, and watching for adverse reactions after his first run-in with a regular flour birthday cake and conventional macaroni. There hadn't been any. Still, many parents of children on the spectrum swore by a diet that cut out both gluten and casein, the protein found in dairy products. Apparently, both proteins had to be eliminated in order to alter the composition of the enzymes in the intestinal tract. Once the enzymic transformation had been achieved, children who had been suffering terrible stomachaches often felt much better.

I believed that this worked for some children, but I was also aware that what worked for one person did not necessarily work for the next. Practitioners of these diets also warned that you might not see results for six months, as the enzymic reshuffle took time. So much change occurs within a child's body in six months. Even if Felix got better, how would I know if it was on account of the diet, or just growth? I did not want to make Felix give up yogurt and milk, not to mention ice cream, all great loves of his, and a significant source of his protein, for something that I did not have an enormous amount of faith in. I asked Jackie what she thought, Chinese Medicine having its own formulations and understandings about the intricacies of diet. Jackie didn't think that all glutens and caseins were harmful, only the types found in mass production crops and cows. She suggested a nonwheat, noncow-milk, nonsoy diet, so we stocked up on goat butter and brown rice noodles, and Emily went about researching recipes, preparing spelt pancakes and cornmeal crusted chicken. I'm not sure if this helped, but the food tasted good, and we were all eating in a healthier manner than we had before.

Neighbors, doctors, relatives, fellow parents, friends also lobbed suggestions. Maybe Felix was particularly susceptible to the change of the seasons? The moon? Maybe it was early onset adolescence? Had I heard of John of God, in the jungles of Brazil, whose touch apparently was miraculous? I sent Felix's pee and blood off to labs in far-off places, checked for allergies, metallic agents, anything that didn't seem downright harmful. Meanwhile Felix flipped back and forth between a bloody, infuriated self destroyer and a pleasant child. I thought of him as Persephone, delighting in flowers and meadows for a month or two, then simply gone, inhabiting a realm I can only describe as terrible. I hated it. I hated that even when he was happy, this dark realm haunted me. I remember an evening in the kitchen, a nice evening with the sun slanting through the windows, and the kids arranged around the table, Miranda chattering, Felix doing his happy torso twist, Happy in my lap. Jason and I were talking about something, when an ambulance passed in the distance. Both of us froze. Our bodies must have reacted to some pitch in the siren, a sound akin to Felix's tritone devil screech, and our muscles had sprung to action. It lived within us, this awareness, this constant alertness, this knowledge that peace could shatter at any time.

The doctors I'd taken Felix to had tried. They had offered their educated guesses, but none of those guesses had hit the mark. My own suspicion was that Felix's autism was at the root of it. By this time, I had started to educate myself in autism and found *Thinking in Pictures*, Temple Grandin's memoir about her life with autism, particularly illuminating. Her autism was her autism, of course. She was a very different person than Felix. But she wrote so clearly about her perceptions and somatic experience that it opened a door within me. One thing that I found particularly fascinating was her experience of emotion. She had only felt four emotions: hate, fear, anger, and joy. Further, these emotions came to her in their purest form, undiluted by secondary feelings. Whether positive or nega- tive, they were completely destabilizing, and she much preferred the quieter, dryer realm of thinking. I knew from Felix's expressions, tones, and gestures that he experienced a far more satisfying palette of emotions than Grandin's, but I wondered if he shared with her a propensity for a single emotion coming at him full throttle. His joy had always been a spectacular thing, so powerful that it emanated out of him, catching other people up in its efflorescence. Could his fits be rage in its purest form, brought upon by a somatic trigger none of us could understand, and that he somehow got trapped in?

Jackie called his fits rages. She interpreted them in a shamanistic light, his spirit separated from his body, caught in a terrifying no man's land.

Grandin wrote about how pharmaceuticals had relieved her of debilitating anxiety and fear, allowing her to become the prolific and admired person she is today. She provided a list of drugs that can potentially help people with autism, an entire family of which we had not tried. When I suggested experimenting with them to Dr. Wells, he looked skeptical. Felix might be functionally autistic, but the cause of his behavior was periventricular leukomalacia, the death of key areas of white matter. "Isn't autism also related to an overabundance or shortage of white matter?" I asked. It can be, he nodded warily. "Even if he is not classically autistic," I suggested, "his behaviors are. Might not a medication that helps autistic people, say, curb uncontrollable fits, also help him?" Dr. Wells pointed out that Felix was very young at the time, just six. And his nonverbal nature meant that he would not be able to tell us if a drug made him feel nauseous, or if it gave him terrifying visions and nightmares. These drugs, Dr. Wells said gravely, can cause serious side effects.

"He's already trying to tear his skin off," I said.

In the end, Dr. Wells gave us a prescription for a light dose of risperidone, an antipsychotic used to treat schizophrenia, bipolar disorder, and irritability in people with autism. But Dr. Wells's unease traveled home with me. What if the risperidone made whatever was ailing Felix even worse? And he wouldn't be able to tell us? I pinned the prescription to the bulletin board in the kitchen, and there it stayed, a neat blue rectangle that I doubted would help anyway, getting lost under school notices and pictures of better times.

. . .

Recalling this time is choppy, the spurts of violence and lack of sleep making mincemeat of my memory. Huge swaths are irretrievable. Apparently, over the summer, I rented an old farmhouse in Chesterfield, Massachusetts, so that we could spend a week with my father, his wife, my brother, and other relatives. Apparently there was a storm. The owner of the house came over to fix the roof. The yard out front turned into a lake. Felix's intestines spewed forth in what Jason tells me the two of us dubbed the "poo-pocalypse." His shit was smeared over multiple rooms of the rental. Apparently I scrubbed it up, but I remember none of it. All that I can recall from this trip is snapping a shot of Svetlana and Miranda on a carousel at the county fair. Both of them are sticking out their tongues, blue from Italian ice. When I dwell on this picture, I can see, as through a scrim, Felix on a carousel, euphoric. But that could have very well have been wishful thinking, a dream, a waking dream. I was averaging under four hours of sleep a night. Felix was getting less.

What I can remember: an afternoon, back in Fort Greene. Felix and I, struggling on his bed, a single mattress on the floor, the sheets undone and stained with blood. He slipped out of my grip, and slapped his eye, already bruised and swollen. He did this sort of thing often enough, yet the rage in his eyes on that particular afternoon, in my particular state of mind, unhinged me. If anyone else had attacked Felix with that level of brutality, I would have jumped them, pummeled them, tried to tear them limb from limb. How could he do this to himself? I screamed an obscenity at the top of my lungs and slapped him across the face. A no-holds-barred slap that stunned us both into silence. Then he went back to hitting himself.

I left his room shaking. It felt as if his violence had seeped into me, but perhaps it was my own violence. Or perhaps trying to distinguish whose violence is whose is moot. Perhaps moods travel, engulf us, possess us. I had known intellectually that violence can get the better of anyone, or at least most people. It's the principle of the tipping point. Given the right amount of pressure, people will turn. And I had.

I remember a night, dark, two or three in the morning. Felix was screaming and I was nursing Happy and someone banged on our front door. Oscar began barking maniacally. Not because someone was trying to get in. Because someone had knocked. Oscar hated knocking. Any kind of knocking. Rapping your fist on a table for emphasis. Dropping a can by mistake. His barks annoyed us all, especially Felix, who would scream all the louder when Oscar started to bark. Two policeman were at the door. They had been patrolling on Dekalb and heard Felix. Jason let them in. Did we need any help? they asked. Yes, we did. But none that they could deliver.

Studying jiujitsu and karate had been good preparation: the holds, the attention to breathing, the separation of fighting from anger. But I was no sensei. After the feeling I experienced when I slapped Felix, I realized that there were times that I should not restrain him. If I was too tired. If I had been wrestling with him too much. If for any reason I felt that the rage could spread into me. But if I couldn't physically hold him, what to do? I had read of blind people in institutions who were not born blind, but who had rendered themselves sightless by destroying their eyes with fists and clawing hands. I could easily imagine such a fate for Felix. A motley parade of homemade straightjackets, boxing gloves, "friendly" looking handcuffs made of bandanas followed. None worked until I happened on oven mitts. Thick, quilted oven mitts from a yuppie kitchen store on Atlantic Avenue. I fashioned them with drawstring closures that could be tied and double-knotted, making them difficult to get off. It wasn't easy getting them on, either. I'd have to pin him to the ground, use my knee to hold down his shoulder as he pinched my thigh, grab him again as he escaped, but there was a foreseeable end to our struggle. It was far better than thirty or forty minutes of holding him to the ground, trying to keep calm in the face of his knife-like eyes, his cracked swollen lips, his bony and furious protest. I could get the mitts on in five minutes. Then I could leave him in his room, relatively certain he'd be safe.

Once we started with the mitts, there was less blood, less swollen eyes, noses, lips. Less of me, on the verge of madness. Even so, even when I was physically separated from him, in another room, the vibrations of his screams made it difficult to breathe, to think, to do anything except stand still, dull and trembling, feeling as if a jackhammer were in my brain. I'd grab at any excuse to get out of the house. The girls had to go to the park. The car had to be moved for alternate side of the street parking. Groceries had to be bought. I would leave with my laces untied, my shirt inside out. Felix's screams would carry all the way down our block. Once I'd crossed Lafayette Avenue and moved on to quieter realms, the still, the peace, was almost surreal. People walked dogs. Children zipped around on scooters. Parents shouted to stop at the crosswalk. There were no bombs dropping. There were, of course, bombs dropping in Iraq, Afghanistan, Pakistan, plenty of places. Families were running for cover, children maimed, minds lost to rage or unutterable sorrow. That kind of violence made more sense than the strange ease of Fort Greene. I would blink in confusion at the couples sauntering about, the homeowners gardening, the tenants taking out the trash. I hated when the milk was purchased and I had to cross back over Lafayette Avenue. How I yearned to linger, to keep walking, past our street, our block, into that drugged haze of peace.

A year before, with Felix exploring the world and Miranda babbling and Penelope a little heartbeat inside me, the great difficulties Felix faced seemed to be social instead of biological. That is, the bureaucratic torment and social frustration that he engendered were a greater burden than his body and brain, which worked, albeit in a way unique to him. In academia, this is known as the social model of disability. Felix was fine. What was blinkered was the society into which he was born, that variegated apparatus of fixers and starers and pokers and pitiers who couldn't deal with the complex multitude of forms that life takes, who suffocated us with suggestions on how to improve Felix, who recorded their incomprehension in truckloads of time-intensive, stress-inducing tests and clunky observations. For many people with disabilities, the social model of disability well describes their situation. A fascinating segment on the NPR radio show *Invisibilia* follows Daniel Kish, a blind man who taught himself how to see through echolocation. Kish convincingly argues that even blindness is not always inherent—it can be caused by a society that coddles its blind, that wants to see for the blind, instead of allowing the blind the tools and behaviors to see on their own.

But when Felix stopped treasuring his world, when he wanted to tear his body right out of it, the social model cracked. Something was wrong. Something was torturing him, and it wasn't, as far as I could tell, his environment. It came from within.

• • •

What do you do when your child is beating himself to a pulp and no one really knows why? What do you do when you can no longer hope that it might be a one-time thing? Well, there's always red wine, which eased me at night, and coffee in the morning, and running through the park, and yoga, and Jason. And the girls. Pregnant with Penelope, I had worried that I might be in for an unremitting period of bleakness. What were the odds that if I had three children, they'd all be doing well at the same time? Wouldn't one always be sick, dejected, whiny, insane? It turns out, no. There were times when a quiet contentment would settle over all three, and Jason and I would steal timid glances at each other, afraid to break the spell. We called these times "nonces," and held them dear. But nonces were rare; the main thing that got me through was focusing on bright spots; and it turns out the more children, the more bright spots. True, Felix might be a bloody mess, but look at Miranda, half-naked, gamboling after the butterfly. True, the baby was howling with diaper rash and had to get shots tomorrow, but look at Felix, giggling and high-fiving the electrician. True, Miranda was kicking and pounding the floor with her fists, refusing to put on underpants even though we were late for preschool, but look at the baby, contentedly snuggled in her crib, her soft sleepy breaths like the gentlest of kisses.

And there were Ozge, Emily, and Svetlana. There are parents who have to deal with the unstoppable violence of their child all alone. They need help, physical help, other people to hold them and hold their children. Even with all the support that I had, there were nights when Felix's fits seemed to go on forever, and Jason and I nearly went mad. I believe that I would have gone mad without Ozge, Emily, and Svetlana. They gave Felix baths, changed his diaper, swung him at the park, took him to Huck, took him to swimming, took him to Jackie, walked him for miles around the neighborhood. And when all else failed, they learned to hold him down. They learned how to put on his mitts. We'd trade him and the girls back and forth, using the girls to restore us when Felix was in a bad spot, using Felix to restore us when his fury passed and his beautiful laugh shot forth.

For Felix did restore us. His joy, when it surfaced, was as powerful as ever. During those long spells when the fits were not claiming him, he continued to grow and explore and delight. One day, changing Happy's diaper, a metallic clatter in the kitchen made me look up. Felix was standing at the kitchen sink, splashing water in a dirty pan. Standing! He must have bunny hopped to the sink, kneeled, hooked his fingers around the rim, and pulled himself to his feet. He'd never pulled himself to standing before. To encourage him to stay in this position (stretching out his calves, allowing for more weight-bearing on his feet, all of which would make Huck happy), I turned on the faucet. He held his hands under the running water, feeling it slip through his fingers, and sang.

Ha-ee buhay oo ooo,
ha-ee buhay oo ooo.
Ha-ee buhay oo oo-oo-oo,
ha-ee buhay oo ooo.

He could sing almost all the words to "Happy Birthday," in a soft melodic voice, far more tuneful than mine.

An Idea

In September, Miranda started at a neighborhood preschool called the Co-op School. I had enrolled her there, hoping to give her, and soon Happy, a safe, stable place away from our home, which could get so chaotic. As the name suggests, it was a cooperative. Each family was required to take on two work shifts a year and join a committee. Up until that point of my life, I had avoided joining committees of all kinds. But the Co-op parents I'd met at Camel Park were so pleased with the school, I figured I could handle a meeting or two, and the more I thought about it, the more attractive the prospect seemed—a guilt-free way to get out of the house. On my way to my first Co-op meeting, I walked down Fulton, shaking off the scene I'd left at home. I wasn't worried. I was relieved, stroller-less, nodding hello to passersby. Words ran through my head: *Felix is sick and he cannot speak. He roars like an orangutan caught in the deep. Like a hyena with no meat, with nothing, nothing at all to eat. Like you if your mind fell out of its keep.* During the Co-op meeting, words kept coming. I borrowed a pen and wrote them on the back of the agenda. I decided to illustrate these words. I would make a book for the girls, a way to help them make sense of, or at least acknowledge, the extremities of our family life.

During those next few months, when Miranda and Felix were at school and Happy was resting, I sat at my computer, drawing pictures of the policemen, the doctors, the scratching and biting, the restraining, the wish to help, the cluelessness, the bliss of quietness, the magnificent happiness of Felix's smile. To give some distance, I named the book's main character Phoenix, and titled the book "Phoenix Is Sick." When it was done, I printed it out on one of those self-publish sites and gave it to Miranda. She liked it. So too, did my friends. Some of them wept when reading it. They urged me to get it published. I doubted that could happen; if I couldn't find a publisher for my novels, how would I find a publisher for something that much more dark, strange, and raw? But I was touched by the way that the book had affected them. I think that they saw something of their own lives in Felix's, that aloneness in the midst of love, that ache of not being understood.

Many of these readers were new friends. That first year at the Co-op School, new friends popped up like mushrooms, inviting us over to dinner in spite of the possibility of Felix's fits, swooping up Miranda on emergency play dates, cheering on my projects. The making of one new friend carries a tang of discovery and surprise, but a dozen, in only a few months? Jason and I were astonished until we realized that Meredith Gray, the director of the school, was an alchemist, creating the atmospheric conditions in which friendships form. Even her version of parent-teacher conference night, in most places a fraught affair, was imbued with possibility. Instead of nervously waiting outside individual classrooms, parents waited their turn in the rec room, which was stocked with beer and wine and children playing on the stage. It was very difficult to skulk off by yourself, talk to your child's teacher for five minutes and leave. It was very easy to grab a beer, chat with other parents, and watch the children play. Up until I met Meredith, I had been suspicious of the phrase "creating community." It seemed like a phrase Chase Bank used to get you to sign up for a checking account. Now I realized that it was a valid activity and quite doable: You gather people in a room, you create a welcoming environment, you celebrate what you have in common.

How I wished there had been something like the Co-op community when Felix was young. How much less alone we would have felt. Even at the Co-op, I'd feel pangs of loneliness when talking about Felix. My Co-op friends were fond of him and wanted to hear about him, but there were times when my words would miss their mark, and whatever I was trying to say could not be conveyed.

Then I met Bliss. Bliss Broyard was the chairperson of the community events committee, the committee to which I belonged. She was also a writer who had served on the board of the storytelling organization, The Moth. She proposed that the Co-op School produce a Moth-like story night, featuring Co-op parents sharing true stories about parenting. They would be coached by storytellers from The Moth. They would have a rehearsal. The result would be a real show, by parents, for parents, no kids allowed. I thought this sounded preposterously ambitious, but she asked me to assist her, and Bliss is not the sort of person to be refused.

Shortly after Christmas, I began meeting with other parents, helping them to hone personal experience into performance pieces, as well as preparing to tell one such story myself, a tale about Felix and his passionate and disruptive love of ice cream. Except for some teaching, I had never performed before, and the thought of it filled me with dread. But it was wonderful when the show did indeed come together, and I stood before a packed and encouraging audience, telling a tale that honored Felix and integrating him into this community of families I had grown to love.

• • •

I loved the Co-op School. I loved our neighborhood. I loved our house. I did not want to move. But our house, beloved as it was,

was one of those old houses typical to Brownstone Brooklyn: narrow, vertical contraptions whose rooms are separated by stairways as
often as hallways. We were continuously ascending and descending
steps in order to get a pair of scissors, find a sock, get a snack, and so
on. With help, Felix could manage some of this. When he was willing and his energy was bright, he/we could climb the thirteen steps
that made up a flight in less than a minute, but usually it took much
longer, and sometimes he couldn't manage at all. In the mornings,
Jason or I (usually Jason) would carry him from his third-floor bedroom down to the kitchen, and from there we'd wheel him out to
the school bus. But he was sixty-five pounds, and growing quickly. A
third-floor bedroom would soon become impossible.

Apartment buildings were out of the question because of the
noise Felix made, but maybe a converted warehouse or garage? On
the first day of looking, a fellow Co-op parent/real estate agent took
me and Happy to a sprawling, graffiti-emblazoned carriage house in
Prospect Heights. Pipes stuck out of the walls and a dented wheel-
barrow hung from the ceiling. The place had once housed hundreds
of horses, later a sculptor, and who knew what in between. It made
me giddy. It delighted Happy, also. She desperately wanted to tod-
dle about, but I couldn't let her loose, as the floors were littered with
rusty nails. She squirmed in my arms as sunlight came down from
the skylights, illuminating a space dizzying in its possibility: twenty-
five feet across, one hundred feet deep with thirty feet tall ceilings. I
pictured a loft where the girls could read, with rope ladders dangling
below that Felix could bat at, swings, a trampoline. I spent the next
few days sketching ever more extravagant layouts. Beehive-shaped
bedrooms that could be piled atop one another and climbed on, an
indoor pool in a glass encased courtyard. The crazy thing was, with
Jason's salary and the sale of our home, such things were possible.
That we could create such an opulent playpen made me a little sick.
At the same time, I couldn't stop fantasizing.

On my second visit to the carriage house, I realized that the excess of my vision would not bother me if those beehive rooms, that sunlit, splashy courtyard, and those swings weren't only for us. What if we made the carriage house into a play space for a whole bunch of families? I imagined the interior strewn with comfy foofs, climbing walls, hammocks, and a tiny, kidney-shaped pool in a courtyard. A place where we could hang out with Jamila and Bashir, and Rebecca, the neighbor who had asked me where I got Felix's walker, thinking it might be good for her son Frank, and whose question had evolved into a friendship, not only between me and her but between our families. More neighbors would come, and more families, families that I didn't know yet, but I knew were out there. I saw them in hospitals and waiting rooms. A shaft of light shot down through the skylight. I laughed out loud.

I don't think that the idea would have popped into my mind if not for the Co-op School. Or had it popped into my mind, it would have just slid right on by, in spite of that encouraging slant of sunlight. It would have seemed like an idle fantasy—but the Co-op School proved that creative community projects could be done. And this project I was starting to envision would be easier than a school. I did not want a school. Schools focus on work, learning, therapy. I wanted a place dedicated to playing, relaxing, being, a place where kids like Felix could, for once, be free of people trying to change them into something else. Schools are also exclusive. They can only admit a certain number of people, often at a steep cost. I wanted a place that would welcome anyone who wanted to join. It wouldn't matter what their disability was, what their age was, what their family income was.

I bounced the idea of a creative community center, designed for families with children with disabilities, off parents at the playground. In typical Fort Greene fashion, they all thought that it was

a great idea and encouraged me to do it. Jason was more sanguine.
Do you have any idea what you're getting yourself into? No. But I
had produced student movies in my early twenties. I had herded
people of diverse talents together and scraped up money, wasn't
that more or less what such a project entailed? He tried to talk me
out of it, but I felt the same sort of compulsion that I feel when
working on a novel—the urge simply took over.

On an errand to YAI, a private nonprofit agency that tries to
help people with developmental disabilities and their families, I
made a detour to the development office. Maybe someone there
would have a clue as to how to proceed? Better yet, maybe YAI
would want to invest? None of the development people were there,
but I talked with a very nice secretary. That night, a man from the
development department called me as I was boiling brown rice noodles for Felix's dinner. You are not crazy, he said kindly. Parents are
responsible for many of the innovative developments within the
disability community, and a pan-disability gym is a good idea. But
YAI would not be able to fund it. You need to start a grassroots
movement for that sort of thing.

Starting a grassroots movement did not sound the least bit
doable. The only public speaking I'd ever done was that one terrifying, exhilarating story night at the Co-op. Merely making a phone
call to a stranger could bring on a mild panic. I specialized in self-
directed solitude. Writing. Art. But I felt it would be polite to keep
the conversation going, so I asked how one went about starting a
grassroots movement. The YAI guy told me about a book, then
went about paraphrasing the whole thing: first, you hold brain-
storming meetings to get feedback on your ideas and generate
new ones. Then, with the help of these groups and their input, you
come up with a tangible goal and a step-studded map to get there.
The more people involved in the discussion, the more momentum,

the more talents and resources available. Each step that brings you closer to your goal will attract more people, making the end goal— the gym—that much more attainable. Good luck! he said.

Five years earlier, I would have never considered asking strangers over to our house to consider a far-fetched dream. But my discomfort with calling attention to myself had been chipped away by Felix. When you are pushing a loudly whooping or biting or giggling disabled child through crowded streets, you attract attention. You get used to it. So I sent out a mass email. Late in March, a couple of weeks after Felix turned seven, a dozen people showed up for what I had dubbed the Brooklyn Funhouse Brainstorm. Neighbors whose children had disabilities. Friends from the Co-op School. Professionals in the field. Ragged screams rang out from Felix's bedroom, where Ozge was trying to calm him, as I talked about the need for a place of our own, a place where the weird was the norm. The parents and professionals at the table beamed and nodded. A couple bottles of wine later, Felix was quiet and ideas flew around the table. I was grateful as I said goodbye, moved by the support and enthusiasm, but I wondered if anything had really been accomplished. Mainly I felt like I had talked, my guests had affirmed, and then we had all started wildly fantasizing together.

But the evening had given me the beginnings of a roadmap: as no one knew how to raise the funds to buy the carriage house, we all agreed that we, that is Jason and I, would rent a temporary space where we could hold family movement and art classes for children with any sort of disability. The classes would be valuable in themselves, but they would also work to bring families together, and perhaps pave the way for a larger movement that would be able to achieve something like my big disability community center. The next morning, with Felix and Miranda at school and Happy napping, I put together a to-do list. That's when I realized the real purpose of the brainstorm. I had announced that I was going to do something in front of a room of people. They had hired babysitters. They had rearranged their lives in order to hear me talk. I couldn't just file away the to-do list, and pretend it never happened.

I began combing through Brooklyn, looking for a wheelchair-accessible space with natural light, high ceilings, an affordable rent, and a landlord willing to sign a contract with a nonprofit start-up specializing in children with disabilities. Those with an understanding of the New York City real estate market may be snorting in amusement. It was a quixotic quest. But you've got to start somewhere. As for our brownstone and its insistent and evermore difficult stairs? I hired an architect. We became friends over the course of the next couple of years as we plotted a renovation that would convert our vertical house into a home where Felix could live forever.

Doctors

Felix's hips had begun to curve inward, resulting in an inward twist of his legs.
When he walked, his knees and feet bumped into each other, hampering forward motion, often tripping him. The doctors told us that if we wanted to keep him mobile, we'd have to do a double hip operation along with some extension of the calves. I could not plunge into my disability community center to-do list right away—March and April were tight with pre-op appointments, including a visit to the Hospital for Special Surgery's Motion Analysis Laboratory on East Seventy-Third Street. The motion analysis lab was an intriguing space that looked like a cross between a gym and a movie studio, stocked with cameras and tripods and grids of electronics. After some struggle, a team of physical therapists and technicians managed to hook Felix up to sensors intended to record the movement of his muscles, tendons, and bones, as he walked his walker in a straight line, as he took a corner, as he ran. This information would be analyzed before the surgery, helping the surgeon to better understand Felix's body. But Felix was not having any of it. He had started in on another course of fits shortly after his seventh birthday, and was not at his most amenable. He roared. He slapped. He would not move his legs. I had brought along some homemade chocolate chip cookies, made with spelt flour and goat milk butter, as a bribe to urge him on. I can see the greasy crinkles of the tin foil and the crumbs falling on the clean gym floor. "Yum! Felix! A

cookie! Come get it!" The cookies were slightly sour due to the goat milk butter, but strangely good. They motivated him, even if they couldn't stop his screams.

The fits were still hitting Felix multiple times a day when we packed up his favorite jingle jangles, keys, and CDs and took him to the Hospital for Special Surgery. Aside from Felix's emergency room visits, the MRI's and EEG's, he'd had an undescended testicle surgery after his first birthday, a couple of ear tube operations, an adenoidectomy, and another undescended testicle surgery at six, when it turned out the first hadn't worked. But this operation, not uncommon in the cerebral palsy world, was like nothing he'd been through before. It entailed breaking his hip bones, then putting them back together. The recovery time was estimated at six months. I dreaded it with every bone in my body.

My one ray of hope was a conversation I'd had with the father of a boy who had been through the procedure. I met them in the waiting room at Nordoff Robbins, a music therapy program Felix attended at NYU. The father wheeled his son off the elevator just as Felix and I were preparing to go. I must have been talking to Felix's music therapist about the surgery. The father took one look at Felix and figured out what we were talking about. He assured me that the operation was not as bad as all that. His son had been back on his feet only a few weeks afterward, and it had radically helped him to stand straighter and move faster. The Hospital for Special Surgery was a wonderful place, the staff was so supportive, and everyone loved his son. But of course they did! His son was amazing! What a brave boy he'd been! The son, a handsome boy with fair skin and light freckles, bore the long-suffering expression of a child pained by parental applause.

Dr. Scher performed the operation on April 13, 2010. The surgery went well. Then Felix woke up. His screams reverberated down the halls and would continue reverberating, on and off but mainly on, for the four or five days he stayed at the hospital. Jason and I took turns being with him: trying to quiet him, trying to stop his hand from flying into his face, trying to console him when he'd let us. Nurses entered apologetically. Aides lowered their eyes. Doctors came up to us in the halls, squeezed our elbows, called us saints. They should not have called us saints. Felix was the one getting mauled by lions. But they were shocked. Felix's fits had shocked me, but I had thought that people working a hospital might see this level of fury more than the general public. Apparently they were more used to patients like the boy I'd met at NYU: heroic, quiet, well-behaved children who understood, on some level, that whatever had been done to them had been done, or at least was intended to have been done, in their best interest. There was no way to explain to Felix, though we had tried, that the breaking of his hips was supposed to be good for him.

We took Felix home with Ziploc bags filled with Valium and Motrin. He cycled between sleep and bouts of screaming and hitting himself. Had Felix not had the operation, it's possible that his fits might have passed by then, for they came in waves and usually receded after a couple months. But the procedure had destabilized him. His physical recovery didn't bode well either. He did not have a cast stabilizing his legs, only bandages, as our surgeon had assured us that movement of the thighs was so painful that people recovering from the operation automatically kept them still, and he didn't want to burden Felix with the further discomfort of a cast. But Felix jiggled his thighs. His screams were the distillation of agony. Day after day, he kept moving those thighs and kept screaming. He may not have been aware of where the pain was coming from. He may not have been able to control his movements. New bone grew as a result of all that jiggling, complicating his joints. But that is another story. Right now I want to talk about doctors.

We had been lucky with doctors. We hadn't come across any of the blustering know-it-all's other parents had told me about, doctors who said things like, "Your son will never walk," or "He has a two-year life span," or "It's your fault." For the most part, our doctors had been kind, open about their ignorance, and willing to scrunch their foreheads in sympathy and try to figure out how they could make things better. That I had begun to question if they could wasn't their fault. It was just the situation. There are no specialists in Felix. Except perhaps Felix, but he could not tell us what to do. So we continued to take him to doctors and healers, and acquired ever more diagnoses. As the years went by, I thought more and more fondly of Natasha's doctors in *War and Peace*:

Doctors came to see her singly and in consultation, talked much in French, German, and Latin, blamed one another, and prescribed a great variety of medicines for all the diseases known to them, but the simple idea never occurred to any of them that they could not know the disease Natasha was suffering from, as no disease suffered by a live man can be known, for every living person has his own peculiarities and always has his own peculiar, personal, novel, complicated disease, unknown to medicine—not a disease of the lungs, liver, skin, heart, nerves, and so on . . . but a disease consisting of one of the innumerable combinations of maladies of these organs. This simple thought could not occur to the doctors . . . because the business of their lives was to cure, and they received money for it and had spent the best years of their lives on that business. But, above all, that thought was kept out of their minds by the fact that they saw that they were really useful, as in fact they were to the whole Rostov family. Their usefulness did not depend on making the patient swallow substances for the most part harmful (the harm was scarcely perceptible, as they

were given in small doses), but they were useful, necessary, and
indispensable because they satisfied a mental need of the invalid
and those who loved her—and that is why there are, and always
will be, pseudo-healers, wise women, homeopaths, and allopaths.
They satisfied the eternal human need for hope of relief, for
sympathy, and that something should be done.

• • •

Tolstoy might have tempered his take on pills and powders had he
lived to see the advent of aspirin and penicillin. But I imagine that
his insistence on the uniqueness of each individual's own particular
disease would remain the same. Surely Felix's constellation of disabilities and abilities, workings and ruptures were Felix's alone and
no one else's.

It seemed that every doctor we saw gave him new diagnoses. I
pictured these diagnoses as yellow sticky notes with Latinate words
scrawled across them, signifying the education, background, pref-
erence, attention, and strategy of each doctor at the moment of
diagnosis. The diagnoses of Dr. Pytlak, with her deep understanding of family dynamics and the inner workings of New York State
and City bureaucracies, were generous, copious, and pragmatic.
Her eyes would light up, as if with a poet's inspiration, when she
hit upon one that should, really should, get us a disability placard
for our car, a home health aide, a night nurse. The diagnoses of Dr.
Wells were cautious and conservative and somewhat otherworldly,
imbued with the dignity of truth sought after. The diagnosis of Dr.
Scher, the surgeon who performed the hip operation, was practical.
Felix's hip bones were curving inward. He wouldn't be able to walk.
Straighten them.

As provisional as these diagnoses were, the obtaining of them
made us feel as if we were doing something. In this way the doctors served their ritualistic purpose, as surely they did in Tolstoy's

day. We were not curling up into a ball and sobbing (well, not always). We were not hiding in work (well, not always). We were strenuously seeking help. We were doing something.

. . .

The shock with which the doctors and nurses at the Hospital for Special Surgery had received Felix's rages had rekindled my need to do something. When we got home, and his screaming and hitting did not abate, I called Dr. Wells, who referred me to Dr. Perry, a child psychiatrist and NYU professor who had done stints at Belleview. Jason and I brought Felix to his office on the Upper West Side. I carried Felix's stroller down the steps. Jason carried him, still sore from the operation, as carefully as he could. Dr. Perry whistled low and hard when he saw Felix's bruised and scabbed face. After an hour and a half interview, he told us in no uncertain terms that the risperidone was safe, and that he strongly recommended trying it.

It worked. Had I filled Dr. Wells's prescription the year before, perhaps we could have saved Felix and ourselves a good deal of anguish. Though it is also possible that I would have discounted risperidone as just another useless drug, for Dr. Wells had given us a light dosage. Dr. Perry put seven-year-old Felix on a full adult dosage. This did not immediately return Felix to his normal happy state, as the pain from his operation persisted. But he stopped expressing his agony through hitting himself and screaming. What does risperidone do? I can only parrot basic science blogs and tell you that it helps to regulate the activity of the neurotransmitters dopamine and serotonin. The mechanics of this are unclear to me, but the results weren't: Those successive whirlwinds of violence that had so traumatized our house stopped.

Once Felix had recovered from the surgery and could again move about, he seemed so well, so stable, so himself, that we tried weening him off. But after only a day or two, we were met by his devil screech and he went back to brutalizing himself. We returned him to his dosage. Peace returned. Part of me grieved. The effect of the drug suggested that Felix's madness did indeed reside in his brain, that it was part and parcel of him and his brain damage. The likelihood was that we would be popping pills into his mouth for the rest of his life. Another part of me melted with relief. Not only did the drug stabilize him, it allowed him to sleep. Through the night. We all started sleeping through the night.

Extreme Kids & Crew

The summer after Felix's hip operation, he could not walk, and so he stayed mainly in his room, on his mattress, jingling elaborate tangles of keys and strings and listening to music. Tribalistas, a Brazilian CD that my father had brought back from a business trip, was the hit of the season. Bob Marley and the Beatles were also popular. When he dozed, or when he was off in his own world, and Ozge was looking after the girls, I would go upstairs and work on the 501(c)(3) application.

Once Jason understood that I couldn't shake off the community center project, he had plunged in, pledging seed money and getting me pro bono help from his law firm. In earlier years, I had bridled at his attachment to his BlackBerry, his nose so continuously angled down to its flickering pixels, but now I found myself with a similar sort of fixation, running to my desk to check my email every chance I got. I ended up purchasing one of those smartphones myself and was soon jumping at each little buzz and twizzle. My main correspondent was Anthony Cerceo, the law associate helping me with the legal part of setting up a company. In June he reserved us the name. I had wanted Brooklyn Funhouse, but it turned out that name had already been taken by a party space in East New York. So walking to the subway, I came up with a new one: Extreme

Kids & Crew. Extreme because Jason and I had a longstanding joke about how raising Felix was a form of extreme sports. Crew because the organization was to bring together not only kids with disabilities, but also their parents, siblings, therapists, friends—that is, their crew.

Incorporating was easy. Acquiring nonprofit status was not. The 501(c)(3) is the initial hurdle the IRS presents to those who would start a nonprofit company. It is a cumbersome, thirty-page document intended to scare away the weak at heart and the legally unadvised. It took months to complete, for it entailed finding a board of directors, articulating Extreme Kids & Crew's mission, and sketching out a business plan. Here my practice of fiction writing finally found a practical application. A business plan, which presents the purpose, operations, marketing, budget, look and feel of a nonexistent company, calls upon the same sort of talents—the ability to transplant an idea on to paper in so convincing a way that it seems real. The difference is that you are intending to make it real, this thing that you have dreamed up.

I felt like a con artist, introducing myself to prospective landlords as the director of a company that only existed on paper, drawing numbers out of the air to create budgets—but it was fun. Companies might start as a solitary fiction, but they are soon populated by flesh and blood people, suspicious of your vision, bantering about mission wordage, introducing you to people who may be of help. Every few days, I'd find myself at a coffee shop, scanning the tables, wondering which person was the one I had come to meet.

In this way I met Patricia Connelly, a special education parent advocate who had two things to tell me. The first was a story. Her maternal grandmother emigrated to the United States from Ireland, leaving behind her sister Kitty, who remained on the family farm. Money was too tight to visit one another, but they kept in touch by

mail, writing of their children, family gossip, and so forth. Decades
passed. In the 1950s Patricia's grandmother traveled back to Ireland,
and discovered that she had a niece that she had not heard about.
Her name was Joan, and she was often found in a rocking chair at
the general store, greeting people and delivering messages. She had
Down syndrome. She loved many, and was well-loved in return. It
was said that she held the town together. Indeed many years later,
when Joan died, the village newspaper—which is published just
once annually at the New Year—was completely devoted to her
obituary. She was the heart and soul of Bohola, but her mother had
never mentioned her in letters.

Patricia's own son had a less visible disability, dyslexia. Because
of him, she had become an expert on New York City's special education system, and now worked to help parents navigate the system, a
system that was so leaky that a great number of children with learning disabilities were not identified as such. The second thing Patricia
had to tell me concerned these children: They might not be as disabled as Felix or Patricia's mother's cousin in Ireland, but they also
needed to be accepted and celebrated. That, unfortunately, was not
the case for most of them. They were being bullied. They were being
sent home from school. They were being put in juvenile detention.
Experts and social workers lectured their parents on tactics, interventions, and therapies that were for the most part unattainable,
increasing parental stress and frustration. Patricia wanted these
families to be included in Extreme Kids & Crew, too. They need
a community center, and, she pointed out, they will increase your
ranks. According to the Census, 5 percent of school-age children
living at home have a disability. But over 15 percent of New York
City school children have IEP's, that is, the Individual Education
Plans the public school system uses to track and presumably help
its students with disabilities. This suggests that most parents don't

report their child as disabled if they have a learning disability like ADHD or dyslexia. Perhaps they feel more comfortable with the term "special needs" that is more often used in the school system. Perhaps the word "disability" scares them.

I agreed with Patricia, but the clunkiness of sentences like, "We welcome all children with physical, behavioral, cognitive, intellectual, emotional, developmental, and learning disabilities," made me cringe. I whittled it down to disabilities, and figured eventually people would get it: We would open the door to anyone who did not fit in. I put up the first website for Extreme Kids & Crew in December of 2010. On the site I included a long letter, sketching out my dream of a community center and inviting people to help make it happen. A steady stream of emails began to arrive in my inbox. Many parents wrote that the letter had moved them to tears. They told me of their lives, their children, and their situations, and I would start crying, too. They wrote how they would love a place like Extreme Kids & Crew, and asked how could they help, and would there really be a pool? I would write back: I want that pool, too, but at the moment, we're arranging parent-child weekend classes in art, clay, or yoga. They will be creative, freewheeling, and process-oriented, appropriate for any sort of ability or disability and any age. They start in late January. Sign up!

The directors of disability arts programs I had met with had all warned me that enrollment was their most difficult challenge. I had shrugged this off. Their programs were located in Manhattan, and steeply priced, sometimes costing as much as therapy or doctors' appointments. We would be offering a sliding scale method of payment, five to twenty-five dollars per class according to household income, and we only needed six families to start. We'd be fine. And yet we weren't. Heart-wrenching missives from parents rolled in, but no one signed up for a class.

By January, I was frantic. I had trained teachers. Andrea, a friendly neighbor who had come to the brainstorm and pledged to help, had found me a sunny room to rent at a local community center. We had furnished it. I had posted flyers and advertised on parent listservs. But only four families, all friends, had enrolled. I was wondering if I'd have to throw in the towel when I got a call from the *Daily News*. One of their reporters had learned about Extreme Kids & Crew on Patricia Connelly's Facebook page and wanted to do a story on us.

I spent what seemed like an entire weekend on the phone with Ben Chapman—I never saw him, just heard his voice. I told him that I didn't know if he had a story, as I wasn't sure if we'd get enough people to run the classes. That's where the *Daily News* comes in, he replied. He seemed as intent to get Extreme Kids & Crew off the ground as I was. We talked strategy and story line for hours. He thought that the best angle would be a discussion of the difficulties involved in taking children with disabilities to regular playgrounds, and made me cough up every cold look or annoying comment Felix and I had ever received. Somewhere in the midst of this, he asked me about my life outside of Felix. I told him that I wrote, but I didn't want to call myself a writer because I hadn't published anything. We had moved on to another subject when the phone beeped. Johnny Temple, the publisher of Akashic Books, was on the other line.

Johnny was a neighbor and a fellow parent at the Co-op School. We had known each other for ages, as we had run in the same circles when we were kids in Washington, D.C. But we had not known each other well. On bed rest, when I was pregnant with Felix, I heard that he had started an independent press and called to see if he'd read my novel. He had politely declined. When you run a press, everyone you have ever met asks you to read his or her novel. He suggested that I send it to his editorial staff. I declined. He had forgotten this conversation by the time that we moved into Fort Greene, and I had no desire to remind him. But when my friends bugged me about trying to get "Phoenix Is Sick" published, I had asked Johnny if he'd take a look at it. He agreed without hesitation. It is far easier getting someone to read a twenty-eight-page illustrated book than a 270-page historical novel about utopian thinking. We met for drinks not long after that. He could not think of a publisher for "Phoenix Is Sick," but he liked it, and asked if I had written anything else. So it was Felix, the wordless one, who finally got Johnny to read my manuscript. He was calling in the midst of my telephone interview with the *Daily News* to tell me that all of the editors at Akashic loved my book. They wanted to publish it the following spring.

I returned to Ben Chapman. "You can call me a writer after all," I said.

. . .

A few days later, the *Daily News* sent a photographer to our house to do a photo shoot. Felix, who had been in a foul mood all day, perked up. He looked at the camera. He appeared to be following the photographer's directions. What was going on? He didn't follow directions, except for those of his physical and occupational therapists. Maybe because the photographer's directions were similar, simple one-step directives? Maybe because the photographer was cute? Maybe because Felix needed to forget his funk for a while? Who knows, but it was a fun shoot, and it led to a full-page picture and story that worked as a kind of baptism. Extreme Kids & Crew now existed. We'd been in the paper. We got a $20,000 grant out of that story. And enough families to run the classes.

Ten families, including ours. Thirty-two people. I had been worried about the prospect of spending ten precious weekends in the company of people I did not know and might not like, the normal trepidation about starting a new school or a new job made stronger by the no exit clause. I couldn't very well drop out of my own classes.

I needn't have worried. The people were lovely. String bean Jack with his hip-hop yoga moves. Ocean, solid ambassadress of goodwill, who had the same haircut as I did when I was a child, brown bangs, all the rest chopped off at the shoulder so as not to get tangled, tripping around the room, insistently high-fiving everyone. Bright-eyed Ethan and his mom, gamely driving around in an enormous cardboard car. Felix, nonplussed by art, would wheel his walker out of the room and through the tiled halls of the community center, investigating broom closets and bathrooms. That was his form of self-expression. Miranda and Happy stayed at the art table, squishing the clay around in their fingers, making blobs and monsters.

We lured Felix in with our first Music & Play concert. One of those work shifts at the Co-op School had had me painting a wall alongside Avishai Cohen, a fellow parent and well-known jazz trumpeter. When I told him how much Felix loved music, he told me he'd had a deep experience playing for an audience of autistic students in Israel and volunteered to play for Felix sometime. I'd never taken him up on this. Now I asked if instead of playing for just one boy, he'd do a free concert for Extreme Kids. He invited his sister Anat, who played the clarinet, and they performed a beautiful duet. Our room in the community center was an unusual, but lovely site for a concert: a simple room furnished with art tables and bean bag chairs, and decorated with life-size self-portraits from our art class. Midway through the performance, Felix pulled at my arms, indicating that he wanted to stand up. Using me as a walker, he approached the musicians. Kate Milford, soon to be a program manager for Extreme Kids, took a picture of him trying to capture the sound waves as they came out of Avi's trumpet.

I asked Karla Schickele to play for us the next month. Her concert was similarly moving. Then Astrograss, a local bluegrass band, volunteered to do a show, and soon Extreme Kids was committed to putting on free monthly concerts. I loved these shows, the freedom with which the children ran around the room and the light in the adults' eyes. It had been ages since I'd heard live music so regularly. I hadn't realized how much I'd missed it.

Space No. 1

Throughout the spring and summer of 2011, a friendly volunteer architect from Kentucky, whose son had a learning disability, would ride his bicycle to meet me at various loft spaces, church basements, storefronts, and garages around Brooklyn. He would take in the dimensions, rejigger them in his mind, and, a couple of minutes later, come up with a beguiling sketch of how they might be converted into play and art spaces. These pictures would bloom in my imagination as I drew up proposals for landlords, but none of them wanted to rent to a start-up nonprofit that specialized in kids with disabilities. Eventually, I gave up on commercial real estate and asked Meredith and the board at the Co-op School to rent us space in the school.

The room at the Co-op School was no carriage house. It was 900 square feet, a seventies cinder-block construction with an ugly drop ceiling and rickety fluorescents. But it had the bare essentials. It was wheelchair accessible, its bathroom was large enough to accommodate a massage table (so that parents could change diapers on 100-pound children), it had windows and two enormous walk-in closets that could be converted into alternative environments. It was well below market rate. Most importantly, it was ours: Meredith and the Co-op board agreed to rent it.

I dubbed the room Space No. 1, in the hopes that it would pave the way for a larger and more beautiful Space No. 2. Kate and

I covered the fluorescent lights with blue filters to mitigate their potentially harmful effects (some epileptics are particularly sensitive to fluorescents), and we lined the floor and walls with carpeted gymnastic mats, which are softer and comfier than vinyl mats and feel good on your toes. In consultation with Huck, I selected equipment that would be intriguing to both parents and children, accessible to any sort of body, and safe. I didn't want to replicate a typical indoor play space. I wanted to create a transformative space that would release both children and parents from their normal patterns of movement.

We kept the main room as open as possible, an expanse of fuzzy mats upon which rolled an enormous red ball four feet in diameter. In one corner stood a 750-pound C-Stand. From this, we hung a large, carpeted platform swing that parents and children could glide or spin on together. The swing accommodated all sorts of positions: It could be sat upon, stood upon, laid upon. Or it could be unhooked and replaced with a hammock swing, a cuddle swing, a moon swing, a squishy tire swing. In the other corner stood a sturdy art table where children could draw, paint, collage, or eat their snack. A dozen colorful foofs lined the walls, waiting to be piled into mountains for climbing and jumping, or arranged into a circle, or turned into caves, or anything else the children dreamed up. We turned one closet into a ball-pit room, the other into a cozy lounge, with lava lamps glowing from a high (inaccessible) shelf and lots of pillows.

By November 2011, we were ready. Up until that time, Extreme Kids had held concerts, parent-child classes, family art projects, and parent meet-ups. When enough people came, these events were shimmering and energetic, but enough people didn't always come. I believed that this was due to the particular strains that parents raising children with disabilities face. Among them: exhaustion—Felix wasn't the only kid known to sleep two to four hours a night; logistics—behavioral or physical disabilities can make public transportation traumatic or simply not possible; money—finances were strained due to medical and therapeutic expenses, as well as loss of income from taking time off work or stopping jobs entirely in order to care for their children; depression—isolating conditions can lead to a hopelessness that saps energy and the wish to connect. Parents didn't believe their children would be able to participate in a meaningful way in a class or event, so why bother?

Space No. 1 came about as a response to these conditions. The room was designed so that there would be something of interest to every child, whether it be tactile, vestibular, visual, aural. The idea was to give parents the tools to explore with their children at their own pace and style; they could do anything they wanted, provided that it was safe. A volunteer therapist might show parents particularly useful ways to use the swing or the ball pit or the squeeze machine, but there was no pressure to do these things in one particular way. Everything could be done in many ways. In terms of logistics, we could not, alas, provide transportation, but we could provide a large window of time in which to get to our space. Parents would not have to worry about reservations or advanced scheduling. They'd simply need to show up somewhere between twelve and four, say, on a Sunday afternoon. They would not be bothered with the ten-page forms that they had to fill out dozens of times a year. They would not have to prove their child was disabled or what their salary was. If they could not afford the suggested donation, they could pay what they could. The only thing that they would have to fill out was a waiver, saying that they would take responsibility for the safety of their child.

It worked. They came. Eighty people on our first day. Seventy families that first week. I wandered around in a haze of exhaustion and elation. A mother half submerged in the ball pit played catch with her daughter. A father spun on the platform swing, his son whooping in his lap. Parents sprawled on foofs, talking with each other. Children ran about laughing. In spite of our blue filters, Abby, a pig-tailed powerhouse of a five-year-old, had a seizure on opening day. But her mother was cheerful about it. Space No. 1, she later told me, was a great place to have a seizure. The other families, used to the unusual, did not overreact, magnifying the effects, and causing further anxiety. They saw that Abby was OK and continued to play. No big deal. A seizure, of course, can be a big deal. But when it's not, why turn it into one?

As the months went by, I became more aware and appreciative of this "good place to have a seizure" atmosphere. The gear was important. Kids came for the gear. We had a little boy from Manhattan who took the C train once a week to sprawl for an hour in the ball pit like it was his own personal sauna. Almost all the kids (and many of the adults) loved the various swings, the squeeze machine, the lava lamps. But the atmosphere really made the place. Andrew Solomon wrote about how disability can push you to the periphery or even expel you from the group in which you were born. You are orphaned in a way. I believe that part of the joy that bubbled up at Space No. 1 was born of that feeling of orphans meeting other orphans. These meetings might be laced with words, but they might not. A glance, a hug, a hum, a hand outstretched, the smallest, quietest motion between a child and his mother could spike within me a recognition that I was not alone, that I had a tribe, and that I liked my tribe.

That feeling started to slip away in the spring of 2012, when a fair amount of families whose children did not have disabilities discovered us. I had wanted "normal" families to come. I had wanted them to see how cool a place for kids with disabilities could be, and disperse some of those wisps of fear and pity that so often accompany difference. But instead of reverse inclusion, these families began outnumbering the families dealing with disability, more or less replicating what was going on outside at the playgrounds. Kids from these families would run right into children with disabilities. Smack!

Like not only attracts like—like *sees* like. In my early twenties, my knee gave out and I had to walk around Manhattan with a cane. To my great surprise, on almost every block I'd see another person with a cane. Where had all these cane walkers been when both my legs worked? Similarly, when I was pregnant, I noticed all the pregnant women. Siblings of children with disabilities saw disability. But so many of the children who did not have that kind of day-to-day familial experience did not. They saw only the "normal" kids. They ran into, or ran around, children with disabilities with barely a flicker of recognition.

These neuro-typical kids also tended to play king of the mountain more, fight more, and, in general, maintain a robust struggle over dominion. It's not that the kids with disabilities were enlightened angels. They were great at having temper tantrums, biting themselves and each other, flailing around in inconsolable misery, peeing in the ball pit. But their mayhem tended to be less about domination than that of the regular kids. This lack of pecking order is not a trait of all people with disabilities, of course, but it is common in kids on the autism spectrum, and we had lots of kids on the autism spectrum. If one is not "wired" for social intelligence, then one is also not "wired" for the social pyramids into which most of us automatically organize ourselves.

I began to see that a neuro-typical child, or adult for that matter, when walking into a room, will, without even thinking about it, assess who is in charge, and what his or her relationship is to this person. Does she want to dislodge the boy standing on the mountain of foofs and take his place? Does she want to align herself with him? Does she want to avoid him and his gang altogether and go quietly draw satirical cartoons of them? A kid on the spectrum is less likely to notice these subtle waves of social power. More likely to pick up a ribbon from the floor and study the way it glistens, feel its smoothness on the skin, taste its texture. If he wants to climb up the mountain of foofs, it's probably because he is interested in the feeling of being so high, with the squishiness under his feet, rather than a desire to dislodge or align himself with its current ruler.

Once, while walking Oscar, a neighbor at the dog park told me a story about her autistic nephew living in South Carolina. This nephew had a best friend who was transgender. After his friend turned from a "he" to a "she," she and her family faced ostracism and outright attacks at church, school, and work. The nephew with autism, however, switched pronouns without a ruffle. He couldn't understand what all the fuss was about. He was good at following rules, and it was a simple rule to follow. His friend's boundary jumping, which was so threatening to the community at large, meant hardly a thing to him, as he was impervious to his community's unspoken, but deeply felt power relations. This imperviousness to unspoken power relations allows people with autism a certain freedom that the rest of us don't often get a chance to taste.

In order to ensure that disabled kids would always be visible and in charge at Space No. 1, we changed the rules. Families with only neuro-typical kids were still allowed, but they needed to come with a family that had at least one child with a disability. The idea was to maintain a good ratio of typical to atypical children. We didn't want the kids with disabilities to be in the minority. And I, for one, wanted to feel more of that strung-out, autistic sense of inquiry and contentment-in-oneself. To be shut up in one's world all alone can be terrible, but to be content in one's world and able to share it is a lovely thing, and something that many of these children are particularly good at, given the right environment.

I became fascinated by environment. On numerous occasions, when families visited the space for the first time, the mother would serve as the advance guard. She would pop her head in the door, study the space with flickering, nervous eyes, and explain to me that she had brought her son (it was almost always a son), and that he had a hard time with transitions and unfamiliar terrains, so she didn't know if it would work. Said son would appear, accompanied by an aide or another parent, walk through the door, and just keep walking, often straight onto the mat, without taking off his shoes. I would scuttle after him, and ask him to take them off, or just slip them off for him. He would sit on a foof, taking in his surroundings with curiosity and approval, for all the world at home. The mother, still by the door, would blink in confusion, unaccustomed to a simple entrance. What was going on?

All children with disabilities were welcome at our space. Thanks to Patricia Connelly, we did not make a distinction between the radically disabled, people like Felix, and that large swath of children, 15 percent of schoolchildren, with IEPs. Some of these children are honors students, some have unaddressed learning disabilities and are lost. What ties them together is that their bodies and minds are particularly mismatched with the methods of instruction that work for the majority. They are outsiders, but not so far outside that they are not expected to comply with standard rules. It is a hard zone to inhabit: to both fit in and to not fit in, to feel pressure to be something that you are not. One of my most treasured notes came from the mother of one of these "disability-lite" children.

> I just wanted to thank you for the wonderful time that [my son]
> and I had at Space No. 1. I hadn't realized how much [my son]
> needed to be in an environment that allowed for, and appreciated,
> his idiosyncrasies until I saw what it was like for him to be free in

a place that offered so much to him and didn't judge him. I try not to judge him myself, but it's odd having a child who can "pass" on some levels. I don't realize, or hadn't, how much time and energy I spend trying to get him to adapt and to control his very impulsive self. He works very hard, all the time, to keep his impulses in check and to find ways to deal with the transitions that are foisted upon him. But after two hours in your space, I realized what unmitigated joy there was for him in being able to follow himself, uninterrupted, for that long. He needed, of course, to be reminded from time to time to be safe with himself and others, but the energy of acceptance in your space is truly like oxygen we didn't even know we needed.

He loved it and talks about it a lot since then. I think there's some weird part of us as parents that tells us subconsciously that if we somehow only cultivate and encourage more "normal" behaviors that our children will be safer, which of course I know from experience of my own upbringing is totally false and unhelpful. It was so refreshing and encouraging for me to be around you and the other parents and kids in such an atmosphere of delight and acceptance and complexity and yearning. Those kids woke me up.

Atmosphere. The feeling in a room. The air you breathe. It's a hard thing to write about, for it is so subjectively felt, and yet most all of us feel it. You walk into one room and you stand up taller. You walk into another and you hunch your shoulders protectively. You teach one class and jokes and analogies burble up without a thought. You teach the same material to a different group and your voice is wooden and your thoughts are numb. Bodies, the bodies of other people in a room, transmit an enormous amount of information that our minds barely register, yet our spines stiffen, our throats

tighten. Or, if you happen to be me at Space No. 1, and its succes-
sors, your jaw loosens, you breathe more deeply, you find it easy to
get down on the floor and talk and babble to anyone and everyone,
whether they understand you or not. What I began to realize is that
the atmosphere that helped autistic kids walk easily into the room
also helped me. It was not just the kids who felt accepted, but me,
too. I began to understand how rare this feeling was for all of us, and
I began to study how to foster it.

For the two years that Extreme Kids & Crew operated out of
Space No. 1, I volunteered almost every weekend, bringing along
Jason and the kids for most of the sessions. Jason excelled at being a
monster, which generally translated as scooping up children—anyone's children—and throwing them onto a crash pad. Miranda and
Happy felt totally at home, balancing on the rim of the ball pit in
capes and boas, drawing enormous murals out in the hall, making
little caves and nooks in the ever-shifting pile of foofs. Felix would
usually bunny hop over to the platform swing and take it over.
Sometimes he'd stay with us for the whole four-hour session, eating
bagels (he was no longer on his nonwheat diet), swinging and jingling his jangle, but usually he'd get restless after an hour or so, and
indicate, with varying levels of intensity, that he had to go out, at
which point Jason would strap him into his stroller and embark on
long ambling explorations of Bed Stuy and Crown Heights. "Oh my
god, you work so hard!" people would tell me, but most of the time,
it didn't feel like work. It was fun. It gave me energy. It was a great
way to be with my family.

Space No. 1 also gave me the opportunity to meet other kids
who reminded me of Felix. There was Hugo, who expressed his
love of music with the same floppy, exuberant twisting of his trunk.
There was the rollicking, toothy might of Eli. And there was Lula.
I met her parents at the beginning of Extreme Kids & Crew, right

after I put up the website. Both of them were enthusiastic and volunteered to help, even amidst the tumult of their lives. Not only had they just become parents, but parents of twins, one of whom was hypotonic, fragile, and had to be fed through a tube. The first time I held Lula, I almost cried, remembering the feeling of holding Felix as a baby. That weight. The weight of the head, the weight of a body when the neural circuitry cannot ignite the muscles, the gravitational pull toward the earth. She smelled so good. Her eyes were beautiful and enormous. They looked up and saw me.

She died in her mother's arms, at eighteen months. People from all over the United States and Europe came to her memorial, crowding the Society for Ethical Culture mansion so full that not everyone could get in. I had prepared some words to say in her honor, but as I watched a slideshow of pictures her mother had taken, I didn't think I'd be able to rise to my feet, let alone speak. I was convulsed in grief. When the time came, however, the strength and yearning in the room flooded into me. I walked to the podium. I spoke. I realized then how palpable it is, the courage we get from each other. Many of Lula's friends and relatives made memorial gifts to Extreme Kids, and with this money, we bought a bubble tube, a gently vibrating transparent column, five feet high, filled with water that bubbles upward and slowly changes colors. It is particularly well suited to children like Lula who can barely move their bodies, but whose sense of wonder and attention is undiminished. But all kinds of children love it. They hug the bubble tube. They stare. They shimmy up it, hoping to remove the top and splash their hands with water.

The Book

In March 2012, Felix was going to the Rebecca School in Manhattan; Happy was in preschool at the Co-op School in Clinton Hill; and Miranda had started at Brooklyn Friends in downtown Brooklyn. We were in the midst of renovating the house for Felix, which meant weekly meetings with architects and contractors, and Space No. 1 was hitting its stride. Almost every Sunday, new parents and children streamed in: single mothers from East New York, gay couples from Harlem, doctors from Chinatown—over one hundred families since we'd started the year before, which translated into ever more meetings with new families and volunteers, philanthropists, parents. In the midst of this, my first novel, *The Mercury Fountain*, came out. The weekend before Felix's ninth birthday, I opened the pages of the *New York Times Book Review* to find a photograph of me, along with a strong, thoughtful, and good review. Over the years, I had conducted many an internal tirade against the *New York Times Book Review*, precisely because I couldn't imagine they would deign to consider anything ever written by the likes of me—but there I was, my picture looking back at me from the flimsy newsprint, my book taken seriously.

In between *The Mercury Fountain* and Extreme Kids, I was introduced to hundreds of new people in the space of only a few months. Parents and children I did not yet know would come up

and hug me. My capacity for recalling names came to a sputtering standstill. Once, gazing fondly at Jason, I blanked out on his
name, too. People kept on congratulating me, and saying I must
be so proud. Mainly I felt confused and frantic, with unexpected
wafts of shame floating around in the mix. I was not used to my
projects coming to light. I was used to storing away my work, sadly
consigning it to closets and file boxes. Now, almost overnight, my
work life seemed to have flipped. I rushed around, meeting with
funders, community activists, local government people, writers.
For the past nine years, I'd done the bath-books-bed routine almost
every night, with the exception of an odd date for an anniversary
or something. Now, two or three nights a week, I went out. There
were board meetings (I had joined the Co-op School's board to
gain experience with running an organization). There were galas,
a completely new thing for me. I had been advised to attend them
in order to meet well-placed people in the New York philanthropic
scene. One night, when my mother was visiting, I came down from
my bedroom prepared to go to one. She warmly complimented my
outfit and told me to have a great time at the party. "It's not a party,"
six-year-old Miranda corrected her, "It's a gala. It's not about having
a great time. It's to make money."

So I dressed up for galas, and I dressed down for readings at
bookstores. It was profoundly disorienting. Neighbors and people I
did not know well treated me differently. I seemed to have instantly
acquired a reputation as a super-mom achiever, instead of someone whose novel had been published after ten years of rejections. I
would explain to people that *The Mercury Fountain* coming out at
the same time as Extreme Kids took off was a fluke of timing, but
the information didn't sink in. Mothers struggling with their own
sense of frustration and entrapment kept asking me, "How do you
do it?" I would tell them that a great deal of "how I did it" rested

on Jason's salary and support, my ability to hire babysitters, and the passage of many, many years. But they didn't want to hear this. They wanted to hear that I ate kale salad for lunch, or that I meditated five minutes a day, some simple, doable thing that would allow them to get their movies made and their businesses started without having to confront money, luck, timing, the unaccountability of life.

If I was embarrassed, Felix wasn't. For someone who could not be relied on to carry out the niceties of one-on-one communications—he still would not return a wave, and only sporadically a high five—he was consistently receptive to the press. A number of photographers had done publicity shots for Extreme Kids, and in each instance, Felix had hammed it up for the camera. This willingness to interact with an audience was not always welcome. During Lula's memorial, he tried to climb center stage during her eulogy. But at other times, it was a delight. Over spring break, we went to visit my mom in California, and I did a couple of book readings. The kids came to the one at Modern Times in San Francisco, a cozy bookstore in the Mission, flush to the sidewalk so that Felix could move his walker in and out. Jason intended to go outside with him while I read, but to our astonishment, Felix wanted to stay inside, and he remained quiet throughout. Afterward, he clattered his walker up to me: Unh!!! I lugged him onto my lap. He must have weighed ninety pounds by then. He beamed at the friendly little audience, still gathered round, his eyes twinkling as if to say, you think she was good? Look at me!

The other reading was in Mendocino, near my mom's house. She had arranged it and invited a ton of her friends who nicely packed the bookstore. We all went to dinner afterward, Jason and I taking turns walking Felix around the restaurant's parking lot, for he was in one of his outdoor moods. I was touched by my mother's pride and her friends' enthusiasm. At the same time, my whole body felt like wincing. I mentioned to Jason how ridiculous it was: I had been humiliated at not being published, but publication made me feel just as uncomfortable. He shot me a skeptical look. Why would anybody ever write a novel if they didn't want their work recognized? He was right, of course. Now, when I think about *The Mercury Fountain*'s reception, I am able to enjoy it. A cell of my loneliness had rubbed up against others, sparking that sense of recognition and connection that art is all about. But I couldn't see that then. I was so harried. I kept wondering why my life had to be so chaotic: the doctors' appointments, the lunches to be packed, the work obligations hitting me from all sides. I could not see the symmetry in the way things had unfolded. Now, the beauty of it astonishes me. My first book and the project inspired by Felix came out together, as if we had been granted our voices simultaneously.

The Beast Returns

July 15: Violent in the a.m., five o' clock bites Jason, etc., but the day is interspersed with calm, collected, sweet Felix. Two or three rages. Come on a dime then disappear.

July 16: Violent on bus and at school. Calls from social workers, etc. We see an hour or two of calm and connection, but the rages keep breaking through.

July 17: Detail—45 minutes with him, just the two of us in his room—went through two very distinct cycles. Calm, connected, wants to be cuddled and sung to, reaches out to touch you fondly—10 minutes or so, very sweet, then he pulls away and a look of a boxer in the midst of a grueling fight appears. And then there's the rush to the door (he always seems to feel that to go outside will cure his woes—or is he trying to escape something?). Then rages when he cannot go outside. (It's 8:30 p.m., bedtime, I'm not going to walk him around in the dark forever while Happy and Miranda sleep.) Followed by slapping and jumping on his knees (20 minutes). Got him through this cycle once and we got back to the beautiful, connected calmness (10 minutes), but then once again the Sylvester Stallone look appeared. I just put on his mitts and let him be. Ozge tried to calm him but didn't succeed. He's been raging now for about two hours.

My notes tell me that Felix's fits came back on the first day of summer, June 21, 2012. I remember the scene. It was dinnertime. Happy, Miranda, and Felix were seated at our kitchen table with their colorful insect plates and their mac and cheese, but Felix wouldn't eat. A thin wail rose from his lips. It grew in volume, its pitch twisting until the unmistakable sound of the devil screech filled the house. The soul-sinking splat of that sound. I hadn't heard it in two years. I had thought it was a thing of the past. Felix grabbed one of his cheeks as if he wanted to twist it right off. He hit the other with a fierceness that stopped time. We were right back where we were in the season of his hip operation. The world that was solid a minute before, the kitchen, the girls, the dog's frantic nose in the nook of my knees, everything seemed to dissolve. Nothing existed except for a howling boy and his determination to tear at his flesh, to rip it and pummel it with every ounce of his strength.

The fits of 2012 felt harder than those of 2008–2010. Felix was stronger. Two years of horseback riding, swimming, and swinging on his walker as a gymnast swings on parallel bars had developed remarkably powerful muscles in his upper body. The blows he delivered upon himself were scary. The duration also increased. When he was younger, the periods of peacefulness had outweighed the periods of violence. Now the ratio turned: for every two weeks of fits, we might have a week of normalcy.

I think of his fits as "coming back," although physiologically they may have been there all along—just tempered by the risperidone. Even in those two years of peace, there had been days when his yells had acquired a dangerous edge, and his slaps of frustration, hunger, impatience had taken on an unsettling intensity. When this happened, we had upped his dosage of risperidone and his moods had stabilized. The first thing I did, therefore, that summer of 2012 was call to Dr. Perry. Once again, we increased Felix's dosage of risperidone, but the fits did not abate. The drug seemed to have lost its effect. I imagined that his fits had outsmarted it, like those cockroaches that figure out how to thwart the traps and poisons with which we seek to eliminate them.

Sleep flew out the window. I was not as good at dealing with the lack of it as I had been. A couple of days of less than four hours of sleep and I felt like a sac being held together by a dried out membrane: one poke, one shriek, one trip on a stair, and I could break open. I learned that if I could pull together five hours of sleep a day, two here, three there, then my mind felt OK and my skin had some elastic to it. How my skin felt—its brittleness, thinness, or thickness—was a good barometer of my internal state. Anything for that elastic feeling. I grabbed on to sleep like an addict, a thief. I would sandwich my head in pillows, trying to diminish the volume of Felix's yells, while Jason restrained him. But sometimes Jason was fried to the bone, and I knew that I had to do my part. I would climb out of my stupor, miserable, instinctual, propelled by an ancient sense of duty. At moments such as these, I thought of death with a sort of longing. I wouldn't have to get up. There would be quiet.

Jason was by far the more heroic of us. I remember the two of us passed out, roused by Felix's dive-bomb of a scream, Jason jumping from the bed with mystifying alacrity, as I lay motionless, eyes closed, pretending that I had not heard. In our division of labor, I generally tended to the girls, which made sense, as the girls generally wanted me, while Felix generally wanted Jason. But it also worked in my favor. When Felix's screaming woke them, I would sing them back to sleep, which meant that I often got to re-fall asleep in Happy's bed, her three-year-old body squished into mine, as Jason switched CDs in Felix's room on the floor below. There were nights when Jason did not sleep at all, when he spent the entire stretch of darkness restraining, then cuddling, then restraining Felix. Dawn would come, and he'd get Felix dressed, then get him on the bus, then take the subway to his law firm, where he would strategize and negotiate with international businessmen on the tax ramifications of countries going bankrupt and companies gobbling each other up.

It's possible that his job renewed him. If he didn't have sleep, then he had twelve hours in an office with nice paintings on the wall and a modicum of quiet. He had access to a somewhat orderly world. There were questions that he could answer. I look at the calendar and I realize that my work may have helped me, too. I had one or two meetings almost every day that July, contractors had begun the renovation, and there was a bunch of prep work revolving around NY1. Each week, New York's local Time-Warner channel airs a segment at the end of their news show called New Yorker of the Week. It is an interview and story on an ordinary citizen working to help other people in the city, and is useful for getting your message across to a wide swath of New Yorkers, and potentially garnering funding. Micaela had nominated me. I had been accepted. I couldn't back out, even though I did not feel one bit like a New Yorker of the Week. I felt like a mother whose son was tearing the flesh from his face.

· · ·

Then Allan died. My aunts Heidi and Scotty were with him, and had been with him all the night before, singing songs and rubbing his feet. I remember their faces in the corridor, that morning when it was over, when we gathered at Norwalk Hospital. Allan's four daughters were there, and me, but not Nancy. Elsie, her caretaker, thought that she was too confused and frail to be moved from her house, and that the trip would kill her. Perhaps it would have. But I can't help but think Nancy might have wanted that. When we came back without Allan, she refused to eat. When Elsie or her daughters tried to spoon feed her, she'd grit her teeth. The spoon would tap against them, uselessly. For days she resisted being fed, until she finally gave in to her family's determination. She would follow Allan a year and half later, so tiny by that time that her bones reminded me of a bird's.

Allan's death had happened too suddenly to bring the children out to see him. The girls seemed to take it in stride. Allan was ninety-five. That is what happens when you get old. Felix made no outward sign that he understood. But this does not mean that he didn't. He may have. I simply do not know. I do know that one of my favorite memories is of Felix lying on a carpet in the living room in New Canaan, with Allan standing over him, swaying on his cane, singing nonsense syllables. Ah-len, said Felix. Once. But Allan heard it and spoke of it proudly years afterward. They would sit together on the couch, not saying anything. Just sitting together, Felix propped up with pillows. Allan believed that they shared a special tie because not long after Felix was born, Allan developed neuropathy. I remember him demonstrating its early effects in his dining room. He was wearing blue jeans and an old sweater, looking down at his feet with a mixture of exasperation and bemusement. He bent his knees a little, he said "Come on, Allan, jump!" Nothing happened. Whatever neural circuitry had allowed the coordinated contraction of the muscles necessary to get both feet off the ground at the same time had disintegrated. No more tennis.

• • •

Right after Allan's death, Felix's fits dissipated, his bruises healed, and his charming nature came to the fore. It was good timing for the NY1 shoot. If you watch their clip about Extreme Kids, you can see him, sprightly in his green shirt and khakis, entering the play space in his spiffy blue walker. Ozge smiles behind him. I try to high-five him, but he disregards my hand and heads straight for the swing. You can see me pushing him as he lies on the platform swing, propped up by an inflatable tire, clapping and whooping. You can see Ozge pushing him and Happy on this same swing and Miranda running up to join me in the ball pit. We look happy. And at that moment, we were.

But a couple of days later, his face was heavy and sullen, and his eyes were dull. I knew his fits were coming back, for he had that look about him, a look that is best characterized by absence, as if a vital part of him had been leeched away. He whined dangerously as I left the house for the studio interview at NY1. I have a copy of that interview and it is strange to watch. I had a shiny new haircut. My face was tan from playground duty. I seemed for all the world at ease, eager to discuss the necessity of a safe space where children with disabilities and their siblings can play and meet one another. You cannot see the apprehension that I felt at the lights and camera and the preposterousness of talking so optimistically when Felix could have been at that very moment doing himself great damage. I am not ashamed of that interview. I believed what I was saying and still do. But I find it odd how good I looked, how confident, when what I remember from that time is misery. Perhaps I was simply grateful at the chance to dwell on something that was working. That's what you see bubbling up: gratitude. And relief that I am not at home at that very moment, tackling my son.

Afterward, NY1 provided a car to take me back. I leaned into the leather seat, looking out the window at the streets of Manhattan and the lights of the bridge, marveling at the discrete, becapped driver, wanting to confess to him, wanting him to know that I did not usually get driven around like this, that the truth of the matter was that my son was being tortured by something I could not understand, and I did not know how to help him.

As it became clear that risperidone, at any dosage, no longer influenced the workings of Felix's brain, Dr. Perry and I began experimenting with risperidone in combination with other drugs, an anxiety-ridden process for anyone, heightened because Felix couldn't tell us how the drugs made him feel. We could only study him and hope that our observations were correct. After checking one or two drugs off our list, we tried Thorazine. The effect was startling and immediate. A single dosage sapped Felix's energy right out of him. He slumped, his expression deadened. Tears ran down his cheeks, and he moaned the most awful moans. I had thought that I would do almost anything for quiet and an abatement of violence, but that moaning, hopeless, beyond protest, was worse. I threw the Thorazine away. I'd known that medicines can be poisonous, but the weight of this knowledge had never been so clear. I could not bring myself to experiment anymore. I took him off everything, including risperidone. The thing about medicines, whether they're "Western" or "Eastern" or natural or synthetic, is that you have to have faith in them. And I was losing mine.

• • •

"Why do we do?" That was Felix's phrase that summer. He did not say this when he was enraged. Words did not form when he was enraged. He only spoke in his normal, lovable mode. "Why do we do?" he would ask, inflecting different words, stretching them, breaking them up, putting them back together.

"Why do we do?"

"I don't know, Felix."

• • •

And what of Miranda and Happy? Happy, at three, didn't think it was fair. Why did she have to struggle to poke her head through neck holes and get her shoes on the right feet when Felix would get his clothes put on for him? Why did she have to use her words, use forks, use the toilet, when Felix didn't have to bother with any of these things? Why did we jump to attention when Felix slapped his face? She started slapping hers, hoping for the same effect. But we didn't drop what we were doing. We just told her to stop. The sight of her, chubby legged and defiant, hitting herself was troubling, but sometimes it was hard not to laugh. Her eyes would blaze with indignity, and she would raise her arm as if for a killer slap. Yet by the time that her hand touched her cheek, it had lost its velocity. It was hardly even a slap, more of a tap. Thank goodness that sane self-protective part of her was stronger than her anger. When she understood that slapping wouldn't work for her, she gave it up, but I heard her once, at the kitchen table, telling Miranda that she wished she were like Felix. Miranda, who had voiced the same thought when she was Happy's age, shook her head. "Don't say that, Happy," she said in a serious voice. "You don't want to be disabled."

I took only one photograph that whole stretch of summer. It's of Miranda, quiet and thoughtful, on the cusp of kindergarten. She's squatting by a brick wall at the playground, her feet festooned with red toenail polish and sparkly flip-flops. In front of her, a cardboard boat she made at art camp. It's beautiful, crescent shaped, with two matching portholes. She painted it blue, white, yellow, green, and orange and attached a flowered flag. Perhaps she dreamed of sailing away on it.

• • •

The Rebecca School took Felix Monday through Thursday and for a half day Friday throughout June and July and part of August. Their therapists trained Ozge and me on the safest means of restraint: how to use a pillow in a nonsuffocating manner, how to cross Felix's arms over his chest and hold his wrists, pulling outward, so as to conserve our strength. They were an enormous help, but some days, when Felix raged and the school was understaffed, or the staff was too worn out, the school's social worker would call, requesting that I take him home. After a few of these requests, I stopped answering the phone. I needed to work. I needed to think about something other than Felix, I needed to hear something other than his raw, ragged voice, the slaps, the horrid thuds when he learned how to bang his head on the floor.

I hate writing about this time. My body shrinks from it and my mind skitters from place to place. I remember my bones vibrating, weird shafts of strength and a continuous jumpiness. We were always in a state of emergency. A 2009 study showed that the level of stress hormones in mothers of teenagers with autism is comparable to the stress levels of combat soldiers. This sounds about right. The intensity and suddenness with which Felix would explode was like a mine going off in a sunny meadow. You are taking a walk on a lovely afternoon, there are butterflies and clouds scuttling across a blue sky, and then Bam! that shriek, that slap, that bite, until nothing exists except for a screaming child consumed with a pure, earth-erasing rage.

And yet it was interesting, also. The purity and power of his rages were such that when I was not exhausted, I sometimes watched his face contort with a kind of fascination. As a student of history, I had studied war, but from the point of view of political science, economics, imperialism, strategies, and tactics. I understood competing ideologies, the seduction of power, the struggle for resources. What I had not been able to grasp was the blow-by-blow execution. As often as I had read accounts of carnage and seen footage in the news and documentaries, the act of hacking a machete or firing a machine gun into another person seemed theatrical, not real. But sitting on Felix's hips, pinioning his wrists, the floor hard beneath us, I could imagine the reality all too well. When I hadn't had enough sleep or was worn down from containing earlier fits, I would concentrate on the banister of the stairs or on the colorful children's rugs that I'd bought from IKEA and nailed to the wall to cut down on the noise. To see the fury of his eyes, the cracked swell of his lips, the vibration of his tongue felt risky. I was all too aware that we were very close to another place, a place of no morality, no conscience, no he nor I.

It was not a place that most would want to visit, and yet sometimes the experience left me feeling scoured and clearheaded. I would walk Oscar around the tennis courts at Fort Greene Park, with neighbors immersed in more placid stretches of life, feeling marvelously free. They were so caught up in the chatter of New York, that never-ending din of self-help gurus, earnest columnists, seekers and shysters, teachers and doctors, believers and players, advertisers and entrepreneurs, whispering, shouting, suggesting, chiding, directing anyone who would listen to be healthier, faster, smarter, younger-looking, longer-lived, thinner, funnier, kinder, happier, stronger, sexier, richer, more generous, more disciplined, more ruthless, more virtuous. Compared to Felix's, these voices were so predictable and transparent, I couldn't understand their allure. I remember a mother confiding to me that she wanted to lose five pounds, and me biting my tongue. She was forty years old. She looked great. Hadn't she outgrown this stuff? Another friend fretted about what to do with her life. I sympathized with her, but I could not commiserate. I knew exactly what I was doing with mine. I was not letting Felix blind himself and not joining him in his fury. In *The Asian Journal of Thomas Merton,* Merton compares the madnesses of America and Calcutta. America has the mad rationality of affluence, Calcutta, "the lucidity of despair, of absolute confusion, of vitality hopeless to cope with itself." There were times when I felt, in all my riches, like a barefoot beggar who had stumbled out of that city and into an American country club. Perfectly astounded, wondering what the hell everyone was talking about.

. . .

Ozge loved Felix and the girls, but she was exhausted. Emily and Svetlana had moved on to graduate school and no longer worked for us. Ozge had taken up their hours. Forty hours a week is fine in most families, but not in ours. The air in our house was taut with things unsaid. One evening, Ozge hesitated in the door of Felix's bedroom. I was on the floor with him. The blood-stained carpet. His pale, spent face. I think I was soothing him after a fit. Or maybe I'd just been changing his diapers. Ozge's face was drawn; her words were unsteady. I interrupted as she started to give notice. What if we cut your shifts to three a week? Her face lit up. She would have no trouble finding work with a family that was easier than ours. She could work for them two days, renew herself, not feel bad about leaving Felix. She would soon have a break anyway. We were leaving at the end of August for a three-week vacation.

I embarked on a search for more help in my typical way, emailing family, friends, colleagues, stopping neighbors on the sidewalk, asking around at Felix's and the girls' schools. I let everyone I knew know that I was looking for an extra babysitter and if possible, a night nurse, for I had come to realize that our house would be significantly safer if Jason and I could get a good night's sleep. This method had always worked before. I didn't interview dozens of people. I didn't write up a questionnaire. I didn't do background checks. I just let it be known that we needed help, and within a week or so, someone would show up at our door. If Felix reached his hand out in welcome, and the babysitter-to-be recognized this and knew how to respond, then he or she was hired. Felix was the genius behind the great line of people who had helped us: He edited out the faint at heart, the lazy, the scared, the bored. But this method of finding help no longer appeared to be working. Day after day, week after week, no one responded. I advertised on parent Listserv and special needs Listservs. I reached out to graduate programs, did they know of a young person interested in working in the field of disability or therapy? I reached out to dojos, looking for a black belt with a heart of gold. Nothing.

Ozge had agreed to stay with us five days a week until I found someone, but I didn't know how long that would last. One morning, after a particularly harrowing night, I told myself I was not going to get off the phone until I found help. I called our social worker at SKIP. They had not been able to find us home health care before, but maybe if I renewed my suit? I explained how violent Felix had become, how we couldn't get any sleep, how we had two young girls who needed attention, too. How our one remaining babysitter was going to break if we didn't find more help fast. The social worker murmured in sympathy, but she did not seem to understand the level of desperation in our house, as much as I tried to articulate it. She checked that we hadn't disappeared from the wait-list for community respite. We hadn't. She asked if I wanted to submit the form that had brought us the sour ladies from CASA. As I had submitted it twice and been denied both times, I didn't see the point. Even if it got approved, it would take months, and I'd still have to find the person to care for Felix. I need help now, I insisted. The social worker said she was sorry. I called every social worker I'd met through Extreme Kids. I called every agency I'd come across in my politicking. I called schools and parent advocates. I learned that New York had no hands-on programs to provide assistance for families living with escalating pediatric violence, no night nurses for children like Felix, no beds available in the emergency-respite programs.

The closest thing I got to help was the nonhelp of having to find child care so that I could attend a parent education workshop on curbing behavioral problems. "I don't need training," I told the unfortunate young man who offered me this workshop. I knew how to tie on Felix's mitts. I knew special massages and acupressure points. I knew how to read Felix's gaze, his tone, his gestures, and get him what he wanted as quickly as possible in the hopes of avoiding a fit in the first place. I knew about redirecting his attention. I knew his favorite music. I knew his favorite foods. I understood the effectiveness of long walks, swimming, swinging, and all kinds of physical activity. I had dozens and dozens of tricks to help him. "I've had training. I need help. What do I do when Felix goes crazy?" Take him to Bellevue, the man said.

Bellevue Hospital, that is, with an in-hospital psychiatric program that has twelve beds for all of New York City's pediatric cases.

Jamila, more patient than I, went to one of those parent trainings. The format was about preventing violence before it happens. This is optimal, of course. One wants to prevent. But most parents figure out how to develop prevention measures pretty quickly. What Jamila wanted to know was what to do when prevention did not work. The psychologist told her to call the police. Jamila's son is African American and nonverbal. Calling the police when he is acting violently did not strike Jamila as a good idea. Just that spring, on February 1, 2012, Stephon Watts, a fifteen-year-old African American with Asperger's Syndrome, became agitated when his father tried to get him ready for school. He had experienced violent episodes for the past two years, and his parents, on the advice of their social worker, had called the police. The previous times, the police had come and sedated Stephon with a stun gun. But on the morning in question, Stephon attacked an officer with a butter knife. Instead of the stun gun, two other officers reached for their real weapons. They shot Stephon once in the leg, once in the head, killing him. They knew he had autism. They knew he was fifteen. It was a butter knife. They shot anyway.

I stopped calling the disability agencies. The conversations I got into with their representatives made me want to start flinging butter knives of my own. I called Dr. Pytlak. What Felix needs, she said, is twenty-four-hour nursing. Twenty-four-hour nursing? How sublime! How unbelievable! Did such a thing really exist? Of course that's what he needed. That's what Jason and I and the girls needed. But how does one attain such a thing? Dr. Pytlak ordered her staff to get us twenty-four-hour care through the Visiting Nurse Service of New York. In the following days, I signed papers and faxed faxes and crossed my fingers. Could we possibly, really be getting the help we needed? There was much back and forth, unreturned calls, requests for more forms, waiting. In the end, Visiting Nurse Service refused to accept Felix. The reason offered: He was a minor. But your nurses look after other children, reasoned Dr. Pytlak's aide. No, they don't, said the agency rep, and hung up, leaving her staring at the phone.

Do bureaucrats know the despair they cause? To dangle the prospect of help, then snatch it away? I would have preferred those insurance, disability, medical reps to say, right from the start: No. There is no help. You are on your own. I wouldn't have felt so guilty. I wouldn't have had that nagging sense that if I'd only called this extension instead of that, or if I'd stayed on hold that extra hour, or if I'd signed up with that other agency, then I would be getting the help Felix needed.

In late July, two agents from Child Services knocked on our front door. We had been reported for child abuse. My blood really did run cold. The Child Services Administration had the power to take away Felix. And what then? If Felix could push Jason and I to our limits, what might happen to him in the care of an overworked aide in a temporary shelter? A foster family with no experience of nonverbal violence? I would not let the agents in. I would not give them the names of my daughters. They came back. That is their job. This time, Felix was sitting in his stroller, yelling, striking the side of his face. I let them in, one woman, one man. Both young, thin, pale. Both weary from the strain of their job. They were formal, sternly writing in their clipboards. They did not relax. They did not joke. But I was no longer scared. Now that they had witnessed Felix's "self-injurious behavior," I didn't think that they would take him away. The girls, who had been running underfoot, pretending to be evil stepsisters, stopped to observe these strange people in our house. We often had strangers in our house, but usually they were friendlier. The agents tried to smile. It didn't come easy to them. My anger faded. These were two young people, concerned for Felix's safety, trying to do right by him.

They gave me a letter, with our case ID number. "You have been identified as the person(s) who is responsible for causing or allowing to be inflicted injury, abuse, or maltreatment to the child(ren)." They told me I could no longer tie oven mitts on Felix's hands. I pointed out that the mitts cut down on the blood and made it less likely that Felix would blind himself. They nodded helplessly. Regulations. One of the Child Services agents asked how they could be of help. What did Felix need? I told her that Felix needed help twenty-four hours around the clock. Well-trained people, who got enough sleep, who were decently paid, who could work in shifts. We can get you Visiting Nurses, she said. Those elusive visiting nurses again. But perhaps this time they would be more than a mirage. Child Services carries more bureaucratic clout than my pediatrician, and in the following days, filling out the required paperwork, I began to think it might really happen. But we were again rebuffed. This time on account of the Medicaid waiver we'd gotten through

SKIP. Visiting Nurses claimed that they only accepted patients with "straight" Medicaid, not a Medicaid waiver.

"They can't do that! A Medicaid waiver is straight Medicaid," sputtered our social worker. Few of the social workers I've met at SKIP last more than a year or two. They are young. They presumably get into the business from an altruistic place. They end up driving around town with their clipboards, brightly suggesting programs that may or may not exist, only to see their clients rejected or put on five-year wait lists. Even when clients get into a program, success is not guaranteed. Some programs are so underfunded and mismanaged as to be worse than no help at all. Jamila, perhaps due to her son's singular diagnosis—he only had autism, not autism mixed with cerebral palsy and irregular EEG's—got into a program that provided a few hours a week of free home care for her son. The first home care worker smoked pot on the job. The second left her son alone in her apartment, then lost the key, so that when Jamila returned she found the worker out in the hallway and her son inside. She stopped using the program after that.

The Child Services agents had hinted that an official from the Department of Pupil Transportation had initiated the abuse investigation on account of Felix's oven mitts. If we wanted to stay clear of Child Services, we'd have to find another means of protecting his face on the bus. I grumbled at the idiocy of this as I searched online for a medically sanctioned alternative. But I must admit that the Posey Double Security Mitts that soon arrived on our doorstep were an improvement. They had more padding and were easier to strap on. While I was in the market for restraints, I also purchased a papoose board, recommended to me by a friend who had been a paramedic. A papoose board is a five-foot, padded plank with heavy duty velcro straps intended to immobilize the most madly flailing arms and legs; it is used as an alternative to sedation during medical procedures. As I had not been able to find extra people to help restrain Felix, I figured that I could use the papoose board instead. I could velcro him down during those times that I felt on the verge of snapping. Then I could leave the room, knowing that he could not harm himself. Surely that would be worth the $500 the board cost. I was wrong. Strapping Felix into that thing enraged him all the more, increased the level of violence in the house, and made me feel like a monster. It didn't even work. If I succeeded in strapping him down, he managed to break loose within five minutes. The board is still in Felix's closet. There may be one like it in a supply closet at Guantanamo Bay. In much of the world, it is considered a form of abuse. The governments of the United Kingdom and several other European countries have banned its use.

I gave up. Help seemed impossible to find. The agencies seemed useless, the doctors clueless. I turned to nature, driving Felix out to the beach as often as I could. He loved the rhythm of the waves, and the feel of the water, wind, and sand on his skin. Often the ocean could calm him. When it couldn't, the wind would mute his yells. The great expanse of sky and shore also helped me, shrinking him down, reminding me that he was, after all, simply one unhappy child. The universe wasn't imploding. Distancing myself from him was hard, and I felt hard, a part of me stony. But I could not dive into his pain and rage. I had to take care of Happy and Miranda. I could not go where Felix was.

Religion

There were moments during that summer that I so emptied myself of feeling that I felt like one of T.S. Eliot's husks. One afternoon, in that hollow sort of mood, I slumped on our lumpy green couch after a long struggle to get Felix's mitts on. He lay on the floor before me, hitting his bloody mitt against his cheek. With each blow, his head knocked against the wooden floor. I pushed him onto the rug to lessen the impact. He wriggled back to the hard planks. Hit-thump, hit-thump, hit-thump. He was yelling, but he had so shredded his vocal chords that only a rattle came out. When his attack subsided, he lay there in the heat of the afternoon, naked except for a white diaper, his body bruised and scarred, emaciated in places, his arms outstretched, his legs twisted, his face beautiful. I gasped, feeling rushing in. The arrangement of his limbs. The expression of his face. He looked like Christ, nailed to the cross.

The analogy was odd, for I am not Christian. And yet the power of seeing Felix in a Christ-like way was undeniably moving. I got up from the couch, took off Felix's mitts, and smoothed his hair from his face. His lips were swollen and cracked with blood. His eyes a sea of pain.

I did not grow up going to church, and we did not have any crosses around the house. My father was an atheist, my mother perhaps best classified as a hybrid animist/God-is-love type person. The friction between their beliefs provided a fertile ground for a home-made type of theology that I have enjoyed since childhood. But I had never aligned myself with a religion and felt a little uncomfortable around those who had. I remember stiffening when Felix was little, and the sidewalk Christians started blessing us.

I called them sidewalk Christians because we encountered them on the sidewalk, as I took Felix to appointments or simply pushed him around on those long walks that he loved. They may not have all been Christian. People of many creeds, even those not sure they believe in a god, say god bless. How else to invoke something greater than ourselves, something beyond human? As Felix's disabilities grew more obvious, so too did the frequency of these sidewalk blessings. It got to the point where I would have thought it unusual if we wandered through Brooklyn, at least the more down-and-out areas, and were not blessed. We were noticed. We were blessed. Particularly by immigrants, African Americans, the poor, the disabled. It's possible that some well-off white people, my people, blessed us, too, but this happened so infrequently as to have been lost to memory. I soon grew to appreciate these interactions. What were blessings but a sort of spiritual alms? In the event that these people's words had any sway with divinity, they simply wished to cast a vote in Felix's favor. How could I object to that? I didn't. I began to realize how kind these people were, when Felix and I had it easier than they in so many other ways. I began to be grateful for their blessings, their nods of recognition, the jolt of energy I could get from the light in their eyes.

Once, in Fort Greene Park, as Felix struggled to push a clattery silver walker up a steep slope, an older gentleman, attempting to jog up this same steep slope, passed, then paused and returned to us. He had a prayer group, he told me, a little hesitantly. He admired my son's determination and wondered if I would allow his group to pray for him. "Sure," I said, also hesitant. I had not until that moment realized that prayer groups even existed. He told me that the prayers would work better if his group knew my son's name. "Felix," I said. "And thank you." He jogged up the hill, pleased with his project. He was wearing a gray sweat suit and the leaves were brown in the branches arching above him. I've thought about him fondly over the years. It was his awkwardness, I think, that I liked so much. His admiration of Felix, pushing his metal contraption up the bumpy path, the ancientness of his offering, his uncertainties bridged by a wish to say hello.

There were times, however, when religious people provoked my ire. Particularly when Felix was in a dark period, and the siren wail of his screaming was raw within me, and some well-meaning blunderer called Felix god's special gift or an angel. I'd want to grab them by their collar. It's a gift to watch my son tear at his skin? To be woken by his slaps? An angel of destruction, do you mean? And what of Happy and Miranda, were they not special gifts? They were children, all three of them as human as could be, and one of them suffering terribly. Damn anyone with a cloying voice insisting on the blessed nature of my special angel.

And yet, and yet. Issa was a Japanese haiku master who wrote upon the death of his young daughter:

This dewdrop world—
is a dewdrop world,
And yet, and yet . . .

His poem and the subject of Felix are inextricably woven in my mind, even though Felix, thank god, is alive. It's those and-yets. Felix is a compendium of and-yets.

The and-yets in this case were those exasperating Christians. Perhaps they were not as foolish and sappy as I made them out to be. Perhaps they overemphasized Felix's blessedness to correct for the many people who perceive Felix to be lesser than his sisters, the unsuccessful child, the one wounded of brain, the one not worthy of celebration. Perhaps the gift they insisted had been bestowed upon me refers to what I have learned from Felix.

For I have learned a hell of a lot from him. Before his birth, I had been more exposed to the fearful, lusty, murderous, hubristic, and domineering sides of us than I had been to the kindness, thoughtfulness, and care that also run through us. He has enlarged and sweetened my view of human nature. He has made me more perceptive, more patient, more aware of body language, physically stronger, able to scoop poo out of the tub without flinching, more integrated with others, and less self-conscious. He, both he and the people he has bound up in his web, have altered me, most would say for the better. Is that not a blessing?

And yet, to rhapsodize about these things begs the question, at what cost? I may crow about how I've grown up raising him, but in the words of my father, "The poor kid!" His simplest movements are a struggle and hard won. He can't tell us what he wants, what he thinks, what is wrong. He assaults himself in violent rages. Is it a gift for him? Wouldn't he trade in what I have learned for the freedom to run, sing, swear, seek out adventures of his own choosing, kick a soccer ball, climb a fence, do any of a thousand things he might choose to do. Wouldn't I trade in what I have learned? Is it a blessing to become wiser at the expense of your child?

Once, Felix and I were on the subway, coming back from swimming. Picture a narrow New York subway car, packed with people coming home from work, who have to crowd more closely together to make room for Felix, his outsized stroller, and the walker dangling from its handlebars. Felix stretched his legs, inadvertently kicking the guy by the pole. He cackled in his unmodulated way. The subway is not usually a place where I am told that Felix is a blessing. But on this particular ride, an older lady in a wig beamed at Felix and gave me an approving nod. She told me that she was part of a friendship circle, which started in the Jewish community, but has expanded from it, a group formed to visit and befriend children with disabilities and do what they can to support the parents.

"One of the women in the circle," she whispered, scandalized, "Her husband left her when he found out the child was disabled. Can you imagine?" Well, I could. Easily. Half the children at Felix's school were raised by single parents, most of them mothers. But this woman with her wig and her hat and her righteous anger could not believe it. "How can he do this?" she asked me. "G-d gives him this, and he runs away?" Her eyes blazed. Her entire being reeled in incomprehension. And Bing! I got it. In her world, a disabled child was not a gift or a blessing, but a holy task, a challenge lobbed by god. How can you run away from that? She could not get over the idiocy of this man for thinking that he could.

My own take on religion is best summed up by Ovid: If the gods didn't exist, they'd have to be invented. I was about to employ the grandiose human "we" and write: We need stories. But if Felix has blasted one thing into me, it is that as much as we have in common, we are each of us incontrovertibly different. Felix doesn't need stories, at least not at this point in his life. He shows no interest in television. He has no patience for books unless they are singsong and rhythmic enough to resemble music. But I, and people with brains similar to mine, love stories. They help to make sense, if only fleeting sense, out of all the impressions, actions, memories, happenings, disasters, deliciousness, weather, and every other little thing and nonthing constantly zooming by us and into us and through us.

The Jewish lady on the subway presented me with a story that honored the disabled baby and the rigors of the parents instead of sentimentalizing the situation. Parenthood was a divine gauntlet.

You couldn't escape, so chin up, girl, and have courage. Her words resonated with me in a way similar to that of the acupuncturist's story about Felix's furies being a sort of a spirit journey gone awry, his soul trapped in a terrible realm. Both stories got something of Felix that the quantifications of the medical and educational experts couldn't get. To them, Felix was a compendium of inabilities and lacks, a problem that needed to be, but clearly wasn't, solved. There was no space in their accounting for his epic nature, no wonder at his mystery.

. . .

Growing up, my mom had taught me that Jesus was a great man, somewhat akin to Martin Luther King, Jr., who had helped the poor two thousand years ago. The way that Christianity exalted his crucifixion, therefore, had puzzled me. Why not show him like Martin Luther King, Jr. noble and thoughtful? Why the bloody joints and green skin? Or the more cerebral but just as blunt crosses? Why linger on him broken in body and spirit? After seeing Felix lying, as if crucified, on the living room floor, I became intrigued by these questions. I had read anthropological accounts, citing an element of human sacrifice at the heart of Christianity. Could some of those sidewalk Christians who praised Felix subconsciously be linking his suffering to Christ's? Was it the torture visited upon Felix that they respected? Did they believe it might in some way benefit them?

At odd moments over the years, I had found myself wondering in a sort of speculative-superstitious way if Felix's hardships lessened the load for the rest of us. Did he suffer so that his sisters could walk, I could speak, Jason could be the kind and stable person that he was? I doubted it. I'd seen too many families at Extreme Kids whose children were all visited with intense difficulty, where the suffering of one clearly had not helped the others. And yet the thought returned at odd moments. The logic of sacrifice is perhaps the logic by which we console ourselves when we are boarding a plane on the day following a terrible plane crash. Surely yesterday's tragedy will protect us. Surely there will not be two such incidents in a row. Perhaps on a grand, statistical scale, there's something to it. If the number of children born with major birth defects hovers at about 3 percent per year, as CDC studies indicate, does each child born so afflicted increase the chances of other children being born into the lucky 97 percent? Is this 3 percent an annual sacrifice to a god, nature, age, mutation, bad luck, unjust policies, mismanaged love, the species as a whole? Is human sacrifice a real thing?

I wrote to my uncle Cam, who many years before had startled my parents by becoming a priest, and asked him why the cross was so central to Christianity. He referred me to the Jewish tradition of the suffering servant, the idea of God suffering with and for us, from which early Christian leaders borrowed when their church was forming and they needed a way to come to terms with Christ's brutal end. He sent me several passages that described this suffering servant, including this from Isaiah: "Surely he has borne our infirmities and carried our diseases; yet we accounted him stricken, struck down by God, and afflicted. But he was wounded for our transgressions, crushed for our iniquities; upon him was the punishment that made us whole, and by his bruises we are healed." There it was, that thread of sacrifice I'd been looking for, that wish to find purpose in pain. But it didn't resolve much, for as interesting as I found the passage, it did not move me, and seeing Felix as if crucified had moved me. That's what I wanted to understand. Why had I been so moved?

Perhaps the answer lies in the words that popped into my head at the time: Christ, too. And Mary, and all the weeping mothers throughout time, and those too hollowed and husked to cry anymore. We were not alone, Felix and I. Others had suffered, just as we had. Earlier that day, watching Felix rake at his skin, I had asked myself: How is such torment possible? Perhaps that image was telling me, *Your question is at the very root of religion and as old as language itself.*

This is the thing about Felix. Who else but he could have torn me so open as to see an image of Christ in my living room? What's more, and quite marvelously, that image did exactly what such images are supposed to do: It healed me. It gave me the strength to get up off of that couch, kneel beside Felix, take off his gloves, love him again, grieve for him again, hope for him again, then get back to the business of wiping the blood off the rug and figuring out what to make for dinner. In the longer run, it let me appreciate the religion of my ancestors in a way that I had not been able to before. I now take those crosses and crucifixes as an acknowledgement of the ineluctable, fundamental suffering that runs through life, right along with joy and beauty. You cannot expunge this suffering. But you can let it in and share it, and it does help to know that you are not alone, that you, I, all of us, are in good company.

Hanging On

By September, our renovation—this hazy thing that had been occurring in the backdrop of Felix's fits—had started to yield results. Phase One, Felix's room, a lovely new bedroom on the ground floor, had been completed. No longer would the morning get-Felix-on-the-school-bus routine include the risky spectacle of Jason, in a sleep-deprived blur, racing down two flights of stairs with a ninety-pound Felix flung over his shoulder.

Everyone who worked on our renovation, from the architect and contractor to the youngest assistant on the crew, seemed pleased with their work. Over the course of the project, they had become fond of, impressed by, or sympathetic to Felix, and I think that it made them feel good to put their talents and time into making a home that fit him better. They would take pictures of his room, or just hang out in the doorway, grinning at how cool it looked. And it did look cool. It was a combination of Space No. 1 and the cabin of a ship, with porthole windows that opened into the bathroom and hallway. The floor was covered with gray, carpeted mats. Ballet bars ran across one wall, for the girls to practice dancing, and for Felix to pull himself up to standing. A grid of rotating hooks hung from the ceiling, from which we could suspend a variety of swings.

I wished that Felix were in a state to enjoy it more, but the girls loved playing in it, and our neighbors' kids loved playing in it, and eventually, I hoped, so would Felix. For now, the room minimized the harm he could do to himself. His furies had led to disturbing new moves: the knee jump, the donkey kick, and the skull bang. The mechanics of this knee jump, the combination of balance and coordination that it required, were utterly beyond him when he was at peace. But in the heat of a frenzy, he could rise into a kneeling position and jump from there, coming down hard on his kneecaps. This, and the donkey kicks, with his hands on the floor, led to bruised and swollen knees and concern that he might do permanent damage to his joints. Then there was the skull bang: an emphatic banging of his head on the floor that would last until an adult shoved a pillow under his head, and recommence the minute he rid himself of the pillow. Having the floor entirely covered with mats eliminated, or at least significantly diminished, the danger of him hurting his head or knees. He could knee jump for twenty minutes straight. He could bang his head on the floor. He'd be OK.

The room also worked prophylactically. At nine at night, when he whined to go outside, but none of us had the energy or will to pack him into his stroller and take him on an after-dark walk, we could put him on his swing, and address his craving of motion that way. The swing was a carpeted platform, large enough that we could ride with him, cuddling him and humming lullabies. It was low enough that he could scramble onto it by himself, and push himself by pushing his feet at the floor. Thus, Jason could lounge in a foof working on memos as Felix propelled himself in circles. Sure, it was eleven at night on a school night, but there was no screaming and hitting. It was a great improvement.

I still hadn't been able to find an extra babysitter to relieve Ozge. Felix's ability to attract great people no longer seemed to be working. In my early twenties, I had briefly worked as a home health aide. I'd found the industry isolating, depressing, and exploitative, and had no desire to go that route, but I could not think of an alternative. I called Felix's school and asked where they found their one-on-ones. The home health care agency to which I was referred did not accept health insurance. They charged twenty dollars an hour. From my earlier experience, I knew that only a fraction of that money went to the aides. It made me ill to think about it. I tried not to think about it, and told myself that if we found a great aide, I'd plump up his or her salary with a bonus.

Our first aide, L., was a likable young man with a wrestler's body who had been through a war in Africa, had a new baby boy, and had been trained in nonviolent restraint. Shortly after he started working for us, he and I took the kids for a movie night over at Kate and Karla's, whose sons Auggie and Emmet were good friends with my girls. They lived in a nearby apartment building that featured a talking elevator and a long corridor that was great for Felix's walker. After supper, Miranda and Happy and Auggie and Emmet took off down the hallway. My heart soared as Felix followed them, racing in his walker, laughing. He hadn't laughed like that in ages. I had forgotten how sweet his laughter could be. Perhaps he was finally coming out of his dark period?

Then, in the midst of this laughter, he fell. I raced toward him, my pulse pounding. His hands had simply released from the handlebars. He had gone straight down. I'd never seen this happen before. I put his head in my lap. His eyes were open, stunned. The floor had been carpeted. He hadn't been hurt. But his fall was so peculiar that I couldn't get it out of my mind. I was afraid it might have been a drop seizure, which meant another seizure could be on the horizon. I talked to Jason. I talked to Felix's doctors. I talked to Felix's school. We decided that whoever was helping Felix would stick close to his side whenever he walked with his walker. We'd cup our hand over his, helping him keep his grip strong, and ensuring that we'd be there to catch him should he again fall.

The next week, L. took Felix to Camel Park. Felix again fell, this time on cracked pavement. When Jason answered L.'s call, he turned white and raced out of the house. I stayed home with the girls while Jason and L. took Felix to the hospital. Felix had broken a tooth, and his jaw had to be wired. We heard no more of that sweet laugh-ter after that. If Felix had been on the verge of coming out of his dark period, the pain from that fall, and the wires that now poked into his cheek, put him right back there.

I had a hard time trusting L. after that, particularly as Felix had begun to shy away from him. I think he held Felix's wrists too tightly when he was restraining him. The agency sent over a new aide. Felix did not retract from her and she performed the duties we had articulated in the contract, allowing us to get through the autumn. But a neighbor or two pulled me aside, their voices low with disapproval. They had seen her pushing Felix around the park, listening to headphones as Felix hit himself. We had all done this: Jason, Ozge, Emily, me. We had all had moments when we pushed Felix as he howled and hit, too tired to intervene. I think it was the blankness of the aide's stare, what seemed to be a refusal to care, that bothered them. In her defense, she was one of the agency's most reliable workers, and they had her doing midnight shifts in Queens. She had three teenage kids of her own. They'd call her on her cell phone, demanding that she resolve their disputes. Her exhaustion may have been as bad or worse than mine.

One spark of the old Felix magic did show up that fall: Arun, the bass player in our neighbor's son's band. I got his email out of the blue. He was taking a year off before going to med school, and heard we were looking for help. When he came over for an interview, Felix grabbed a shock of his curly hair and pulled him down to investigate his stubble. Arun laughed with pleasure and I felt my bones go soft with relief. He had come from a big, extended family in Sri Lanka. When he was eight, his parents had moved to New York, fleeing the civil war. Now they had relocated to South Carolina, and he missed his younger brother.

He could only work on Sundays, but those Sundays were splendid. We would all go to Space No. 1. Arun would push Felix on the swing. Jason would play foot monster with the girls and lob math questions at Arun, pleased to have someone from the sciences in our menagerie. After an hour or so, Felix would whine or slap, wanting to go outside. Arun would help him to his stroller. Felix's fits could often be avoided if he were walked for hours and hours, and Arun liked wandering around, exploring new neighborhoods. He liked Felix's company. He had a strong back. He would return to us with reports on the funny things that Felix did. Sometimes Felix had fits in spite of these walks, and Arun learned to force on his mitts and hold him down so that he couldn't hurt himself. But even on bad days, Arun didn't seem eager to leave, and he would return for his next shift with admirable promptness and a spring in his step. He had a wonderful ability to restore himself. And a little bit of this ability worked its way into us.

Discovery

I met the Kittays on one of those blind dates at the beginning of Extreme Kids.
Jeffrey was the former editor of *Lingua Franca*; Eva was a professor
of philosophy interested in the intersection of philosophy and disability. They had an adult daughter with developmental disabilities
who had lived with them until she was thirty-eight, but now resided
at the Center for Discovery, a school, home, and clinic for people
with disabilities in upstate New York. Jeffrey was on the board there
and invited Jason and me up for a tour and to meet with the director. The school's curriculum was organized around agriculture and
nature, as was the physical infrastructure. Modern green buildings
and old farm buildings bordered a sprawling biodynamic farm and
dairy. The farm provided work for the residents, hands-on teaching
for the students, and healthy food for the entire community. The
clinic had a climbing wall and geothermic heating. Over a lunch
prepared by residents, the CEO, Patrick Dollard, told us how part-
nerships with MIT and Harvard were underway to monitor existing treatments and foster new ones. Another project, still in development, used new technologies to remotely monitor children's vital
signs, allowing them to live at home, and giving their parents direct,
twenty-four-hour access to the doctors and therapists. Jason and I
drove home, energized and bemused. The disability services we'd
seen in the city were so piecemeal and frustrating. I'd blamed this on

the bureaucracies that governed these projects, replacing flexibility and unscripted talk with forms and regulations, and not providing enough money to fix basic needs, like a dripping ceiling. But the center had to deal with these same bureaucracies. They hadn't been strangled.

Jeffrey had brought Patrick to visit Space No. 1 in July. When Jeffrey asked after Felix, I burst into a passionate response, which included the word "psychotic." Patrick gently advised me to be more careful with my language. Tossing around words like psychotic could hurt Felix. Programs that might be able to help him would turn him away. I hadn't thought about that before. I knew that parents whose children have less visible disabilities often try to keep their child's records "clean," as diagnoses of cognitive, emotional, behavioral, and learning disabilities can affect their children's futures, limiting their chances of getting into college or acquiring a job. When I first applied for Early Intervention, the social worker had assured me that Felix's enrollment in the program would not go on his permanent educational record. It hadn't occurred to me to worry about this. His disability wasn't something I wanted to hide. Perhaps she was trying to tell me that I should not be so dense. Now I saw that even within the disability community, some diagnoses and descriptions could leave you out in the cold. Others wouldn't.

I called Patrick. I told him that Felix's fits showed no signs of abating, and I did not know what to do. The fantasist in me imagined him replying, why don't you bring him to the center? We've got an extra bed. Felix would be swept away from the wreck of a raft we had him on, to that beautiful farm with its good food and well-trained, well-rested people. Patrick did the next best thing: He invited Felix and me to the Center for Discovery's clinic for a three-day intensive medical-psychological evaluation. Maybe his doctors and therapists would be able to see something that our New York people hadn't.

Meanwhile, the Rebecca School requested that Jason and I come in to meet with Felix's team, a group of therapists, teachers, and assistants, most of them women in their twenties and thirties, usually smiling, but now looking at us with big, pained eyes. Many of them had worked with Felix for years. They loved him. They wanted to offer solutions and guidance. But they had none. They wrung their hands, saying something had to be done, he was too miserable, it was too awful, they couldn't get through to him, he was driving everyone in his class mad, too. Jason and I sat on our folding chairs, listening, nodding. We had gone to the doctors, tried the drugs, followed the behavioral plans and diets. What else did they want us to do? Something. They wanted something to be done. They could not stand their uselessness, our uselessness. They had been brought up to think that there is always something that can be done to make things better.

A few weeks later, Tina McCourt, the director of the Rebecca School, requested a meeting. When I went in to see her, the look in her eyes reminded me, if I had ever doubted, how little I would want to run a school. She had known Felix since he was four. She had known me for five years. We liked each other. But all through the summer and into the fall, Felix's yells had been echoing through the hallways, disrupting classes, and breaking down morale. She looked at me frankly. She was responsible not only for Felix, but all of her students, all of her staff. The school could not teach Felix anything in his present condition. They were mainly holding him, keeping him safe, consoling him when he'd let them. They could not do that forever. I'll look for another placement, I promised. Just let him stay until the end of the year.

Find a way to stabilize him, she said.

. . .

Felix and I arrived at the center on a cold November evening, the first bits of snow whipping around in the wind, and spent the next couple of days shuttling around the campus, frost crunching under the wheels of Felix's stroller. We met with almost a dozen specialists, all of whom were used to the unusual, none of whom seemed intimidated by Felix. In the three days that we were there, Felix balked, yelled, and hit himself, but not once did I struggle with the superhuman strength that characterized his furies. This was remarkable. By that point, we very rarely got three days without an incident. I wondered if his receptivity and lucidity had to do with the place. He responded particularly well to the evaluating therapists as they spent hours swinging him, swimming with him, and helping him pedal on an adaptive bike. At one point, the evaluating OT took me aside and whispered, "Your son has so much potential. He's smart!" I thought so, too, but no one at his New York City schools had used this word in reference to Felix before. She told me that thirty hours of school, supplemented by extra therapy here and there, could not compare to the 24-7 aspect of a good residential program, where trained staff could work around the clock and in concert with each other. The physical therapist told me that the way Felix walked, supporting most of his weight with his upper body, propelling the walker along on his toes, would not work as he grew. His wrists were already compromised. They would not be able to sustain the weight of an adult body. If we wanted to keep him walking, he needed significantly more intervention than he was currently receiving.

On the third morning, the speech therapist, who had been trying without success for days, found an iPad app to which Felix responded. The icons were large and easy to swat. They took up the whole screen. They came in a sequence instead of side by side. "Felix, what do you want?" the therapist asked. First came the icon for pencil, then toilet, then pretzel. Felix took in the order. The next

time pretzel came around, he swatted it. I gasped. I'd been trying
to get Felix to use an iPad for years—maybe the apps I had been
using required too much hand-eye coordination? Maybe the icons
had been too small? For the rest of the session, Felix kept waiting
for pretzel to appear in the sequence, selecting pretzel, then eating the pretzels that we gave him, responding so consistently that
we were all convinced he understood. It was an amazing moment,
like in *My Fair Lady*, when Eliza Doolittle first employs correct
pronunciation—"The rain in Spain falls mainly on the plain"—
after which she and the professor and his friend leap around the
parlor, singing and dancing. She did it! By George, she did it! Felix
had done it, too! And what if he went beyond pretzel? What if we
could get him to use symbols to communicate? The implications,
the possibilities of such a thing . . . I realized that I hadn't let myself
hope for ages.

The drive home from the Center for Discovery was quiet, Felix
listening to music in the back seat, me alternating from praying that
his contentment would last (please, god, no fits on the highway) and
pondering our experience at the center. The evaluation had ended
with an hour-long meeting, during which everyone who had seen
him presented a short report. My head spun from the recommen-
dations. Some of them were simple—a new stroller, a new walker,
a new type of cushioning for his seat at the kitchen table. I could
check those off the list without much difficulty, but others left me
feeling hopeless, in particular the Botox injections in his calves that
were to be followed up with a specialized physical therapy twice a
week for two months. How could we fit that into his schedule? And
who could I find to do it? There's plenty of Botox in New York City,
and plenty of physical therapists, but finding a therapist who knew
the procedure and could effectively work with a resistant and most
likely infuriated boy like Felix? I was afraid I'd have to go back to

the Hospital for Special Surgery. The Hospital for Special Surgery is a good hospital, and the doctors, nurses, and aides I met there were smart and capable. But as much as they may have understood Felix's body, they didn't understand much about his mind. This had been made clear during Felix's hip surgery, both in the doctor's airy assurances that Felix would not need a cast, as the pain of moving his hips would be enough to keep him still, and in the shocked way the staff had reacted to Felix's furies, the way they kept calling Jason and me saints. Felix was weird at the Hospital for Special Surgery. He wasn't weird at the Center for Discovery. I wondered if that was why he had been so engaged and receptive at the center, so much less fitful than usual. He fit in. He belonged.

Placement

When I was born, in 1968, doctors routinely recommended children like Felix be taken from their families and raised in institutions. In ninth grade, I visited one of those institutions. On a field trip. I was taking an elective in child psychology. I don't remember the name of the institution that we visited, just the general impressions—sterility, surveillance, a deep well of shame. I felt guilty swinging my arms and chattering with my classmates, free in the presence of children who were not. Through one-way mirrors, we spied on them, these other children, in their beige rooms with hospital beds and white-clad nurses moving about. They were not presented to us as children, but as objects in a cabinet of curiosity: that's Downs, that's the Chiari Malformation, that's a genetic disorder, that one you think is an infant is actually sixteen years old! We could not talk with them. They were untouchable. I do not recall what our teacher intended with that visit, but I know what I took away from it: Don't get a strange illness, don't be different, or you'll be locked up.

My fear, awaiting that first appointment with Dr. Wells, must have been predicated on that field trip. If Felix were deemed neurologically defective, he might be thrown into a place like that.

I don't think that I knew about New York State's Willowbrook School until after Felix was born and I became interested in the disability movement. But it's possible that we talked about

Willowbrook in that ninth-grade child psychology class, and that the field trip was meant to show us the state of Maryland's humane treatment of abnormal children, as opposed to that of New York. Willowbrook was still in operation then, though in the process of being dismantled. It was built on Staten Island in the 1930s, although it did not open its doors as a school for mentally retarded children until 1947.

It was misleading to call it a school. It was an enormous locked cage in which were kept thousands of children and adults, some with cognitive disabilities, some misdiagnosed, some of normal intelligence who had cerebral palsy. Soon after its opening, miserable health conditions and the lack of such basic human-care needs as toothbrushing and bathing led to hepatitis. In the 1950s, doctors from NYU and Yale used the site for medical experiments, later deemed illegal, including injecting children with the hepatitis virus and reportedly feeding them infected feces. By the 1970s, the experiments had ended, but the dehumanizing conditions continued, including the sexual and physical abuse that appears to be axiomatic when people are not treated as people. In 1965, when Bobby Kennedy made an unannounced visit, he found over 6,000 people crammed into a facility meant for 4,000. In a televised interview he called the place a "snake pit" and described how children were "living in filth and dirt, their clothing in rags, in rooms less comfortable and cheerful than the cages in which we put animals in a zoo." The photographs of these children are reminiscent of those who have suffered unspeakable human rights abuses the world over: jutting rib cages, bruised, scabbed faces, the lost expressions of spirits that have absented themselves. In 1972, Geraldo Rivera toured the facility with a hidden camera. The resulting exposé fueled a national movement, led by parents and disability activists, to shut down state institutions across the country, for Willowbrook was not alone. The abuse, overcrowding, and underfunding of state institutions was endemic.

In 1975, Congress enacted the Education for All Handicapped Children Act (now IDEA), which mandated that children with disabilities were entitled to a free and appropriate public education. No longer would they be routinely shipped away. They would live with their families, with the sun shining down on them and fresh air to breathe. They would be provided with the therapy and equipment they needed to learn. Whenever possible, they would attend local schools. This was a humane and good law, intended to integrate people with disabilities into their community, and not lock them away. I am grateful for it. And yet, our home, and our community, as loving as they both could be, were failing Felix. We had not been able to educate him to the best of his abilities, and as he grew bigger, and we grew more tired, even our basic care for him was falling apart.

By the fall of 2012, I had begun to wonder if Child Services was right to have investigated us for child abuse. All the harm done to Felix had been done by himself, but the conditions in which he lived, in which we lived, were dangerous. I lived in fear that my mind might snap while I was restraining him. Even if I didn't harm him, my exhaustion was such that I was a threat to the public health whenever I got behind the wheel. Yet I had to drive. There was no other way to get Felix to his appointments. After seeing Felix at the Center for Discovery, I was convinced that he'd have a better chance of walking and of learning to use a communication device if he lived there, and that it would be safer for everyone. But it is one thing to think such thoughts, quite another to actively go about sending your child away.

Especially after seeing Dr. London. We met Dr. London at the Center for Discovery. He had given me his card and offered to see

Felix at his private practice in Staten Island. Right before Happy's birthday, I drove Felix over the Verrazano Bridge to his office. Midway through our interview, Felix had a fit. I grabbed his wrist and tried to put on his mitt. He got away from me. I grabbed both wrists. He leaned down and bit his knee, carrying me with him. I hunched over, greasy with sweat, trying to appear calm, trying to get his mitt on. He kept getting out of my grip, slapping the side of his face, pinching me, yelling. Dr. London sat behind his desk, watching. His face was frustratingly composed. What was he thinking? Did he see this sort of thing often? I had not seen Felix's level of fury in the other kids at Extreme Kids, but presumably few parents would bring them in if they threatened to get in that state. Dr. London suggested a heavy dosage of Zyprexa, a drug in the same family as risperidone that he had seen work when risperidone no longer did. Felix started taking the pills on December 2, 2012. They took effect almost immediately. Felix still had his temper, but not the spiraling madness of his fits. His laughter again rang through the house.

A few weeks later, his people magic kicked back in, too: A judge whose twins had volunteered at Extreme Kids, and who, years before, had lost her first daughter to Rett syndrome, emailed. The nanny who had cared for this daughter was a bright, loving, remarkable woman in need of work. Did I know someone who might want to hire her? When Yvette came to meet us, Felix immediately reached out his hand. She took it with a wide, open smile. There it was again: that instant connection. I let our exhausted home health aide go. Yvette was not as strong as Arun and could not manage the hours-long walks, but she loved Felix. She read to him every night, sparking his interest by her rhythmic delivery, or not sparking it, but persisting anyway, not giving up. With her, Ozge, Arun, Jason, and myself, Felix finally had enough people, and the right people to help him, and Dr. London's pills had stabilized him.

How could I send him away? Particularly as he had stopped asking: "Why do we do?" And he now said: "DOH-NT leee meee." Don't leave me. "DON'T leeeeee me," in an undertone or whine, declarative, yelled, or sobbed.

"We're not leaving, you, Felix," I'd say, feeling like the lowest sort of traitor.

. . .

The problem was education. The public schools that I'd toured were absurd for Felix. Even in the classes reserved for the most disabled, Felix would have to take math, English, an altered suite of academics. There were no foofs, no swings, no music. There was nothing that would engage him or mean anything to him. There were no changing tables in the bathrooms. Even with his new pills, he would go insane. The privates I'd looked into would not accept him. Rebecca School wouldn't renew his contract. Aside from a residential school, there was only homeschooling. Part of me, the part of me that did not want to send him away, thought I should try this, though the prospect scared me. It is a torment being trapped in your house if you have an adventurous soul, which both Felix and I have. I figured that we might be able to do it without destroying each other if we left the house. I could drive him around the city for various therapies. Maybe we could have picnic lunches in Central Park? It wouldn't be so bad; it might even be fun, provided that the Zyprexa kept working.

But it was so frustrating! Extreme Kids kept growing, getting more and more complicated, more and more busy. I enjoyed the networking and strategizing and juggling that this growth entailed. I was good at it. On the weekends, watching the families play, I reaped the rewards of it. How aggravating to give this up for a job I felt doomed to botch on a great many levels. Felix is great at teaching me, but the reverse has not applied. The day after he and I returned from the Center for Discovery, I had gathered Jason, Ozge, and Arun to the kitchen for a demonstration of the sequential communication app that Felix had used with the Center's speech therapist. "Felix, what do you want?" I asked, offering him the chance to swipe at pretzel, water, stroller, hoping for another *My Fair Lady* moment. But Felix would not acknowledge the iPad. "Come on, Felix! You did it at the center. Please!" Jason, Arun, and Ozge looked at me doubtfully. I showed the app to his teachers at school, but they met with no success either. After a week of pleading, bribing, withholding treats, I gave up. I knew that he had done it at the center. There were notes, there were witnesses. But he was not going to perform such tricks for me. I knew that it was possible to arrange homeschooling with a teacher other than the parent, but where would I find this teacher? The special education teachers that had visited with him in Early Intervention had been nice people, but they didn't seem to make a dent in Felix's consciousness. Unless some kind of Anne Sullivan walked into our lives, and I'd been looking for an Anne Sullivan for a long, long time, I didn't see Felix learning a damn thing.

I called the Center for Discovery. I found out that you can't apply privately. You go through the DOE. You request an IEP meeting where you show that your child has been regressing in a traditional thirty-hour school week. If the IEP team agrees, then the DOE moves your case over the Center Based Support Team (CBST), which sends the application to the Center for Discovery. Because the DOE does not like placing children in residential programs—they are very expensive—I was advised to back up my arguments with professional opinions and seek advice from a special education lawyer.

Our lawyer greeted me with a box of Kleenex. She did not think that it would be difficult to establish that Felix had regressed.

As children typically acquire new skills each year, and hone ones that they had before, regression simply means not developing or building on academic skills. That was easy. Felix did not have academic skills. Testwise, he scored in the six- to twenty-four-month range, as he had for the past four years, and his mobility had measurably regressed.

In March, soon after Felix's tenth birthday, the Rebecca School social worker, Jason and I, and his IEP team convened in a badly lit Board of Education building. I presented the report from the Center for Discovery. Rebecca School teachers spoke from a speakerphone in the center of the table, affirming that Felix needed a more specialized program, that even though the Zyprexa had quieted him, they could not get through to teach him. The CSE special education teacher and school psychologist agreed. Felix was approved. The meeting took less than an hour. Jason and I stumbled out of there, blinking at the traffic on Seventh Avenue. I had expected something more dramatic, something commensurate with the pain I felt inside.

But the reason for pain had not yet arrived. Getting approved for residential schooling is simply that: an approval. Your dossier is put into another file cabinet. Later, a nice woman from the CBST would call to explain the process. Felix's dossier would be sent to residential schools in New York State. If any of the schools had an opening, they would contact me. If I toured the school and did not like it, I did not have to send Felix there. I could wait until a more appropriate placement opened up. If there were no placements available in New York, CBST would look out of state. Were there any schools in particular I was interested in? The Center for Discovery.

But the Center for Discovery did not have an opening. Only two New York schools did. In late spring, a woman with an officious voice called to tell me that she had received Felix's file. Did I want to do an intake interview? The school was a five-hour drive from

Brooklyn and it was operated by the same organization that ran the preschool that had strapped Felix to the chair. It is unfair to judge every program in a national organization by one bad experience, and perhaps I would have traveled to Utica had I liked the woman's voice, but I didn't. When I googled the school, I found a bunch of employees complaining about working conditions. When I google it now, I discover that one of their counselors has been arrested for abusing a student. Allegedly, he "dragged the victim, who was in a prone position, down a hallway and stepped onto his back leaving a footprint on his body. Bruises on his face, neck, and arms were observed by his teacher the following day."

The other school was on Long Island, only an hour and a half away. When Felix and I visited, the school was not in session, so we toured the home where the residents lived. It was a cute little ranch house that fit into its suburban surroundings, the bedrooms decorated by the family of each child. The staff seemed friendly, smart, and caring. They specialized in autism, not cerebral palsy, but they had a partnership with a nearby hospital. Felix would receive the required physical therapy. It was not ideal. There was no biodynamic farm, no rolling hills, no health clinic designed for people as unusual as Felix. But it was nearby. I'd be able to pop in on him in the middle of the week. Felix could come home on the weekends. I said yes, but they said no. Some of their kids were prone to violence. They didn't have the staff to protect Felix. He'd be too vulnerable, they explained, in his chair, unable to defend himself or get away.

I geared myself up to homeschool, which meant interviewing potential new directors for Extreme Kids. As luck/fate/the grace of god would have it, Caitlin Cassaro, our volunteer bookkeeper, who had a background in nonprofit management and a great set of tattoos, wanted the job. She knew what she was getting herself into. She'd done our accounts. She wanted the job anyway. Extreme

Kids had been there for her son and her family. She had cried with gratitude on her first visit. She was hired in June 2013, and I spent the summer training her.

Meanwhile, a representative from a school in Pennsylvania called. The school had been around for one hundred years. It had the right sort of website that said the right sort of things. It was not a dumping ground. It was a place dedicated to helping people with disabilities lead full, self-directed lives. It was only an hour and fifteen minutes away. I made an appointment to tour the facility alone, and for the admissions officer to visit Felix at the Rebecca School. I hung up feeling hopeful. Then I did further research. The facility served over a thousand people. Two students from New York State had died there in the past two years, one in an incident I had read about in the papers. A twenty-year-old boy with autism locked in a van for five hours in ninety-seven-degree weather. He had been baked to death.

The next day, a woman called from a school in New Hampshire. She was warm and bubbly, but I was becoming wary. As crappy as homeschooling might be, I didn't want to kill Felix.

"I'm sorry," I said. "New Hampshire is too far away."

"Oh, that's too bad," she said. "Your son looks like he was made for us."

I leaned into the phone, doubting my hearing. No one had ever said that about Felix. The place was called Crotched Mountain School. It had a lake front. Felix could swim in the lake every day in the summer. In the winter they had a heated therapeutic pool. They had adaptive skiing. They had a hospital. They specialized in autism, emotional and behavioral disabilities, and complex medical conditions.

We visited in September. Felix no longer said, "Don't leave me." He now said, "Don't worry about it," and seemed excited about the journey to New Hampshire. He whooped as Jason strapped him in and whooped through most of the drive, a four-and-a-half-hour drive that stretched into six with lunch and pit stops. The country became particularly beautiful after Brattleboro, when we turned onto Route 9, a two-lane highway that curved by frozen waterfalls and trees laden with snow. By this time, however, Felix was sick of the car. He howled with impatience. Jason, in the back seat, held down his slapping hand and tried to shift his attention with pretzels.

As its name suggests, Crotched Mountain School was located on top of a mountain. The buildings were nestled between the ever-present New Hampshire trees, which here and there gave way to views of snaking rivers, imposing banks of clouds, and the great ponderous hump of Mt. Monadnock. The students who lived there, about sixty, resided on a lane lined with bungalows, their lawns strewn with blueberry bushes and picnic tables. Each house had four bedrooms, a common area, a kitchen, a sunroom, and two bathrooms equipped with enormous, upward tilted bathtubs, with doors that opened and seats molded right in, so that the bather could not slip underneath the water. At the corner of this lane was Happy's favorite thing: a wheelchair-accessible tree house, designed by one of the student's parents, as cozy as a hobbit hole, but nestled in the branches and trunks of a cluster of trees, with a winding wooden ramp leading up to it.

The school itself was a large brick building, built in the utilitarian style of the fifties. Jason and I watched Felix wander about its wide hallways in his walker, his expression open and curious. "Don't worry about eet," he said to a ponytailed teacher in charge of a sunny classroom filled with art and communication devices. Her face lit up in delight. "I'm not worried, Felix." He nodded. "DON'T," he repeated, as if to remind her.

The teachers and therapists, children and aides, everyone I met and observed at Crotched Mountain suggested that the DOE bureaucracy, that bungling tangle of acronyms that I so often railed against, had directed us to a school as hopeful, supportive, and understanding as the Center for Discovery. Felix seemed to like it, too, and the admissions team liked him. Now we just needed New York State's bureaucracy to stay on our side a little longer, for the state had to give its seal of approval before Felix could be enrolled. Week after week went by. I called our social worker at Crotched Mountain. She told me not to worry; they had plenty of kids from New York. I called our agent at the DOE. She told me to pray. I worried that Crotched Mountain might be another mirage, like those damn visiting nurses. We hammered out a provisional deal with the Rebecca School. They would take Felix on a month-by-month basis until December. September ended. October came and went. My hope faded. Then one November night, as I was putting Miranda to bed, I saw that the answering machine was blinking. The message was from Crotched Mountain. The paperwork had been cleared. Felix could start school next week.

I think I jumped in the air. I know that I whooped loud and full just as Miranda burst into tears. Uncontrollable, gasping-for-air tears. I hadn't ever seen her cry like that. Chastened, I held her on my lap as if she were a baby. Her seven-year-old body trembled as I rocked her, kissing away her tears. I couldn't talk, I could only feel her grief passing into me. The next morning, as gently as possible, I told Felix that his new school had called and they really were going to take him. He whooped, too. I wonder if the prospect of me homeschooling him had depressed him as it much as it depressed me? Happy didn't understand, no matter how clearly we tried to explain. For months after Felix left, she would ask, "When is he coming home?"

Diminishment

I can remember preparing for Felix to go: buying him a new CD player at Target, snow boots and wool socks at the Fulton Mall, gathering together his jingle jangles and the framed family photographs that Emily had given us as a Christmas present. But the moment of departure? The knot in my chest feels as fresh as ever, but I cannot summon one image. Who strapped him into his safety belt? Jason? Me? Or was it Emily Brooks, a lovely young woman who worked at Extreme Kids and was particularly fond of Felix? She rode in the back seat with him, feeding him snacks, while Jason drove and I stayed home with the girls. Jason is the one who informs me of this. I had blocked it out.

Felix was assigned to a house called Hawthorne. He had a roommate who liked Elmo. His teacher was the friendly young woman with the ponytail with whom he had conversed on his visit. Only a few days after he had been away, I received an email from Hawthorne's house manager: a photograph of Felix, flanked by an aide and one of his housemates. He was wearing an "I'm a keeper" T-shirt and grinning. According to the staff, he was adjusting very well. The same could not be said of Jason and I. We washed the dishes in an unseemly quiet. We slept, but it did nothing for our spirits: We woke feeling gray and empty. We clung onto the girls. I did not feel myself again until a week later. We were driving to pick up Felix for Thanksgiving, winding up the road that leads to Crotched Mountain. The narrow lanes, the close trees, the nearness of him. The pain melted away, and there I was again, humming. When we arrived at Hawthorne, Felix looked great, cleaner than we had managed to keep him, with glowing skin and bright eyes. I hugged him, greedy for his smell, his warmth. I wanted to burrow into him.

We packed Felix and his gear into the minivan and drove up to Maine, to celebrate the holiday with my father and his wife. Driving back on Sunday, I worried that Felix would balk when we reached Crotched Mountain. Instead, he clapped as we parked outside Hawthorne. As we milled about in the living room, discussing our weekend with the staff, Felix looked meaningfully in the direction of his room. His aide wheeled him down the hall, and he giggled. We left him lying on his bed, listening to the soundtrack of *Cabaret*, not a bit distraught at our goodbyes. The staff had not overstated their case: He had adjusted well. More than well. He was thriving. When we picked him up for Christmas break, his eyes sparkled with a pride I remembered from when he was much younger.

I had been expecting, in a guilty kind of way, to secretly rejoice at my newfound freedom. I did not have to homeschool. The great logistical challenge of overseeing Felix's day-to-day care had been lifted from me. Time no longer had to be minutely calculated. There was, quite suddenly, enough. I could sleep, I could read the notices that came home in the girls' backpacks, I could develop Extreme Kids & Crew's board of directors, I could write this memoir, I could have friends over for dinner. I could even check out the podcasts and television shows people had been talking about. I could read the editorial page of the paper. I could get caught up. I thought I would appreciate it. Instead, long, dark, dull day followed long, dark, dull day. I did my work. I read the editorials. I drank like a fish.

I lightened up when I took the train to New Hampshire or we drove up as a family. I lightened up even when it was Jason's turn and I stayed home with the girls, just as long as one of us was up there with him. I lightened up when Felix laughed on the telephone, or simply when he breathed, when I could hear him snort.

I had not forgotten how hard living with him was. He had been crabby for much of Christmas break, and we had all been relieved when we squished into the car to take him back to New Hampshire. But when he was happy, the world sparkled. He didn't need to be in the same room. He just needed to be near. He could be downstairs with Ozge or Yvette, and I could be upstairs, toweling off the girls and getting them into pajamas, wondering if he would sleep or if he would spend the night in mirthful laughter. His unpredictability, his audibility, his difficulty illuminated all that we had: the girls' springy movements as we cuddled under the covers, the sweet softness of their skin, their shared understanding of the story unfolding in the book on my lap. His absence diminished all of us.

My thoughts became woefully quotidian. One day in yoga class, I tucked my right foot to the left of my knee and began to twist, only to find that I was being blocked by something. A roll of fat. My abdominal muscles, once taut from lifting a 117-pound person multiple times a day, had softened. So much for that marvelous sense of freedom I'd had as I walked around the tennis courts, wondering at my neighbors and their agonies over waistlines. Take away Felix, and those voices that I thought I had long since outgrown piped right back up. I yanked down my shirt, as embarrassed as a *Cosmo* reader, and solemnly vowed to cut out my Nutella toast.

Thank goodness for Extreme Kids. An older relative had advised me to spend more time with "normal people," now that Felix was in New Hampshire. She didn't understand that what she found comforting, I found itchy. I could no longer volunteer every weekend, what with the trips to New Hampshire, and the girls getting older and wanting to do their own things. But I'd drop in when I could. I loved being amidst all those children, children in walkers, in strollers, in wheelchairs, loping children, barreling-down-the-hallways children, spinning children, children clutching lanyards or holding their ears, children who talked a mile a minute, children who had never spoken a word in their lives, children who loved music (one so much that he tried to eat a trumpet). Children who might seem strange outside on the sidewalk, but who seemed perfect and brilliant exactly the way they were at Extreme Kids. I never freaked out about a roll of fat when I was with them.

By this time, Extreme Kids & Crew had moved from the Co-op School. Our new headquarters: AMP Space, short for Art Music Play, had been secured by Caitlin. It consisted of two sunny rooms connected by an accordion door on the first floor of P.S. 15, a public elementary school in Red Hook. One room was a sensory play space, the other an art/music studio and office. From there, Caitlin and a staff of three or four part-timers presided over an expanding program. P.S. 15's students with disabilities and their therapists used our sensory gym during the school day, after school we ran a free program for them, and on the weekends, families from all over the city came for open play, concerts, art projects, classes, birthday parties. We also had a satellite. The Parks Department had lent us a building within the Crispus Attucks Playground in Bedford-Stuyvesant, not far from the Co-op School. It was too small for big kids, but perfect for toddlers. I had painted it with Melinda Burke, an Extreme Kids mother from our very first art class. A big crew of workmen from our renovation and other parents from Extreme Kids had hauled in the C-stand, the swings, the mats, and the ball pit from Space No. 1. Micaela had converted a walk-in closet into a magical Lula Universe, with stars revolving around the ceiling and the bubble tube burbling. Yvette worked there on Sundays. I'd run over to pay her and be greeted with her wide smile. She loved it when new families came: their expressions when they opened the door and saw what was waiting for them. They had not been forgotten. There was a place for them, too.

Crotched Mountain

In the spring of 2014, for the first time in forever, Felix met his IEP goals. This should not be taken to suggest that Felix had turned into an avid student. The new, more advanced goals that his team drew up included benchmarks like "being able to tolerate science for five minutes." And, according to one of his progress reports, "The challenge at times is remaining within a nonfamiliar group activity for the entire time without screaming." But still, Felix was more engaged in school than I'd ever seen him. He was learning how to ride an adaptive bike with his physical therapist. He pressed—willingly—a yellow button to vocally participate in morning meeting. At speech therapy sessions, he selected meaningful icons on the iPad with 80 percent consistency, providing quantifiable proof that he was capable of symbolic thought and expressive language.

This was real growth, real movement. People kept on asking how I got Felix into such a great school, and I kept having to admit that I didn't do anything except follow the official procedure. The same New York State and City bureaucracy that for years had left me feeling strangled and oppressed had found Felix the placement and paid for it, complicating my relationship to the DOE, and making it impossible for me to indulge in the sorts of full-throttled rants that I used to enjoy.

How to account for Crotched Mountain School's success? What did it have that our family didn't have, that New York City, with all its resources, didn't have? Some of Felix's development may have arisen precisely because Felix was no longer in New York City. He no longer had to cope—or not cope—with its stress, competition, and hurry, its staircases, curbs, and narrow aisles. He wasn't in a school that no longer fit him. He wasn't jangling keys in his family home, which, for all its comfort and familiarity, was perhaps too familiar. He had a whole new world to explore, and he could explore this world with a modicum of independence.

When I was his age, my parents' presence weighed on me. I was always hiding out in tree branches, in forgotten, stuffy nooks in the attic, in moldy storage areas in the basement, anywhere I could be alone, breathe my own air. Perhaps Felix felt like this, too. How frustrating to yearn for some space from your family, at the same time as you are completely and utterly dependent on them. He had needed us to wipe his butt, to puff his pillows, to change his CDs. He would always need others for these things, but perhaps when these people weren't us, he felt freer—more his own person.

Not long after Felix moved there, the head of Hawthorne House sent back his mitts. They weren't using them. Felix still hit himself, but not as often and not as fiercely. They could slip a pillow between his hand and his cheek, and usually he'd stop. His increased peacefulness surely was related to his increased help, and the quality of this help. His aides worked in shifts, so no one would get too tired. The day shift started at 7:00 a.m., when his school aide came to Hawthorne to dress him and bring him to his classroom. A second shift started at 3:00 p.m., when his residential aide picked him up from school and walked home with him, or took him swimming, or tried to get him interested in bowling (yes, Crotched Mountain has a bowling alley). The third shift started at 10:00 p.m., when two night aides arrived to oversee the house, quiet now, at least in theory, its boys all tucked into bed. If the night aides ever needed assistance, a crisis intervention team was on call twenty-four hours.

Everyone in his class at school got this sort of help. Two special education teachers oversaw a half-dozen aides and a half-dozen students, many of whom, like Felix, were in wheelchairs. The class came together for circle time and group projects, but most of the instruction was done one-on-one, by the aides, which meant that children at different academic levels could share the same classroom without hampering one another. Some of the children in Felix's class could read and were working at a third or fourth-grade level. On any given day, they might be memorizing state capitals or honing their computer skills. Felix, on the other hand, was working on his prelearning skills, skills like tolerating "a nonpreferred activity" and learning how to wait. How do you teach waiting? One day I got to watch Cindy, one of Felix's school aides, at her job. She used a tablet and her own animated self. She would tell him that they had to wait a minute before, say, eating a snack or listening to a song on the iPad. She would activate an app: a second hand turned around a featureless white circle, spreading a field of red in its wake. When the circle was fully red, a minute had passed. She would stay with Felix, watching with him, and sometimes for him, as the red slowly, incrementally, and yet predictably and reliably spread. When the minute was over, she would cheer. Yay! You did it. You waited a minute! And Felix would get his chip or his song. He got the concept pretty quickly.

To develop his number awareness, Cindy used plastic cubes a little bit bigger than dice. "One," she would say, holding a single cube on the palm of her hand. Felix's job was to take it, then place it back in her other hand. If he refused, she would take his hand and guide it along. "Now, two," she would say, two cubes on the palm of her hand. She would joke when he resisted. She would not let him off the hook. She could cheerfully keep up her end of this cube exercise until Felix couldn't stand it anymore. When he started hitting himself, she would take him for a walk. Then they would return, and he would have to face those damn cubes again. "Come on, Felix, you just have to do five more minutes of math, and then you're free." In this way, he learned that he could not escape.

Did Felix understand the correlation between the spoken number and the quantity of cubes in his hand? It didn't matter. Over time, Cindy assured me, he would. I understood her reasoning: teaching through repetition, creating connections through force of habit. What I marveled at was her unflagging energy. When I taught English 101, I was instructed to repeat everything three times. Apparently, that was the average amount of repetitions necessary to make an impression on the average brain of an average college student with average attention. I found repeating things three times very difficult. When I am interested in a subject, words tumble out, often at a confusingly fast pace, building on themselves, leading to unknown places. I want to follow where they take me. To go back and calmly reiterate my initial point is a torment. A brain like Felix's might need 300 calm reiterations of a point to sink in. It delighted and impressed me to watch how well Cindy could do this. It is no small skill to stay fresh and attentive, repetition after repetition after repetition.

In New York, so many of Felix's teachers had been young, filled with theories, confused about what to do when Felix did not respond as he was supposed to—to ABA or Floortime or whatever pedagogy they'd been trained in. But there is no Felix methodology. The best you can do is experiment, improvise, see what sticks. The teachers and therapists at Crotched Mountain, many of whom were older, had worked with a good number of students whose brains were as unusual and uncharted as Felix's. Their faith that these children could be reached was based on their experience. They had seen amazing things in the past and trusted that they would continue to in the future.

Julia, the speech therapist, was as intrigued by Felix's language processing as I—in particular, the discrepancy between his receptive language abilities, which to her seemed relatively intact, and his barely existent expressive language. Happily for us, she was also an expert in assistive technology, and began immediately experimenting with different devices—a variety of tablets and communication boards and eye-gaze machines, in which the energy of the eye activates the screen, rather than the pressure of a finger. The field of assistive technology, she told me, was changing at a breathtaking pace. The combination of the computer gaming industry and brain-injured veterans had led to an efflorescence of devices that can capture the inner energy of the brain and translate it into words or images or prosthetically assisted movements. "Prepare yourself," Julia said. "The equipment is evolving at such a pace that by the time that he graduates, Felix may be able to express himself and manipulate his environment in ways that we cannot imagine."

I sometimes feel that Felix's greatest challenge is his own resistance, but with people like Cindy and Julia so strenuously and compassionately urging him on, with all the space and technology and time that Crotched Mountain gives him, his resistance may give way. Who knows what he is capable of? Lots. I know that much. Certainly their faith in him has already made its mark. You can see it in that pride that so cheered me. You can read about it in his files.

Once, visiting Felix at Hawthorne, he and I hung out in the sunroom while the staff gathered around the table for their weekly meeting. I was not allowed to listen in when they discussed Felix's housemates, but when Felix's turn came, the house manager opened the door and let me snoop. His residential aides, his teaching aide, his therapists, the house manager, and the staff from nursing compared observations, made suggestions, and joked about funny things he had done. In New York, I had considered it a success simply to get one of Felix's doctors to talk to another on the phone. Here, almost his entire team discussed his case with each other, face to face, regularly. From previous visits, I had gathered that there were rifts within the staff, sometimes between the aides, many of whom have not been to college, and "know-it-all" professionals who are getting paid more and could have attitudes. On the day I observed, however, they all sat around that table, eating pastries, and listening to each other with interest and respect. I imagine that meetings like this are part of what makes the place so lively. The staff—all of the staff—are being listened to. They are part of a larger conversation.

In New York, at home, at school, even at Extreme Kids, Felix was usually the most disabled person in the room. At Crotched Mountain he lived with a half dozen housemates as odd and mysterious as he: G., skinny and bearded, protected by a white helmet, jump-dancing hour after hour in the sunroom; Gangly P., striding down the hall, attempting one more time to slip out of the house; J., stiff where Felix was floppy, presiding in his enormous reclining chair, his feeding tube suspended like a bulbous antenna. J. was Felix's new roommate. His first roommate, the lover of Elmo, had moved into a single. Felix and he had not had a conflict, but they hadn't had much of a connection, either. J. and Felix, on the other hand, had a thing. They listened to bluegrass and show tunes together. They set each other off in loops of laughter that kept them up way past bedtime.

Once, arriving at Hawthorne, I released the girls from the car and went inside, eager to see Felix. The girls, who had been talking nonstop for an hour, trailed me, their hands on my clothes, still chirping, chattering, interrupting each other's interruptions, their words a barrage of nonsense. They had nothing to say. They just wanted to be heard. I shooed them away, desperate for quiet. How nice it must be, I remarked to Felix, living with people who don't always have to be talking. He threw back his head and clapped. Yes, indeed.

. . .

The summer of 2014, the girls and I spent nearly two months in rented houses near Crotched Mountain, seeing Felix most every day. In the mornings, I wrote. In the afternoons, after Felix's school day ended, the girls and I picked him up from Hawthorne. Sometimes we took him hiking. Crotched Mountain has two wheelchair accessible trails, one that circles boggy wetlands, one that ascends a gentle summit. We soon discovered that the wetlands were buggy in the summer, and that Felix had no patience for black flies. The summit was better. The path wound through pine forests and meadows filled with wildflowers. At the top were blackberries and blueberries that the girls loved to pick and cool winds that made Felix giggle. When it was hot, we'd go swimming. By this time, Felix weighed 125 pounds. On our first trip to the lake, it took four tries to get him back in the car, and we both almost fell in the process. After that, I brought along an aide to help me with transfers. We'd all bump over the dirt road to the waterfront, then the aide or I would change Felix in the car, help him into his chair, and push him down the ramp to the shore. My stomach muscles popped right back into place, guiding him over the sand, and into the water. Once he got in, he was again light, mobile, free. With me holding him, he could jump. We jumped together, sending big sloshy ripples into the lake. When I got tired of jumping, he would gulp down the water. I would shout no! He would laugh and ignore me, while the girls splashed around on inflatable rafts.

If this sounds like an idyll, it was.

And yet.

One Sunday morning, picking up Felix from Hawthorne, I arrived to the ancient and awful sound of his fury. I rushed into his room. Amber, his weekend aide, and the weekend manager hovered over him. Amber had tears in her eyes. Felix had been hitting himself for twenty minutes, roaring with rage. She'd been trying to stop him, but he was so strong. She didn't understand. She'd worked with him for months. They'd always had a good time. I held Felix, his shoulders shaking, his cheeks red with slap marks. I put my mouth to his ear: "It's all right, it's all right." The words were meant for Amber as much as for Felix. I was almost pleased that he had had a fit at Hawthorne, relieved that it didn't happen only at home. He quieted down. Amber remained pale and trembling. The house manager hugged her, then turned to me, her expression earnest. "What should we do when he does this?" She and Amber looked at me. They were both so serious.

What was I supposed to say? They were doing everything they could, more than we'd been able to do at home.

"Despair?" I offered. The women looked at me blankly. But J., Felix's roommate, who had been lying so quietly in the bed that I didn't know he was there, burst into a belly laugh. He had gotten my joke. The women started giggling, even Felix snorted. And there we all were, the five of us, bound together in laughter.

• • •

In September, with its cooler nights and the trees already beginning to change, the girls and I drove back to Brooklyn. No more fields of ferns waving to us as we pushed Felix up to the summit, no more afternoons at the lake. An end-of-summer sadness settled over me, but it was a sweet sadness, the kind that you treasure. The ache that I had carried around with me all winter and spring was gone.

The last remnants of it had lifted when J. laughed at my joke, when Felix snorted. He was not alone. He had friends of his own making. How could I grieve? My grief was gone, and in its place, a spark of gladness.

We came back to Jamila and Bashir, who had volunteered to dog-sit. I had been wary, thinking of Felix grabbing his skull in agony every time Oscar barked. But Jamila had insisted that Bashir loved Oscar, and on our return, she was still in a pro-Oscar mood. They had taken him for long walks in Fort Greene Park, Bashir holding Oscar's leash, and Oscar, who is usually balky, agreeing to be led. What is more: Bashir, who speaks so rarely as to be classified as non-verbal, talked to Oscar. "No, Dog! Come!" More words to Oscar in a day than he had said to Jamila in a week. Jamila kept shaking her head and laughing, as if she couldn't believe it. No, Dog! Come! Equally surprising, Oscar, impervious dog that he is, obeyed. No, Dog! Come! Three words and the wag of a tail. Perhaps it was not for naught that Oscar came up from Alabama. Perhaps he was also where he was supposed to be.

Epilogue

I am often told that I'm a good mother. I wonder if anyone who has read this book would use so glib a phrase. People who call me this mean well, and I prefer them calling me a good mother rather than sneering at my parenting techniques, but I find the judgment capricious. Consider the past: What if I had snapped while restraining Felix? What if, driving the car while he raged in the back seat, I had run over another child? What if Child Services had not judged in our favor and taken Felix away? Any of these things could have happened. If they had, I would be more or less the same person I am now, but instead of being applauded, I would be despised. Perhaps in the very act of writing this, I am condemning myself.

I am a mother. I love my kids. I try to do my best by them. This makes me wholly unremarkable. Surely the great majority of mothers, and fathers, too—surely the great majority of parents love their children and try to do their best by them. Our bests may be different, shaped as they are by resources, character, history, culture, but the urge to protect, feed, and love one's child is one of the great commonalities that binds people together, as is the pain parents feel when they can't.

It is a commonality that would seem to extend beyond people. A spring day, years ago: Miranda was maybe four months old. I was nursing her in the backyard, cradling her in my lap, her soft, downy head in my arms, the warm sun on my skin. I was aware of a shift, a sudden, uneasy silence followed by squawks of terror. I looked up to see a cat, running along the top of the chain-link fence that divided our lawn from the neighbor's. A tiny bird dangled from its mouth. Two blue jays dive bombed this cat, then circled it, madly flapping their wings. The air churned with their distress. I leaped up from my chair, still nursing Miranda. But how could I enter the fray with her in my arms, and how could I put her down when she could not yet sit? By the time these thoughts had fully registered, the cat and its catch were gone. The blue jays, shrieking, disappeared into the boughs of the trees. I heard them for hours afterward, their raw keening piercing through the leaves.

Were they good parents for having tried to fight the cat? Were they bad parents for having exposed their fledgling in the first place? These questions are absurd: They were blue jays, frantic and heart-broken. I identify more with those birds than with the idea of a good mother or a bad one. Perhaps I resist "good mother" because of its corollary and the social condemnation, shame, and foolish-ness heaped upon women whose offspring are in one way or another deemed lacking. One of the more notorious mother bashers was the mid-twentieth-century professor Bruno Bettelheim, who popular-ized Leo Kanner's idea of toxic parenting as the root of autism, sin-gling out "refrigerator mothers" as the cause of their children's dis-tance. While Bettelheim's theories have been roundly discredited, our own age is ripe with columnists, bloggers, and parenting experts eager to shine a light on their own view of good parenting, indirectly and sometimes directly questioning the virtue, decency, and fitness of parents who might not agree with or be able to act upon their advice. Parents do, of course, play an important role in shaping their children. They influence them with their genes, their behavior, their discipline, their food, their wit, their gestures, their stories, and so on, but how each child interprets and ingests these influences is magnificently anarchic. Don't we all know brilliant people who came from miserable families and kind, responsible people who birthed scalawags?

Parents are too often judged on the slightest skim of knowledge. To be fair, I doubt that the people who "good mother" me necessarily approve of, or are even aware of my parenting techniques. More likely, they are saying, Bravo! Your son is odd and you love him anyway. They don't mean to be condescending. They are just cheering on love in its many forms. And yet, and still, I resist. The problem is the singular.

Whatever goodness I have, as it were, is integrally connected with the people surrounding me. I remember a morning during a sleepless week, my eardrums numb from Felix's yelling, Happy howling with teething pain or hunger, Oscar butting me with his bony head. I stood at the sink, trying to screw the top of a leaky baby bottle, when ding! I remembered that bottle of gin in the freezer. I had never had a drink at nine in the morning. It would be egregious, yet pleasingly rebellious . . . How much more adventurous and fun the day that stretched out before me might be . . . Or maybe I could just pass out? Get some rest. It seemed like a great idea. But I couldn't do it, not with the workmen tromping up and down the stairs, the babysitter due to arrive in a couple of hours. The workmen and the babysitter were not aware of their influence, but they guided me. I drank coffee instead of gin, and I am glad that I did. But this decision had more to do with them than any virtue sewn into my DNA.

People. Other people. The interconnectedness of my life. During the summer of 2012, when Felix's rages returned full blast, other people were instrumental to my sanity. I remember being awoken by Felix's devil screech, lying in bed, prostrate, knowing that I had to get up. That terrible sound of his first slap. That terrible knowledge of the struggle that would ensue. That terrible vision of his lips, peeling and bloody from so much screaming. In those middle of the night and early dawn moments, life felt so merciless and exhausting that I could not understand why people clung to it. Death seemed benevolent. You wouldn't have to get up. You could dissolve into quiet and peace. Why did anyone want to live to be ninety-two?

My newfound appreciation of dying might well have warped into something more proactive and troublesome, were it not for those surrounding me. I had Jason, too decent and beloved a person to die on. Miranda and Happy, clamoring for bedtime stories, their squirmy warm bodies and insistent kisses. Felix, when he was lucid. Ozge taking the girls to the park, giving Felix his baths. Karla lugging her bass over, trying to reach Felix through the vibration of the strings. Huck appearing regularly at our house or Space No. 1, treating Felix free of charge. My old friend Diane, who lost her place on the Lower East Side, and moved in with us, along with her son. She would bring back fresh baguettes from the Essex Market, cook big meals of spaghetti and meatballs and roast chicken, sew doll clothes for the girls and keep me company those long nights when Jason didn't get home until eleven or twelve. Help came from people I didn't even know: pedestrians, running after me on the street, shouting Ma'am you forgot your wallet, your keys, your groceries, your phone, restocking me with the items of daily life that I was continuously dropping or leaving behind. And help came from those families who played at Extreme Kids, parents and children who had no idea of the powerful effect they had on my psyche. They showed me that if I could not make life better for my son, I could at least help people like him. That was huge. The feeling of helplessness is crushing. Seeing those other children and parents happy, if only for a moment, and knowing that I had played a part in bringing that about, broke through my heaviness, allowed me to see possibility in the world again.

I am only as good a mother as all the people helping me to be one, and I am helped more than most. So much more than most.

Bruna's words come back to me often. "We all think that we do so much for Felix, but he does even more for us." How can anyone be so wise at twenty-one? But that's part of what Felix has taught me: how different each one of us is, how uniquely outfitted with our own oddities and obsessions, delusions and insights. None of us fit precisely and perfectly into those neat charts of development I memorized all those years ago in ninth-grade child psychology. Bruna was precociously wise at twenty-one—and Felix, who knows what he will be like? He might be reading these words, for all I know. More likely, he will be jangling some combination of strings and shiny metal bits, as disdainful of language as ever, but he will have changed. He will have grown in some way of his own. I imagine, no matter how old he is, that he will always remind me of how little I know. That if ever I presume to come up with a unified theory of him, he will demolish it with a hoot of laughter, a slap across his face, a poop in the pool.

I love the thoughts and associations that he sparks, the sociability that he engenders, the bigger and stranger world that he has allowed me to inhabit. There are those who count lives like Felix's as losses. There are philosophers who question Felix's very humanness. I admit that when I am with Felix, I often feel closer to the rest of nature, more aware of the wind, the smell of the air, the organelles in my cells, the bugs in my eyelashes. I often feel a sort of cultural lifting, a release from language and babble of opinion. I love this about Felix, but he is as human as anyone reading these words, and the web of humans he has woven around him is impressive. He brings out the best in many. He inserts himself into dreams. That many of my friends have dreamed about Felix is not surprising. What intrigues me are those others, neighbors I barely know who have approached me somewhat uncertainly, their happiness overcoming their timidity. Usually they have dreamed of Felix walking and talking. Perhaps it is this transformation they find wondrous and necessary to report. But what I find wondrous is the way that he affects their psyche, now, as he is, the way that he reaches them through language and care, dream and yearning.

• • •

I leave you with a vision, the seed of which was planted back in the carriage house in Prospect Heights. As Felix has gotten older, and I have become more immersed in disability culture, my initial dream of building a creative community center that would honor children with disabilities has grown to include adults, too: the child with autism, the vet with no legs, the mother recovering from a stroke, the grandfather with Alzheimer's. So here it is: The Perceptorium. Imagine an experiential museum and cultural center that would serve as a portal, a place where people first stumbling into the world of disability will see that they are not alone, and that this new world that they are entering, though hard and painful, can lead them to new perceptions and experiences, deeper connections with those they love and the world around them. Imagine a constellation of synapses twinkling on the ceiling, neuronal tubes to crawl through, the seaweedy splendor of ganglia. Virtual exhibits would illustrate what happens when the brain does not work as it is expected to. In one room, the sighted could feel what it is like to be blind. In another, the steady keeled could experience the world-tipping cacophony of sensory dysregulation. Imagine showcasing art by people with these unusual brains, both famous and unknown.

Imagine a place dedicated to fostering the dynamic potential of disability—its affinity for invention and discovery, for dissolving conventional viewpoints, for bridging the cultural barriers that so often divide us. Disability is deeply interwoven with life; it is not something that can be escaped. Better, then, to get to know it, to begin to learn from it, not alone in one's cracked fortress, but in the company of others.

Acknowledgments

This book would not have come into being without two neighbors who have become good friends and for whom I am immensely grateful: my editor Jeanann Pannasch who got me to try my hand at memoir and guided the manuscript through its iterations, and my agent Jill Grinberg who stuck with me through a tsunami of rejections, championing our project with humor and grit. I am also indebted to Rebecca Mead, Sarah Weir, Johnny Temple, Nina Collins and Maureen Langloss for their readings and responses, and, of course, to Rachel Neumann and her thoughtful crew at Parallax. Thank you all for your encouragement and faith.

Neither would this book have been possible without Felix's army of courageous and warm-hearted helpers, some of whom appear in the pages of this book, but many of whom don't. Were I to write each individual name, the list of those who have aided and abetted Felix would stretch into another chapter, and perhaps beyond that.

You know who you are. You are our babysitters young and old, male and female, Swedish, Finnish, American, Tibetan, Turkish, Russian, Caribbean, Sri Lankan, Brazilian. You gave your time, your kindness, your muscle, your humor and your compassion, and increased our family's capacity to love and be loved. You are Felix's therapists, healers, doctors, nurses, teachers, singers, musicians, yogis, waitresses, volunteers, high-fivers. You are Felix's aides and one-on-ones, who put aside your own struggles and showed up day after day after day, with patience and energy and cheer.

You are the people who helped start Extreme Kids, who shared your experience, who prepped me for interviews, who helped raise money and awareness, who helped paint walls and schlep equipment, who played your instruments, told your stories, danced your dances, and took your pictures. Who came with your families and embraced me when I needed it most. You are those who continue to make Extreme Kids flourish.

You are also those whose names I do not know: the city bus driver who carefully strapped Felix's stroller into the wheelchair supports, the bus riders who cheered instead of groaning at the delay. You are the hundreds of people who grabbed onto the bottom of Felix's stroller and assisted me in getting him up the subway stairs. You are the teenage girl, stretching her arm toward me, asking "Can I help?" when Felix was screaming and slapping himself at the corner of Carlton and DeKalb.

And you are those whose names I know so very well, my family, my friends, my parents, my children. One person, however, must be named, for without him, there would be no Felix, Miranda or Happy. Thank you, Jason, my co-conspirator and confidante, my funder, my parenting partner, my most precious companion, who daily sweetens and deepens my life, and makes everything possible.

PARALLAX
PRESS

Parallax Press is a nonprofit publisher, founded and inspired
by Zen Master Thich Nhat Hanh. We publish books on
mindfulness in daily life and are committed to making
these teachings accessible to everyone and preserving
them for future generations. We do this work to alleviate
suffering and contribute to a more just and joyful world.

For a copy of the catalog, please contact:
Parallax Press
P.O. Box 7355
Berkeley, CA 94707
parallax.org